Enduring Success

Enduring Success

What We Can Learn from
the History of Outstanding Corporations

Christian Stadler

STANFORD BUSINESS BOOKS
An Imprint of Stanford University Press
Stanford, California

This edition not for sale in the USA (and dependent territories), Canada, South and Central America.

Publisher's note
Every possible effort has been made to ensure that the information contained in this book is accurate at the time of going to press, and the publishers and authors cannot accept responsibility for any errors or omissions, however caused. No responsibility for loss or damage occasioned to any person acting, or refraining from action, as a result of the material in this publication can be accepted by the editor, the publisher or any of the authors.

First published in the United States in 2011 by Stanford Business Books, an imprint of Stanford University Press.

First published in Great Britain in 2011 as a co-publication of Stanford Business Books, an imprint of Stanford University Press, and Kogan Page Limited:

Kogan Page Limited	Stanford University Press
120 Pentonville Road	1450 Page Mill Road
London N1 9JN	Palo Alto, CA 94304
United Kingdom	USA
www.koganpage.com	www.sup.org

British Library Cataloguing in Publication Data

A CIP record for this book is available from the British Library.

ISBN 978 0 7494 6359 5

Typeset by Bruce Lundquist in 10/15 Sabon
Print production managed by Jellyfish Print Solutions
Printed and bound in the United Kingdom by CPI Antony Rowe

Für Mama, Papa, und Florence

CONTENTS

My father told captivating bedtime stories. As a history teacher he was able to take me back to the streets of ancient Rome, the dramatic battle for a nearby castle in 1504, or the adventures of Andreas Hofer, a 19th-century freedom fighter who tried to throw the mighty armies of Napoleon out of my home state. (He lost, but I can assure you that he put up quite a fight.) No doubt these tales set the stage for my interest in history. But these stories also taught me that history holds more than entertainment value: it's an endless source of lessons, and each of us can learn anew by traveling into the past. Now, I realize that is perhaps not such an unusual insight. Nonetheless, it marked a profound turning point for me and provided a lesson worth reminding ourselves of from time to time.

In business we often forget about history. Or worse, we discount it as something that is no longer relevant. While history might not repeat itself in exactly the same way, such a view of history disregards the sheer endless opportunities to learn from the past. Sure, we do not struggle with exactly the same issues as the men and women of the Industrial Revolution faced. But once we look below the surface, we notice that there are still many similarities. How should we react when a competitor enters our market? Which type of leadership is most suitable in times of trouble? Is innovation the only way to ensure future success? These questions are as relevant today as they were 150 years ago! Throw any question you can think of at "history," and you will receive a number of answers that will enrich your understanding. The tricky bit is finding the stories in history that are most useful for addressing the issues in question—which brings me to why I wrote this book. I tried to identify relevant answers provided by history. I tried to capture what we can learn from the history of outstanding corporations.

Who Should Read the Book?

Executives who are interested in managing for the long term should read this book. I hope that they will be able to learn from the history of the outstanding corporations featured in the book, but also be inspired to investigate the past of their own companies. The data, diagnostics, and stories should help them in answering the following questions: (1) How should we balance innovation and operational excellence? (2) Are we over- or under-diversified? (3) Which mechanisms can help us to capture some of the lessons we learned? (4) Should we be bold or conservative? (5) How can we successfully transform our organization? (6) Who is the right person to succeed me? Investors, analysts, and consultants should also find this book useful when they try to assess the long-term strategies of corporations.

My Promise to the Reader

In his outstanding book *Profit from the Core*, Chris Zook notes that in any given year about two hundred business tools and frameworks are in use. What's most surprising is how short-lived many of those are. It's almost as if one fad hunts the next one. New tools are by nature not yet tested. They promise the ultimate solution, but once they turn out to be more shine than substance, they quickly disappear. This books promises *not* to deliver another magic cure, a solution to all your problems. Its offer is stories and insights from history. Each of its propositions has been tested for more than 100 years in different settings. And even if the ideas put forward are not suitable for your organization, they will stimulate discussion. In fact, since this book and I are outsiders to your particular situation, this is all that we can offer: food for thought to help you develop ideas that work in *your* organization.

Thank You

This book was made possible through the help of many, and I want to express my sincere thanks. Professor Franz Mathis and Professor Hans Hinterhuber from Innsbruck University, Professor Gianmario Verona from Bocconi University, and Davis Dyer from the Winthrop Group all shaped the book profoundly by listening to my ideas, challenging them, and sharing their own experiences. I am equally indebted to the project team members who spent months, some of them years, working with me on the book. In their doctoral dissertations Daniel Blum analyzed the financial performance of our companies, Evelyn Muth studied failing companies, and Philip Wältermann concentrated on German insurance companies. Stephan Höger, Mathias Höglund, Alex Neulinger, Patricia Pedratscher, and Christine Raschke labored through some of the tricky issues while compiling their master's theses.

Throughout the project we were able to rely on the advice of many accomplished experts. I want to express my gratitude particularly to those who joined our advisory board: the late Alfred D. Chandler, from Harvard Business School; Arie de Geus, author of *The Living Company*; Edgar Jones, who wrote the fascinating history of Glaxo;[1] Michael Mirow, the former head of Siemens's strategic planning unit; Jerry I. Porras, a coauthor of *Built to Last*; Peter Schütte, from Nyenrode University; and Risto Tainio, from the Helsinki School of Economics.

Next, I want to thank the top executives who agreed to be interviewed by us. I know that their schedules are very busy, and we appreciate that they took the time to support our efforts: Régina Boullié-Gugliemi, Ciments Français (Director of Finance); Keith Daton, Lafarge (Senior Vice President, HR); Marc Desgranges, Ciments Français (Director of Strategy and Development); Heinz Dürr, AEG[2] (CEO 1980–1990); Hermann Franz, Siemens (Chairman 1993–1999); Jean-Pierre Garnier, Glaxo (CEO 2000–2008); Stephen Green, HSBC (Chairman since 2006,

CEO 2003–2006); Jean-Pierre Herbinier, Ciments Français (Director of Formation and Development); Cor Herkströter, Shell[3] (CEO 1993–1998); Christian Herrault, Lafarge (Board Member since 1998); Arno Junke, Cologne Re (Board Member 2003–2007); Klaus Kleinfeld, Siemens (CEO 2005–2007); Christian Kluge, Munich Re (Board Member 1998–2006); Martin Lord, HSBC (Head of Government and Community Relations); Peter Lütke-Bornefeld, Cologne Re (CEO 1993–2009); Mark Moody-Stuart, Shell (CEO 1998–2001); Alexander Nieuwenhuizen, Lafarge, (Senior Vice President, HR); Jorma Ollila, Nokia (Chairman since 1992, CEO 1992–2006); Heinrich von Pierer, Siemens (Chairman 2005–2007, CEO 1992–2005); David Prosser, Legal & General Group plc (CEO 1991–2005); Hans-Jürgen Schinzler, Munich Re (Chairman since 2004, CEO 1993–2004); Henning Schulte-Noelle, Allianz[4] (Chairman since 2003, CEO 1991–2003); Sara Ravella, Lafarge (Board Member since 2008); Edzard Reuter, Daimler Benz (CEO 1987–1995); Peter von Siemens, Siemens (member of family who founded company); Reinhard Siepenkort, AEG (former Company Secretary); Peter Stileman, Standard Chartered (Head of Corporate Development); Richard Sykes, Glaxo (Chairman 1997–2002, CEO 1993–2000); Jeroen van der Veer, Shell (CEO 2004–2009); Lodewijk van Wachem, Shell (Chairman 1992–2002, CEO 1985–1992); Gerrit Wagner, Shell (CEO 1972–1977); Phil Watts, Shell (CEO 2001–2004); Claus Weyrich, Siemens (Board Member 1996–2006); and Günter Wilhelm, Siemens (Board Member 1992–2000).

As in any project of this magnitude, we relied on people both within and outside the companies to help us gain access to crucial data and improve our understanding of their business practices. I would like to thank Chris Allen, Raphael Sagalyn, the late Gover Boeles, Matt Nixon, Bjorn Edlund, Frank Wittendorfer, Klaus Wigand, Christina Schmöe, Winfried Wittman, Reinhardt Siepenkort, Tina Staples, Edwin Green, Christian Devilliers, Michel Albert, Jean-Paul Berquand, André Boutiron, Jean-Pierre Naud, Olivier Gosset, Phillipe Fabres, Géraud de Fontanger, Jean-Claude Le Berre, Stephan Doumenc, Zoran M. Andric, Dirk Johannsen, Kim Lindström, Blandine Eminyan, Barbaresco Gabriele, Jules van Well, Monika Bergström, Micke Hovmoller, Barbara Eggenkämper, Gerd Modert, Professor Peter Borscheid, Götz Denzinger, and Sabine Denné.

I would also like to thank my colleagues from the different institutions where I resided during the research for their support: Professor Kurt Matzler, Andrea Mayr, Dagmar Abfalter, Margit Raich, Sandra Rothenberger, Lukas Siller, Professor Birgit Renzl, Julia Hautz, Irina Kapavik, and Julia Müller at Innsbruck University; Chris Allen, Professor Geoffrey Jones, and Walter A. Friedman at Harvard Business School; Professor Ludovic Cailluet at Institut d'administration des enterprises Toulouse; Professor Constance E. Helfat, Professor Alva Taylor, Professor Richard D'Aveni, and Professor Robert G. Hansen at the Tuck School of Business at Dartmouth; and Professor Michael Mayer, Professor Klaus Meyer, Professor Edmund Thompson, Sara Dixon, Felicia Fai, Ajit Nayak, Rekha Rao, and Helen Xia at the University of Bath.

The research was funded by the Austrian National Bank's Jubiläumsfonds für die Förderung von Forschungs- und Lehraufgaben der Wissenschaft. I express my sincere gratitude for this support.

I would also like to especially recognize some of my closest friends. As in any project, there are days when nothing seems to work. These people provided the support network that helped me on those bad days. Likewise, they made the bright days brighter: Priscilla Chandrasekaran, Andreas Müller, Andreas Paulhuber, Michael Duregger, Angelika Hummel, Hellen Gikaria, Bernadette Loacker, Hannes Wiesflecker (to whom I am particularly indebted for making my homepage http://www.enduringsuccess.com), my brother-in-law Murimi, my sister Carolin and her husband, Simon. I am honored and grateful to be your friend.

Finally, I am deeply thankful to my parents and my wife, Florence. You went through all the different emotions together with me and sometimes felt them stronger than I myself did: hope, disappointment, triumph, failure. I know it is not always easy to put up with the stress I go through, and I do not have sufficient words to express my feelings, so let me simply say I love you.

Enduring Success

I   THE QUEST FOR ENDURING SUCCESS

There is no such thing as perpetual success.

Life is a constant struggle and we would be fools if we made ourselves believe that some people always succeed. To be honest, life would be dull and boring if we did not face occasional struggles. Success, after all, is a relative experience—relative not only to failure but also to the mediocre and mundane. Overcoming major barriers is part of the fun and makes victory so much sweeter.

For corporations the story is very much the same. At this writing, the world is struggling through a severe financial crisis. This has happened before, of course, and it's a reminder that cycles of boom and bust are endemic to capitalism. A few years ago, following the burst of the New Economy bubble, shareholders, managers, and employees went through similar motions when they became painfully aware that the promise of easy riches remained just that, a promise. What most experienced hands had known all along became obvious to the general public once again: companies that we celebrate one day might stumble and fall before the sun rises again. Armed with natural curiosity, most of us would like to know whether things really have to be that way. Is there the occasional company that avoids or defers this fate? A company our great-grandparents were able to admire? A company we can admire today and feel reasonably confident will be still around when our great-grandchildren grow old?

Brooding on these issues after the completion of my doctoral dissertation,[1] I made a trip to Guildford, a small town an hour outside London, early in 2002. I had been looking forward to this trip, as I was going to meet Arie de Geus, the former head of Shell Planning, who had published a celebrated book on long-lived companies.[2] Arie, I was sure, could answer my questions. But as is often the case with experienced senior managers who move beyond daily operations and reach a certain state of wisdom, Arie raised more questions than he answered. He made it quite clear that we know very little about the long-term development of large organizations. Other than Arie's book, there is only Jim Collins and Jerry Porras's best-selling *Built to Last* (1994), which concentrates on long-lasting corporations. While their work is on U.S. companies,[3] there is no comparable research on European companies, some of which happen to be older than their American cousins due to the different timing of the arrival of industrialization on different continents. European companies therefore remain generally (or relatively) unexplored, and a detailed analysis of them is bound to add to our understanding of how corporations may develop over time.

I am not sure if it was Arie's intention, but he managed to plant the seed for this book. Although I started to work for a large strategy consultancy in Germany shortly after our get-together in Guildford, the questions continued to haunt me. In the summer of 2003 I finally decided that the subject deserved more than a little thought. I returned to the University of Innsbruck to join the strategy department and set up a team to explore long-term success in Europe. Some of the world's leading experts on the subject, such as Arie, Jerry Porras, and the distinguished (now deceased) historian Alfred D. Chandler, agreed to advise us. With their help we were ready to attack three main questions:

How is it possible for some companies to succeed for more than 100 years?

What distinguishes these companies from others that fall by the wayside?

What can we learn from the experiences of these long-lived companies?

Corporate Landscape in Europe

Before the team felt justified in leaping into the specifics of the project, we wanted to gain an overview of the genealogy of European corporations. How old is the average corporation in Europe? Is there a relationship between success and age? The apparent simplicity of these two questions is misleading. First of all, it is not all that easy to determine exactly what constitutes a company. Some large corporations actually consist of scores, even hundreds, of small companies. In each case where one firm owns a controlling interest in a second firm, we considered it to be one company. There are also companies where a family or an entrepreneur owns a controlling interest in other companies, and therefore what appear to be separate and independent organizations in reality should be considered as one unit. Unfortunately, the structure of the publicly accessible data[4] makes the consolidation of the family-owned firms impossible.

A second issue concerning publicly available data is related to the registration of corporations. Rules in different European countries vary, but in general small corporations run by an individual are not required to sign up in the public registry. This creates a distortion in the data set, as smaller companies are missing.

A third issue has to do with mergers and acquisitions. Following a merger, companies sometimes register as a new corporation. For example, DaimlerChrysler appeared as a new firm after the merger in 1999, although Gottlieb Daimler started with the production of automobiles in the late 19th century.

Despite these concerns, it is possible to draw a relatively robust picture of the age of European corporations today. We used the Amadeus database, a platform that aggregates data from local companies, compiling records from public registrars.[5] In 2005 the database listed more than 7 million companies based in Western Europe.[6] Of the total, 2.4 million companies were classified as independent corporations in which no shareholder accounted for more than 25 percent of direct or total ownership.[7] In such a large sample the effect of a family's controlling apparently independent organizations and the new registration of some companies following a merger bears limited statistical significance. The same is true for

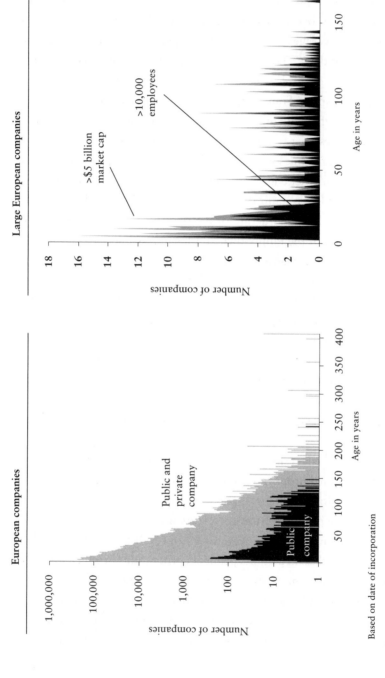

FIGURE 1.1. Age of Corporations

SOURCE: Data from Amadeus database.

the sample of 3,139 publicly traded companies. For the 238 companies with more than 10,000 employees and the 154 companies with a market capitalization of more than $5 billion, we manually checked the data and made corrections where appropriate. The only distortion of the data set that might be of significance is the fact that smaller companies are not always required to register publicly and therefore no records are available for those companies. Since a number of scholars have shown that on average smaller companies also tend to be younger,[8] inclusion of these companies would most likely decrease the average age of European corporations.

The average age of companies in Europe is 12.3 years,[9] though this figure may be slightly lower if smaller companies are included. Publicly traded companies fare a little better, as they have weathered the first storms and reached a certain size that provides them with a safety margin against catastrophes. They are 28 years old on average. Large corporations with more than 10,000 employees or a $5 billion market capitalization are 48 years old on average. This makes them almost twice as old as other publicly traded companies.

For starters, these findings are hardly surprising, as no firm begins life as a giant. This is another way of saying that it takes time to grow, and therefore older companies tend to be large. Economic history in fact suggests that markets and industrial sectors become concentrated at least to a certain degree over time, dominated by a small number of major corporations.[10]

More recent studies added another perspective by explaining that mortality rate decreases as size increases[11] and therefore large companies are more likely to survive. In times of poor performance, large firms are able to retrench by reducing the size of their operations. Large companies also have the means to build counter-cyclical units, so that when some are struggling others are booming. In Europe the imminent threat of a hostile takeover, particularly from abroad, also decreases with size. In 2006, when Mittal Steel, a company traded on the London Stock Exchange and owned by an Indian entrepreneur, sought to take over Arcelor, a Luxembourg, French, and Spanish company, it stirred up heated controversy over foreign ownership of "national champions."

Mittal Steel eventually prevailed, as takeovers have become simpler (or more straightforward) due to new European Union (EU) competition policies. Still, there are countervailing examples. In 2006, Germany's EON tried to buy Spain's Endesa, but the forces of national independence eventually prevailed when EON pulled out of the bidding war in early 2007. Also, on a national level the takeover of large corporations is tricky. In the 1970s Standard Chartered, for example, became a takeover target, but the regulator made it clear that it would not grant approval. In Germany large cross-shareholding of big corporations created the often-referred-to "Deutschland AG," which is only slowly starting to falter as efficiency gains the upper hand. Small organizations do not enjoy the same protection by the state and have less room for maneuvering. Once their fortunes decline, they may not be able to cut down their operations or they may not have the financial strength to weather the storm.

Still, even the comparatively long average life span of large corporations is not especially remarkable. Using the analogy that Arie de Geus proposes in *The Living Company*, we are able to understand how desperate the situation is. Throughout the evolution of the human race, average life expectancy has increased. While the average life expectancy in the Stone Age was around twenty years, modern humans live well into their seventies (78–80 years).[12] According to *Guinness World Records*, the oldest human being, a French lady named Jeanne Louise Calment, lived to be 122 years old before passing away at a nursing home in Arles in 1997.[13] Assuming that 122 years is our maximum life expectancy, we enjoy around two-thirds of our potential today. In the Stone Age—when living conditions obviously were considerably worse—people were able to reach only 17 percent of this potential.[14]

For corporations, the maximum life expectancy is well above the human potential. The world's oldest family business, Kongo Gumi, started to build and restore temples in 578 in Japan.[15] Europe's oldest business is a winery in France, Goulaine, which set up shop around the year 1000.[16] The oldest corporation run in a more sophisticated way, comparable to large corporations today, is Stora Kopparberg,[17] a Swedish mine that was granted a charter from King Magnus II of Sweden in 1347. Older records allow us to date its first copper mining activities back to 1288. Today it is a pulp and paper corporation and recently teamed up with the Finnish Enso Oyj to form StoraEnso.

Kongo Gumi, Goulaine, and Stora Kopparberg are very rare creatures. For several reasons, a more realistic potential life expectancy for corporations is somewhere between 200 and 300 years. First of all, international trade and industrialization started to gain momentum in the 18th century. Modern production methods started in Great Britain and spread to continental Europe and North America. Second, most of the older organizations were not able to function in the new age of capitalism, and third, new legislation such as the Royal Charters provided a new legal framework for corporations to flourish. A number of surviving companies from the early days of capitalism formed exclusive clubs. Membership in the British Tercentenarians Club, for example, is open only to firms that have been trading continuously for at least 300 years while also retaining links to the founding family. The club, founded in 1970, currently has 11 members.

A similar club in France, Les Hénokiens, has 40 members that boast at least 200 years of history.

If 300 years is used as the potential life expectancy of a firm, the average European corporation reaches an embarrassing 4 percent of its potential, while large corporations reach 16 percent. In terms of potential longevity, companies therefore remain in the Stone Age. Even more worrisome is the fact that there is no sign of improvement. More than 10 years ago de Geus and his team[18] calculated an average life expectancy of

TABLE 1.1. British Tercentenarians Club

Company	Industry	Country	Founded
John Brooke & Sons Holdings, Ltd.	Woolens	UK	1541
Whitechapel Bell Foundry, Ltd.	Bell foundry	UK	1570
R. Durtnell & Sons, Ltd.	Construction	UK	1591
Peter Freebody & Co.	Boat restoration	UK	1642
C. Hoare & Co.	Banking	UK	1672
James Lock & Co.	Hatmaker	UK	1676
Toye, Kenning & Spencer	Weavers	UK	1685
Shepherd Neame, Ltd.	Brewery	UK	1698
Berry Bros & Rudd	Wine merchants	UK	1699
Folkes Holdings, Ltd.	Real estate, engineering	UK	1699
Fortnum & Mason plc	Retail	UK	1707

SOURCE: Data from Tercentenarians Club.

TABLE I.2. French Les Hénokiens Club

Company	Industry	Country	Founded
Hoshi	Innkeeping	Japan	718
Barovier & Toso	Glassmaking	Italy	1295
Jean Roze	Textiles	France	1470
Baronnie de Coussergues	Wine	France	1495
Fabbrica d'Armi Pietro Beretta S.p.A.	Firearms	Italy	1526
Mellerio dits Meller	Jewelry	France	1613
Augustea S.p.A.	Shipping	Italy	1629
Van Eeghen	Shipping	Netherlands	1632
Toraya	Confectioneries	Japan	1635
Gekkeikan	Sake	Japan	1637
Hugel et Fils	Wine	France	1639
Friedrich Schwarze	Distillery	Germany	1664
Okaya	Trading	Japan	1669
Viellard Migeon & Cie	Iron making	France	1679
Maison Gradis	Wine	France	1685
Cartiera Mantovana Corp.	Paper	Italy	1690
Delamare et Cie	Packaging material	France	1690
De Kuyper	Liqueurs	Netherlands	1695
Akafuku	Shopping center	Japan	1707
Amarelli	Licorice	Italy	1731
Fraterri Piacenca Corp.	Woolens	Italy	1733
William Clark & Sons	Linen	Ireland	1739
J. D. Neuhaus Hebezeuge	Hoist manufacturer	Germany	1745
Fonderia Daciano Colbachini & Figli	Bell maker	Italy	1745
Monzino1750	Musical instruments	Italy	1750
Lanificio Conte S.p.A.	Woolens	Italy	1757
Möller Group	Metal products	Germany	1762
Editions Henry Lemoine	Music publishing	France	1772
Giobatta & Piero Garbellotto S.p.A.	Cooperage	Italy	1775
Ditta Bortolo Nardini	Distillery	Italy	1779
Confetti Mario Pelino	Candy	Italy	1783
Banque J.P. Hottinguer & Cie	Banking	France	1786
Revol Porcelaine	Craft pottery	France	1789
Falck S.p.A.	Steel, electricity	Italy	1792
Louis Latour	Wine	France	1797
Industria Filati Tessuti Crespi	Cotton	Italy	1797
Lombard Odier Darier Hentsch & Cie	Banking	Switzerland	1796
D'Ieteren	Car distribution	Belgium	1805
Pictet & Cie	Banking	Switzerland	1805
Thiercelin	Spices	France	1809

SOURCE: Data from The Henokiens, http://www.henokiens.com/index_gb.php.

12.5 years for European and Japanese corporations. While mortality rates have continuously declined in the course of human evolution, there is no indication of similar improvements for corporations in the past decade. Around 10 percent of all companies disappear each year.[19]

If one subscribes to a Schumpeterian logic of creative destruction,[20] it may seem that this is the natural course of business life, as new entrants arrive and incumbents disappear. From the perspective of theory the pattern seems plausible, although it comes with costs. In some cases, such as Lehman Brothers, Enron, Worldcom, and Tyco, shareholders lose substantial investments. This has wider implications if life savings and pensions evaporate and the drama of the hour obliges public officials to step in while at the same time forgoing tax revenue previously provided by the company and its employees. In other cases, when companies are taken over, the situation may be quite different. Studies show that shareholders of the takeover target in many cases receive a premium, while shareholders of the bidding company usually have to book losses.[21] The synergies that the merger is supposed to generate are hard to realize. Different corporate cultures turn integration into a substantial issue, and all too often the share price eventually falls.

Meanwhile, for employees the situation is generally bleaker. Theory tells us that finding a new assignment should present little challenge as long as new jobs are being created elsewhere. In practice, however, finding work often involves dislocation and the uprooting of lives. Families may break up when economic needs force one parent to move while the second one stays behind to avoid a change of schools for the children. Arrangements that seem unavoidable at the beginning have the potential to cause irreversible harm to individuals and families. Entire communities face declining prospects and difficult transitions.

An additional consequence of the destruction of a corporation is the loss of tacit knowledge and company-specific capabilities that may not be transferred to new settings. Negative effects are certainly less drastic when companies disappear from the statistics by being taken over. Staff might be able to carry on in their jobs with limited disruption. To deliver on promised cost savings, however, management often resorts to layoffs—in which case employees once again find themselves on the receiving end.

For a national economy as a whole, the negative effects of disappearing corporations might also be more pronounced than expected. One of the

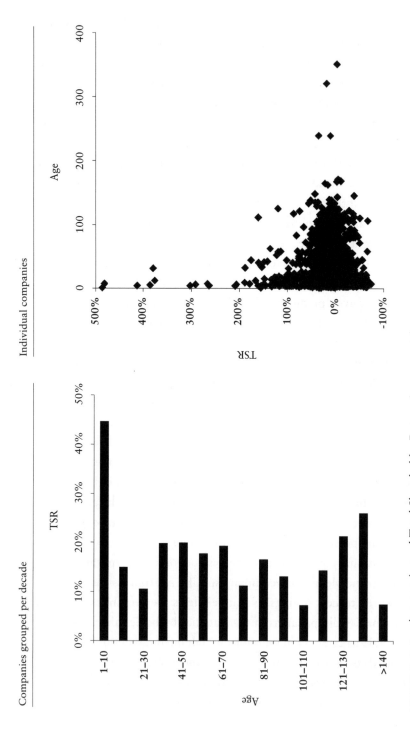

Companies grouped per decade

TSR

Individual companies

FIGURE 1.2. Average Annual Total Shareholder Return (2002–2004)
SOURCE: Data from Thomson Worldscope and Amadeus database.

relevant questions revolves around location. If a corporation ceases to exist, it is unlikely that new jobs will be created in the same region. Even in the case of a takeover, a location move sometimes falters. For a large corporation this situation can also cause great damage to suppliers. Their alignment to the needs of their former customers—in terms of location, products, and processes—makes the acquisition of new customers a challenging task. In fact, many suppliers also pull up roots when their major customers move.

Despite all the negative effects of premature corporate death, there would still be some sense in this painful reality if new companies were more efficient, if they could guarantee higher returns for their shareholders. Unfortunately, a century of economic research has not been able to come up with a conclusive answer to this question. While some economists support Schumpeter, others argue that companies build up capabilities worth their preservation. An analysis of a sample of 3,207 companies in Europe[22] shows that on average, younger firms display higher performance (measured by total shareholder return, or TSR). This, however, is gained at the price of higher volatility, and thus higher risk for investors. The median performance tends to be better for older firms. Older companies that have proved themselves in the past and possess both the capital and the experience to avoid major mistakes are a safer bet, so to speak, but they offer less hope of major gain.

The European business landscape poses an interesting challenge. The passing of corporations causes negative effects for all stakeholders. While a performance analysis supports the argument that some young corporations have a higher upside potential, it also shows the risks attached to them. Likewise, there is no evidence that older firms secure superior return for their shareholders. Nonetheless, the question remains of whether it is possible to have your cake and eat it too. What distinguishes the companies that manage to survive and outperform the market from their peers?

Clearly stakeholders benefit if companies grow steadily and successfully. To avoid the social costs of disruption, companies today can learn from the experience of those corporations that managed to survive for long periods of time. An exploration of how they battled on through difficulties and managed to adjust to a constantly changing environment identifies some of the lessons learned and may help more companies to endure.

Sample Selection

In a carefully designed selection process (see Appendix B), we created a sample of very large European corporations that meet both survival and performance criteria. Although our objective was similar to that of *Built to Last*, we took a slightly different approach. Collins and Porras selected their sample on the basis of a survey of 700 CEOs in America. They asked the executives to name up to five companies that they perceived as "highly visionary" and then focused on the 18 corporations that the executives named most often. Although such a list includes reputable companies displaying strong performance over time, a bias toward more recent performance is inevitable. A similar list for Europe—based on *Fortune* magazine's Global Most Admired Companies 2006[23]—for example, ranks BP ahead of Shell despite the better long-term performance of the latter, does not include

TABLE 1.3. Europe's Most Admired Companies in 2006

Rank	Company	Industry
1	Tesco	Retail
2	BP	Oil
3	Nestlé	Food
4	Safeway	Retail
5	Nokia	Network communications
6	BASF	Chemicals
7	Siemens	Electronics/power generation and engineering
8	L'Oréal	Personal care
9	Shell	Oil
10	Areva	Energy
11	BMW	Automobiles
12	Novartis	Pharmaceuticals
13	J. Sainsbury	Retail
14	Ericsson	Network communications
15	HSBC	Banking
16	Carrefour	Retail
17	Total	Oil
18	Edison	Energy
19	Norsk Hydro	Metals/oil
20	Royal Philips Electronics	Electronics

SOURCE: Data from *Fortune* magazine, http://money.cnn.com/magazines/fortune/globalmostadmired/full_list/.

some strong performers such as Glaxo, but does include Royal Philips Electronics and a number of retailers that boast relatively low TSR over time.

Rather than asking other people which companies they deemed to be successful over time, therefore, we decided to use a more objective approach, basing our selection on two easily controllable variables:

Survival: They have survived for 100 years or longer

Companies that have survived for a minimum of 100 years in Europe proved themselves in the early industrial age, colonial times, two world wars, the Great Depression, the postwar boom, the decline of the 1970s, and more recently, globalization. They have clearly demonstrated that they are able to operate under very different circumstances and prosper despite all challenges.

Performance: They have outperformed the major markets (Dow Jones, DAX, FTSE) by a factor of 15 or more over a period of 50 years (this translates into an annual performance advantage of 5.57 percent[24]), and they are among the top three performers in both their country and their industry.

We faced a potentially large set of performance metrics. In the end we decided to use TSR, a measurement that allows comparison across countries and time. Collecting the data we needed to make this estimation was trickier than we had expected. Centralized financial databases for British companies go back only to 1964; for continental European companies, they extend only to 1972. By visiting libraries, stock exchanges, and corporate archives, we were able to find old reports and newspapers containing most of the information we sought. Finland turned out to be particularly tough. It was only when Seppo Ikäheimo from the Helsinki School of Economics kindly pointed us toward Kim Lindström, an elderly investor who is often referred to as Finland's Warren Buffett, that we were able to obtain the necessary numbers.

Through our selection process, we were able to identify nine corporations that met our criteria. Our intention was not simply to find out what these companies had in common. As Jerry Porras advised us, such a correlation exercise would be of little value, since any other company that did not display outstanding performance could also display the same characteristics.

Perhaps that would not happen, but it would be impossible to tell without a control group. The only way we could make a valuable statement was by selecting a comparison company for each of our chosen top performers. One way to compose such a group of comparison companies would be to select complete failures. But then again, what would our findings be worth? The characteristics that we would identify based on a comparison of great companies and complete failures would probably be obvious banalities. However, companies that had been strong corporations at least throughout the greater part of their history would provide us with an opportunity to identify those areas that distinguish good companies from great ones.

As we trod this path, our analysis showed that the comparison companies occasionally fared better than our selected companies during certain limited periods. There were certainly times when we could learn from them as well. For example, BP (a comparison company) was an exemplary energy producer during the 1990s and early 2000s under the leadership of John Browne. In many respects during these years BP was more successful than our selected top company, Shell. Yet BP encountered a rough stretch in the middle of the 2000s, Browne departed under a cloud, and it remains to be seen whether the company can turn around under his successor, Tony Hayward. BP had great times before under an outstanding leader but failed to sustain success. While early signs were promising, the current struggle with America's largest environmental crisis caused by an oil spill in the Gulf of Mexico introduces major concerns. In the long run, Shell has clearly outperformed BP. The difficult times that Shell has passed through seem less severe, and it has proved able to work through troubles faster and with lasting positive results.

In short, the comparison companies also have excellent records. Indeed, they should be considered elite performers, too. A useful way to describe the champions and the comparison companies is to say that they are gold and silver medalists.

It is also interesting to note that different companies would have made it onto the list, had we chosen different time periods. Particularly striking is the decline of Daimler in the past decade. An exemplary corporation for most of its long history, the company was badly damaged by the poor decisions and leadership of two consecutive CEOs.

Investment in both the top companies and the comparison companies guaranteed superior returns, well above those of the general market (Dow Jones, DAX, FTSE). Assume that an investor has 3 currency units in 1953 and invests 1 currency unit each in our selected top companies, the comparison companies, and the general market. Each time one of the three portfolios returns money to the investor—for example through a dividend—that money is reinvested. Fifty-five years later our investor takes out his initial investment. The investment made in our gold medalists is now worth 5,504 currency units, 115 times what the general market generated. The investment made in the silver medalists is worth 780 currency units, 16 times the general market return. And the general market is worth 48 currency units, well below our chosen study sample.

After constructing the composition of our study sample, we embarked in 2004 upon the lengthy journey of exploring what distinguished our top companies from the comparison group. In a first step we read the corporate histories for each company (in the case of HSBC, for example, this encompassed four impressive volumes totaling 3,114 pages) to gain a good understanding of the development of our study sample. We then created nine categories covering everything from markets to technology (see Appendix B). In our further research, the categorization of thousands of pages of documents ensured that we did not miss any crucial developments. We tried

TABLE 1.4. Gold and Silver Medalists

Gold Medalists	Silver Medalists	Industry	Country
Allianz	Aachener und Münchener	Insurance	Germany
Glaxo[1]	Wellcome	Pharmaceuticals	UK
HSBC	Standard Chartered	Banking	UK
Lafarge	Ciments Français	Building materials	France
Legal & General	Prudential	Insurance	UK
Munich Re	Cologne Re	Reinsurance	Germany
Nokia	Ericsson	Mobiles and networks	Finland
Shell	BP	Energy	Netherlands
Siemens	AEG	Electronics, power generation, and engineering	Germany

[1] Today GlaxoSmithKline

TABLE 1.5. Best-Performing Companies after 10, 20, 30, 40, and 50 Years

After 10 years	Investment performance of 1 currency unit
Lafarge	66
DaimlerChrysler	45
Royal & Sun Alliance	32
Michelin	20
Munich Re	19
Allianz	19
KarstadtQuelle	14
Rwe	9
Nokia	9

After 20 years	Investment performance of 1 currency unit
Lafarge	88
DaimlerChrysler	77
Royal & Sun Alliance	66
Banco Bilbao Vizcaya Argentaria	65
Michelin	61
Nokia	37
Ericsson	23
HSBC	22
Legal & General	22

After 30 years	Investment performance of 1 currency unit
Royal & Sun Alliance	499
DaimlerChrysler	487
Lafarge	321
Legal & General	145
Shell	106
Glaxo	86
Ericsson	80
HSBC	80
Allianz	80

After 40 years	Investment performance of 1 currency unit
Royal & Sun Alliance	3,399
Lafarge	3,335
HSBC	1,388
DaimlerChrysler	1,035
Glaxo	927
Shell	713
Legal & General	696
Prudential	533
Allianz	508

TABLE 1.5. *(continued)*

After 50 years	Investment performance of 1 currency unit
Nokia	8,269
HSBC	5,110
Lafarge	5,048
Glaxo	2,326
Legal & General	2,251
Shell	1,808
Allianz	453
Siemens	417
Munich Re	315

Cumulative stock returns of 1 unit of currency invested 1953–2008

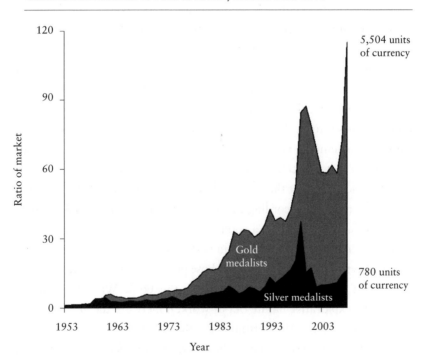

FIGURE 1.3. Performance of Gold and Silver Medalists

SOURCE: Data from Thomson Datastream, European stock exchanges, corporate archives, Hoppenstedt Aktienführer, Kim Lindström (private investor).

to collect as much material on the companies as possible. To meet this goal we read articles in scientific and managerial journals, business magazines, and newspapers. We visited archives, and over the years we talked to hundreds of analysts and scholars with expertise in the companies we studied. More formal interviews were conducted with 19 active and retired CEOs and chairmen of our study sample. In addition, we interviewed 15 board members and senior executives, and 10 experts who had knowledge in areas where we developed a greater interest, such as transformation periods.

Despite the great amount of data that we used, the reader needs to be aware of the explorative nature of our study. We were trying to develop propositions based on the history of successful companies; we were not trying to test hypotheses. This is an important distinction to make. The latter requires a rather different approach, which does not allow the prior selection of strong performers and focuses on more narrow questions. Nonetheless, even in an explorative study we need to be aware of the dangers of mixing up cause and effect. For example, when we interview a manager in a successful company and he or she stresses the importance of culture, it would be rather hasty to conclude that a strong culture is a success factor. It might be the case that a strong culture emerged as a result of the performance or that the culture is not quite as strong and important as the manager imagines it to be. In other words, data that is derived retrospectively with this outstanding performance in mind has a bias. Some of our data, particularly that collected from interviews, certainly falls into this category. To avoid such a bias we therefore collected data from annual reports (which have to be reported according to specific standards) and used descriptive, fact-based accounts such as a company's history written by respected historians; then we compared this data with sources that were likely to result in retrospective sense making. Only those propositions that were confirmed in the light of such data were included in this book. While this does not change the explorative nature of our work, it increases the likelihood that our ideas are robust. The bottom line is that we present interesting stories from the histories of some outstanding corporations and offer an interpretation of these events. Even if you do not agree with our interpretation, the events we describe will give you plenty of food for thought.

Results

Let me start with a comment on the companies that we studied. Despite the superior performance of the companies we selected, it is important to note that our intention was not to claim that these were the greatest European corporations in history. We simply noticed that they have an impressive track record. Likewise we were not in the business of forecasting and did not wish to make any predictions about how these companies will fare in the future, though there is no reason to believe that they will not be around in our great-grandchildren's time. Our intention was to learn from their history. Presuming that they continue to apply the characteristics that they have displayed in the past, the chances are high that they will also continue to put a smile on the faces of investors. These are the lessons we learned:

WHAT—A FRAMEWORK FOR
ENDURING SUCCESS (CHAPTER 2)

When the Vikings settled in Greenland around 980 A.D., they tried to live in the same manner they had in Iceland. Never quite suitable, this approach turned out to fail entirely when the climate cooled in the 14th century. Not a single Viking survived in Greenland. Companies face the same kind of challenge. They need to align strategy and organization with the business environment in which they operate, but the environment changes constantly.

In some cases the shift in the environment can be gradual, extending over a long period of time. Globalization is such a phenomenon. It requires a continuous renewal of the business model on which a firm relies. On some occasions, though, more fundamental changes are necessary. For example, in 1984 AT&T had to embark on major changes following the settlement of an antitrust suit brought against it by the U.S. government. The old monopoly ended and AT&T had to prepare for serious competition. While the value of the framework for enduring success is easy to see, it is less obvious how companies can continuously match their resources and capabilities with environmental opportunities and challenges. The next section will explain this in detail.

HOW — STRATEGIES TO IMPLEMENT
THE FRAMEWORK (CHAPTER 3)

This core section of the book provides proven strategies to implement the framework for enduring success. Ensuring the alignment of the three elements of the framework encompasses a wide range of tasks, and only the most skilled executive teams are able to guide the companies entrusted to their care in such a way that they manage to perform every one of them. They have to generate resources, find the right ingredients, and make adjustments in a suitable way. We identified five strategic choices or approaches that allowed our gold medalists to achieve this: (1) exploit before you explore, (2) be conservative in and beyond your finances, (3) remember and share both mistakes and triumphs, (4) diversify into related businesses, and (5) change in culturally sensitive ways.

Exploit Before You Explore (Chapter 3)   Companies need to explore new ideas to prepare for the future. At the same time they need to exploit existing business to generate income. Exploration and exploitation require different processes, structures, and strategies. Some companies are better at the former, others at the latter. To a certain extent the companies that we found to be most successful over time manage to do both things at once. But—and this is a very important but—exploitation clearly takes first position. If companies are less successful at exploring for new business, they buy other organizations that perform better in this respect. Outstanding explorers, on the other hand, will eventually fail if they do not find a way to exploit their knowledge.

Be Conservative in and beyond Your Finances (Chapter 3)   Most of us act fairly conservatively when it comes to our personal life. We simply know that it is necessary to avoid putting all our eggs in one basket. This is particularly obvious in our finances. We save money to prepare for major expenditures such as home, health care, college, retirement, or the occasional lean time. Likewise, we want to be able to make a significant purchase if an unexpected opportunity arises. For companies the story is exactly the same. Those who fail to build up reserves are hit hardest in times of recession. Opportunities are often missed if lengthy discussions with banks are required in order to secure funding. Companies also run into trouble when they fail to be smart about the risks they take. A certain level of conservatism ensures that they have several suppliers for important components and can avoid political dependency.

Remember and Share both Mistakes and Triumphs (Chapter 3)   Knowledge transfer is a challenging task in large corporations. Transporting knowledge over time is even trickier. Successful corporations take a great variety of actions to internalize capabilities. They learn how to learn. They use core values and visions to provide a lasting framework. Stories of great achievements and, even more importantly, great failures are used as learning opportunities. Leaders see themselves primarily as teachers or trainers. Besides the informal paths, they also take care to create formal opportunities for learning. While this strategy is nothing spectacular today, outstanding corporations did so earlier than others.

Diversify into Related Businesses (Chapter 3)   Companies have finite strategic options. They can concentrate on one single product or technology, have a dominant business, or diversify. If they diversify, they can turn to related technologies, products, and markets or to unrelated fields. From the examples of our top companies, the right thing to do is to diversify into related areas. Concentrating on a single or dominant product can work for a while but threatens future success, while a diversification into unrelated areas is usually disastrous. A company simply lacks the ability to play different games at the same time and win. Over time, related diversification can result in dramatic change. Nokia, for example, originally started in forestry, moved into electricity to generate the energy for its sawmills, then moved into electronics and eventually network communication—a long process involving many small steps.

Change in Culturally Sensitive Ways (Chapter 3)   Finding the right balance between continuity and change is a challenging task. Most companies see their culture—an element that draws them toward continuity—as the single most important contributor to their success. In our study, we noticed that while culture and tradition function as safeguards against change for the sake of change and preserve certain aspects that are useful for a firm, the existence of a strong culture alone does not distinguish the good companies from the great ones. Culture can become a problem if it prevents a corporation from adjusting its strategy and structure to a transforming environment. A company needs a culture that embraces change. If that is the case, its success will depend on the leadership's ability to change in a way that is acceptable in the firm's culture. Only if top executives take a culturally sensitive approach will they be able to succeed in their attempts to guarantee success over time.

WHO — A COMMENTARY ON LEADERSHIP (CHAPTER 4)

The days of the larger-than-life personalities at the top of great companies are not over. They never existed. In hindsight we tend to see those leaders who were successful as charismatic superheroes. In reality only some of them were. What really distinguished the most successful leaders of outstanding corporations was their ability to listen to their organizations, act in a culturally sensitive way in times of change, facilitate learning, and acknowledge their own limitations (e.g., prepare a successor, since they wouldn't be around forever). Charismatic leaders were more difficult to control, since people followed them when they led the troops into the abyss as well as when they led them to the heights. Indeed, charismatic leaders often presented greater risks to the survival and well-being of their organizations than did their lower-profile counterparts who clearly put the interests of the institution first.

The book is structured according to the three themes: WHAT, HOW, and WHO. To show how outstanding companies were able to apply these ideas, each chapter will lay out a combination of detailed stories of a chosen company and shorter snapshots of other companies. An illustration of how great companies behaved differently from their comparison companies will highlight crucial details. At the end of the chapters on WHAT and WHO as well as at the end of each strategy introduced in the chapter on HOW, the main points will be summarized. At the end of the book, our findings will be compared to the insights provided by others who have studied the long-term development of corporations. For those readers who want to learn more about our methodology or gain an overview of the histories of our gold and silver medalists, Appendix A and Appendix B will provide additional details.

2   WHAT—A FRAMEWORK FOR ENDURING SUCCESS

In his 2004 best seller, *Collapse: How Societies Choose to Fail or Succeed*, Jared Diamond tells a compelling story about the fate of a Viking colony in Greenland.[1] A formidable and hot-blooded Viking, Erik the Red left Iceland with 25 ships around A.D. 980 to start a permanent settlement in Greenland. For the next 500 years a population of around 5,000 Vikings lived off the land; then they completely vanished. About the same time, another society, the Inuit, settled in Greenland; they still live there today. Comparing the different approaches of the two societies allows Diamond to present us with some interesting conclusions.

For almost 500 years the Vikings were able to withstand the harshness of the north. Essentially, though, they were always bound to decline in an environment that was not suited for a European pastoral society. By cutting trees, stripping turf, and overgrazing, they caused soil erosion and a slow depletion of their resources. When the climate started to cool, around 1300, and plunged into the so-called Little Ice Age in the early 1400s, the Vikings were doomed. Hay harvest declined dramatically, until animals and people starved to death. Icebergs started to block the fjords. This ended trade with Europe and the regular trips to gain timber in Labrador. The consequences were ultimately fatal. Despite these environmental changes, the Vikings could still have survived had they adapted their

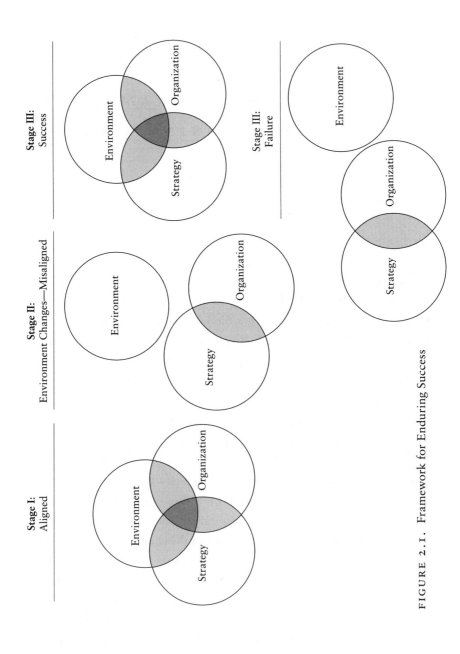

FIGURE 2.1. Framework for Enduring Success

ways to the new conditions. The Inuit's survival is proof of that. They concentrated on resources that were readily available in Greenland: fish and whale. From the Vikings, the Inuit learned useful technologies such as crafting European-style knives or saws. There is no proof, however, that the Vikings learned any new skills from the Inuit. In essence, the Viking society in Greenland collapsed because of their unwillingness to adapt to a changing environment.

The challenge for corporations is no different than the challenge a society faces. Companies must find ways of operating in harmony with their environment. They need to match their resources and capabilities with environmental opportunities. As the business environment is constantly changing, companies must modify their strategies and organizations. If they fail to do so over extended periods of time, they will face the same fate as the Vikings in Greenland: they will cease to exist. Businesses, in other words, will be successful over the long term only if they manage to keep strategy, organization, and environment in balance.[2] This process can be viewed as a series of different stages. In Stage I a company's capabilities are aligned with the environment in which it operates. At some point (Stage II), the environment will change and the company will no longer achieve a strategic fit. Whether the firm will succeed in the long run depends on its ability in Stage III to change its strategy and organization to once again achieve this alignment.

The task of finding the right balance of strategy, organization, and environment is relatively easy during periods of stability, as essentially the firm will remain in Stage I. In a dynamic environment, however, the same task may be significantly more challenging, and of course, getting the timing right is tricky. But even in a stable environment corporate leaders need to be on their toes. A stable environment can be just as challenging and dangerous as a dynamic one. While people (and leaders) get used to change and develop the necessary routines to adapt if they compete in a constantly changing environment, a stable environment can create a false sense of security. Firms may start to relax and feel too comfortable, thus opening the door for competitors. When the environment finally does change, a complacent corporation may not know what to do. Panic may take hold, leading to a deadly downward spiral that may be hard to stop. That is exactly what happened to the Vikings in Greenland. For several centuries they had no obvious competitors. Their strategy and organization seemed to work despite the difficulty of the environment. They avoided experiments with different approaches, since such innovation was likely to have deadly consequences in the harsh environment of the north. When the environment changed and the Inuit started to "compete" with the Vikings, the Vikings were locked into what seemed a perfectly reasonable conservative outlook. The Inuit, on the other hand, were ready to adapt, to learn new technologies and strategies from the Vikings. An important factor, though, was their understanding that the adaptations had to be made in a way that also fit with their own society. They never intended to copy aspects of Viking life; they took only the bits and pieces that made sense for them. For example, they chose to adopt Viking tools and techniques that enhanced their way of life rather than trying to completely implement a model that had not been made for them. The story from Greenland tells us not only that any form of organization needs to adapt to its environment but also that changes are not quite as radical as they sometimes seem in hindsight. The Vikings did not vanish overnight. They had time to adapt. They had time to experiment and slowly find the right way to balance their strategy and organization with the environment. But they did not use their time well.

The imperative to adapt holds true for companies competing in today's fast-paced environment. Change is a constant, but it has to happen in small, incremental steps in order for processes, people, and culture to follow the adjustments without being derailed. When Nokia turned itself into one of the greatest corporate success stories of the 20th century, the leadership team was also aware of the necessity to have flexible structures. As their CEO, Olli Pekka Kallasvuo, likes to point out, the organizational chart is drawn "only in pencil, because it changes all the time."[3] His former colleague Pekka Ala-Pietilä, the former head of strategy, describes the importance of a flexible structure as follows:

We say "Strategy = Structure = Implementation." That means you can have great ideas, but the only way you can get those things implemented is if you change your structure—rapidly, swiftly. But you don't make complete changes, because then recovering from those changes will take time, so that means making small changes.[4]

This flexibility and ability to adapt is not something great companies picked up only during the 1990s, when liberalization of markets brought the terms to the forefront. Munich Re, for example, started out with the intention to become a reinsurance company in Germany. The company's founder, Carl Thieme, and his team quickly realized that the market was small and immature, so they decided to fabricate their own customer. Founding the vibrant and fast-growing Allianz—a company that also features in our research—Munich Re created its own market in Germany. In addition, the firm went to Russia and generated about a third of its premiums there.[5]

On the following pages we will explore the need to keep strategy, organization, and environment in constant alignment. We will start with the contrasting stories of HSBC and Chartered Bank; next we will turn to a glimpse at the early days of the oil industry; and finally we will look at the French cement producers Lafarge and Ciments Français in the 1960s.

HSBC and Chartered Bank—Same Environment, Same Strategy, Different Organization, Different Results

In the 19th century, trade between Europe, India, and China flourished. A number of specialized British banks[6] were established to meet the financial requirements of the European merchant houses, which traded between the colonies and Europe.[7] The two institutions that emerged as the strongest were the Hongkong and Shanghai Banking Corporation[8] (which later became HSBC[9]) and the Chartered Bank of India, Australia, and China[10] (which later merged with the Standard Bank of South Africa[11] to form Standard Chartered[12]). HSBC and the Chartered Bank competed in a tough business environment regularly shaken by crisis. Trade was a risky business in the 19th century, and their main customers, the merchant houses, lacked the financial reserves to prosper in desperate times. They could not afford to tie up their funds, and those who invested in shares borrowed against them. Once a company stumbled, it usually failed to put up further collateral. Banks like HSBC and the Chartered Bank then had to jump in. Relying on their "permanent deposits" rather than on equity shares, trade bills, or gilt-edged securities, they faced considerable risk, as the 1884 downfall of the most prominent institution in the region at the time, the Oriental Bank, showed. Both HSBC and the Chartered Bank were able to prevail through this harsh business environment, but HSBC did considerably better than the Chartered Bank. Their radically different approaches toward organizational design explain the difference. HSBC's approach was aligned with its strategy and the environment, whereas Chartered Bank's was not.

Thomas Sutherland, a local superintendent of the Peninsular and Oriental Steam Navigation Company, brought the Hong Kong business leaders together to set up HSBC in their own town. In contrast, Chartered Bank, under the leadership of the talented James Wilson, who was also the founder of the *Economist*, took the more common approach of keeping top management in London. This made a certain amount of sense: the London base allowed top management to be close to the world's most important financial market at the time and therefore able to find opportunities to raise capital for its business in the Far East relatively easily. At the same time, management's distant location from the banks' core business created coordination problems and resulted in failure to take advantage of some of the most lucrative opportunities in the Far East. A good example was a discussion in the exchange business concerning the period of time allowed for payment of finance and trade bills in the mid-1860s.[13] London- and Paris-based banks like Chartered wanted to shorten the period, as they felt that the current arrangements encouraged speculation and over-trading. As far as the finance bills were concerned, such a view was hardly controversial. The story was somehow different for trade bills, which were supposed to be tailored according to the specific needs of the business. The mind-sets of the European bankers were shaped primarily by their experiences in India, which might have been better served by the proposed four-month usage period instead of the existing six-month rule. For the China trade, however, the new agreement was inappropriate, since it did not fit with the periods required to cover the movement of goods from Hong Kong and Shanghai. Bankers in the Far East were very much aware of that, but such knowledge was of limited value in London-based banks like Chartered. The China-based bankers tried to delay the implementation of the new policy and attempted to change the minds of those at headquarters in faraway Europe. The corporate leadership was not able or willing to understand the significance of such a decision in China, and eventually the local managers had to follow headquarters policies and ignore the needs of their customers.

HSBC's top management was the only leadership with firsthand experience in the region. The role of the merchant community on the board of the bank provided not only local knowledge but also willingness to take the customers' needs into consideration. In addition, the remoteness from the City provided the necessary distance to escape pressure from influential European banks. HSBC therefore decided to keep a six-month period for payment of trade and finance bills. This way the bank was able to pick up considerable new business. Customers who joined because of the trade bills arrangement stayed with the bank subsequently. As a contemporary observed, the bank was even able to purchase "six months' paper, and sell its own drafts on London at four months' sight to its competitors at a good profit. . . ."[14]

As the example illustrates, the HSBC system with its Eastern center of gravity rendered great benefits. At the same time, it was not without drawbacks. These became apparent in the late 19th and early 20th centuries. By this time the bank had grown into a major operation. While just over 50 percent of shares were on the Eastern registers, London had gained more weight. In an imperial age, the importance of London had to be taken into account. As HSBC was the official banker of the British government in Hong Kong and the leader of large loan consortia to the Chinese government, the nurturing of government contacts in the capital was of great importance. Major loans also materialized in London at the time. Was the current structure still appropriate? Should headquarters move to London? The situation was indeed quite tricky, as the Eastern business remained vital to the bank's success. Its main source of funds continued to flow from the region. Intraregional trade was only partly financed from London while other places, like Lyons, Hamburg, San Francisco, and New York, also rose in importance.

In essence, HSBC remained a regional exchange bank. But still, the changing business environment required an adaptation of the organization to keep the three elements of enduring success—environment, strategy, and organization—aligned. HSBC was well prepared for such a shift and did not require a radical overnight solution. In 1875 it had already established the London Committee, which had a limited role to "examine the Bill Schedules sent home and those sent out and to give me the best information about the names etc. and also the general working of the London office,"[15] David McLean, the manager of the Shanghai office and one of the most senior officers in the firm explained. While there were occasionally voices advocating that the London Committee should be transformed into the proper board, the bank always resisted such a temptation and remained true to its local roots, enhancing its strengths in the region. Instead, the London Committee was allowed to raise its profile in line with the growing importance of the City for the firm's business.

The genius of the arrangement that HSBC established with the London Committee was its flexibility. When London was rising in importance—e.g., during the two world wars when most of the East was in disarray—the London Committee was able to take on a greater role, whereas it automatically had less involvement in times when London was less significant—e.g., in the interwar period, when the eye was on the declining empire and business in China was of greatest importance. It operated not so much as a formal structure but primarily through the appointment of board members who had an intimate knowledge of the bank and were also highly regarded in the City.

The final step in the transformation of the board followed the retirement of legendary chief manager Sir Thomas Jackson in 1902. He was appointed as chairman of the London Committee and received a handsome salary of £1,500—six times the basic remuneration of the chairman of HSBC itself—but was no longer a staff member.[16] In other words, the board in London was set up as an independent authority with a special expertise in London affairs. Outsiders frequently mistook the chairman of the committee as the chairman of HSBC. This was a useful misunderstanding at times, as it provided the person with the air of authority required to be taken seriously in the City.

Meanwhile, at Chartered Bank, the system changed little. It remained a successful bank but lagged slightly behind HSBC. It also remained a bank that tried to run affairs from London, through directives and the inspector of branches. The distance from London proved beneficial, though. In fact

Chartered's success occurred not because of but in spite of a centralized system. For example, at the end of the 19th century Thomas Whitehead, the Hong Kong manager, had to fight the suggestion of the London directors that he should resign as a member of the colony's legislative council. While London was afraid of a conflict of interest, Whitehead explained that things looked quite different from a local perspective. His membership provided him with access to official information and advice otherwise not available to the bank.[17] On other occasions the local managers were not able to escape misguided London directives. An ethos of orthodoxy and specialization prevented them from providing lucrative loans to the Chinese government, for example. The 1899 minutes of a meeting of the directors state that loans for railway construction, river improvements, or similar development projects are "outside the province of an exchange bank and should not be entertained."[18] HSBC, on the other hand, enthusiastically signed China loans. Not only did this provide a substantial return, but it also allowed the bank to develop its own merchant banking expertise.

In the postwar period the picture remained pretty much the same. In a world where both banks had to find a way to deal with the decline of the British Empire, HSBC was much more efficient in extending its reach by acquiring other banks. Relying on its strong Hong Kong base, HSBC provided new acquisitions with financial resources and advice but essentially great local independence. Considering the diverse culture of Hang Seng Bank in Hong Kong, the Midland Bank in the United Kingdom, Household Finance Corporation and Marine Midland Bank in the United States, CBF in France, and others, HSBC's approach was the best way to ensure successful operation. By the time the rule of Hong Kong was handed over to China, HSBC was a global diversified bank ready to compete in the new business environment it faced. In recent years the bank has even proved able to make significant acquisitions in China, returning to its country of origin.

Chartered Bank, on the other hand, for most of the postwar period remained a London-based exchange bank. Most worrying for Chartered—which could not rely on a strong "home market" as HSBC did in Hong Kong—was the situation in the United Kingdom. Attempts to establish a reasonable UK domestic presence were long overdue when the bank finally showed initiative in the 1970s. This extended delay was a serious draw-back in an era of global banking. The bank lacked a British deposit base, which meant that it had to buy money on the open markets. Interest rate fluctuations therefore constantly threatened profit margins. From a tax perspective, UK earnings would have been desirable too, as British corporate tax law allowed companies to offset overseas earnings from British profits against foreign income.[19] In essence Chartered was overexposed to countries no longer under the rule of the British crown. A merger with the Standard Bank increased its geographic diversification but changed little in the sense that the majority of its business remained in the developing world. An initially successful attempt to establish business in America by purchasing Union Bancorp of California in 1977 and the United Bank of Arizona in 1985 was short-lived, since in 1987 Third World debt provisions caused large losses and forced Standard Chartered to sell its American banks. Standard Chartered's situation has remained similar since then. It is a mid-size bank that acts too conservatively for dynamic emerging markets, although it does not have the clout to take such a cautious approach, an avenue that is open to the much larger HSBC. Rumors of a takeover continue to surface, although large investments by sovereign wealth funds in recent years might be sufficient in the near future.

The stories of HSBC and the Chartered Bank are not exceptions but illustrations of a phenomenon that we observed across our sample: companies are most successful when they manage to align their strategy and organization with the business environment in which they operate. Another interesting example is Shell and BP, which had similar strategies and organizations but tried to apply them in radically different environments. In Shell's case this was a fit; in BP's, it unfortunately was not.

Shell and BP—Same Strategy, Same Organization, Different Environment, Different Results

At the end of the 19th century and early in the 20th century, Shell (then Royal Dutch Petroleum) and BP (then Anglo-Persian) tried to survive in a market dominated by an aggressive Standard Oil. Each chose to create an integrated oil company. From an organizational perspective, they also

chose a similar approach, bringing in management agents to head their respective sales and marketing divisions. The fundamental difference between
the companies was the environment in which they applied this particular
organizational solution. While Shell operated in the Far East, where its
business approach was common in the late 19th century, BP set out with
the same approach more than a decade later in Persia. Not only was BP's
approach inappropriate for the region, but it was also implemented just as
other companies, including Shell, were developing new approaches. Thus
BP was doubly wrong—wrong time, wrong region.

BP entered the industry in 1901 when the Shah of Persia granted
William Knox D'Arcy a concession to explore and exploit oil resources
throughout the country, with the exception of five northern provinces that
bordered Russia. D'Arcy sent George Reynolds, an experienced engineer,
into the region. He faced the arduous task of setting up operations in a difficult terrain under extreme weather conditions. A lack of infrastructure,
a shortage of skilled labor, and the influence of local tribes that enjoyed
great independence from the central government added to the challenge.
Year after year the young enterprise failed to discover oil in commercial
quantities. D'Arcy, who was primarily an investor and not interested in
building an organization, was unable to carry the financial burden of the
ongoing operations by himself. At the end of 1903 he had an overdraft of
£176,548 with Lloyds[20] and started to look for a partner. In 1905 Burmah
Oil Company agreed to buy in.

Three years later Reynolds and his team finally struck oil in Masjid-i-
Sulaiman in southwest Persia. Not only was this a great moment for the
investors, but it also represented the first commercial discovery of oil in
the Middle East, the beginning of much bigger things to come. In the year
following the Masjid-i-Sulaiman discovery, BP was incorporated to develop the oil field. The vast majority (97 percent) of the ordinary shares
of the corporation were held by the Burmah Oil Company. The remaining 3 percent were held by Lord Strathcona, the firm's first chairman.[21]
D'Arcy, the initial investor, remained on the board but played no significant role in future dealings.

Charles Greenway, who had already been involved in the syndicate
formed by D'Arcy in 1905, became the new managing director. In the

words of a distinguished historian of BP's early years, Greenway "did not have the prestige of a proprietor not the panache of an entrepreneur. He was no hired hand offering his labor. He was a transitional figure in the managerial evolution, resembling more the image of a professional man, from the law, accounting, or banking, but possessing the shrewdness of a successful merchant and some of the opportunism of the politician."[22] Theoretically these talents positioned him well to guide BP through its start-up years. But perhaps his background as a senior partner in a firm of Indian managing agents also led him to misjudge the requirements of his times.

Prior to his new engagement in BP, Greenway had been the managing agent in charge of the distribution of Burmah Oil products in India. Rather than recognizing the trading houses as becoming anachronisms at the time, he viewed them as the ideal solution to organize BP's operations. He engaged Lloyd, Scott, and Co. to manage the company's business in Persia and the East in general. In addition to this responsibility, they were authorized to act as merchants, bankers, traders, commercial and general agents, ship owners, carriers, and dealers in a wide range of commodities. They could set up branches, trading stations, factories, stores, depots, and docks and could start business with any third party engaged in a similar business.[23]

In outsourcing to Lloyd, Scott, and Co., Greenway failed to understand the business environment for the fledgling oil company in several important ways. In the old days of the British Empire the managing agents conducted business in a "gentlemanly" way. Confidence and collaboration rather than cutthroat competition marked their doings. This fit the pattern of trade in an era of slow communication and limited competition from outsiders. By the end of the 19th century circumstances had changed dramatically. Britain was no longer able to claim a sheer monopoly on maritime trade, as American and continental competition was becoming more active. Most trading houses failed to adjust adequately. Greenway's decision to choose a system of managing agents was particularly odd in the Persian context. The culture of the trading house reflected the values of imperial India and alienated the Persian employees. In fact, the attempt to hire Indian personnel led to serious conflict with the local tribes and forced the company to revise this decision.

The most damaging effect of Greenway's approach was the imposed schizophrenia in a company that was relatively small at the time. The agents represented an additional layer of management responsibility between those doing the work on-site in Persia and those on the board in London. The agents, moreover, were not employees and thus were free to pursue their own agenda, which may or may not have coincided with BP's interests. They differed, for example, on the question of commissions paid for their services.

The agents also lacked technical knowledge and expertise, which was of secondary importance to their own dealings but crucial to the success of the new oil company. That they were supposedly managing processes and practices they did not understand proved extremely frustrating to the operators on the ground in Persia. Reynolds, who had remained in charge of the field, had been able to make steady progress between November 1908 and June 1909. After that, however, the agents' intervention slowed down operations.

A power struggle erupted when a new agent, John Black, arrived in Persia with a different technical, administrative, and personal agenda from that of Reynolds. Although he lacked real technical knowledge, he still meddled in affairs outside his competence in a self-righteous way. He outmaneuvered Reynolds and promoted himself as potential general manager, and Reynolds eventually resigned. Black's lack of expertise almost ruined the company, as the refinery continuously failed to turn out acceptable products. By 1913 current liabilities exceeded current assets. If only a quarter of BP's creditors had asked for their money, the firm would not have been able to deliver. Despite these obvious drawbacks, the system of managing directors was not formally abandoned until 1923.

Greenway's unsuitable structure had long-term consequences for BP. His ambitious initial strategy to build an integrated oil company had to be modified because of dismal financial performance, and the corporation was forced to enter an arrangement with the government in 1913. This saved it from a potential takeover by Shell but at the cost of becoming a state-owned and inherently political institution.

At Shell, management agents also played a vital role through the early 1890s. Operating in the dispersed markets of southeast Asia, Shell followed common practice in relying on management agents to handle sales. Though this arrangement was not ideal, companies lacked the resources and knowledge to manage a direct sales force in each country. In 19th-century Asia agents were part of the business environment. At Shell—and in contrast with BP—however, they had no influence on technical aspects of the business. None of Shell's agents had a say in the exploration, development, and production of oil fields.

With the arrival of new communications technology, a new era dawned in Asia. The pace of competition increased, as did pressure to keep costs low. New organizational solutions were required if companies were to remain competitive. At Shell, a fresh approach emerged shortly before the turn of the century when the managing director, August Kessler, hired Henri Deterding, an ambitious young sub-agent of the powerful Nederlandsche Handel-Maatschappij, a Dutch banking house.

Deterding immediately showed his talent for understanding the crucial connection between strategy, organization, and business environment. At the time, trade in the East was dominated by a number of European merchants—the very same community that was playing such an important role in the rise of HSBC. The trading houses had sophisticated knowledge of the local market, understood the language and customs, and had built up networks to reach the hinterlands beyond the harbors. To close out potential competition, they relied on high barriers to entry: a complex market, close ties with local financial institutions, willingness to cooperate when new competitors arrived, keeping close ties with shipping lines entering the various ports. For commissions averaging 2.5 percent to 5 percent, they took charge of the oil firms' distribution throughout the East. Upon arrival of a cargo ship they handled the unloading, the sales, and the remitting of the oil packaged in tins or barrels. The trading houses did not, however, deal with consumers directly—an assignment handled by local Chinese merchants. These arrangements could trigger conflicts of interest. The European merchants were often able to increase profits upon the consignments beyond the commission they received. In Bangkok and Rangoon, for example, oil had to be transported upriver by steamers. Depending on the state of the river, prices and availability could vary dramatically. To take full advantage of this would have required complicated arrangements with a number of buyers. From the perspective of the agents, however, an arrangement with one single buyer was more convenient.

Deterding understood that the business environment was changing and the services of the agents might no longer be needed. His strategy was to build up the company's own distribution network. Having a sales force of its own, Shell would no longer have to worry about potential conflicts of interest. In one of his first letters as head of commercial activities in the East, he wrote: "The first step I wish to take is to replace the Straits agents by employees of our own. I think I am not too optimistic in saying that this measure will save $2000 a month—not to mention that I also have in mind bigger and better regulated sales."[24]

While this idea does not seem revolutionary today, it was almost unthinkable for general merchants importing oil at the time. Under the proposed arrangements, Shell would cut out the agents and sell directly to the Chinese merchants, who would then continue to sell to consumers. Considering that about 10 percent of the proceeds were spent on commissions at the time, Deterding's idea had great potential. The implementation took several years and was completed only after Deterding became managing director in 1900. Given the logistical complexities, the whole endeavor proceeded quite rapidly, particularly when compared with BP's struggles. Deterding's grasp of the right response to new circumstances is impressive.

Lafarge and Ciments Français: Same Organization, Same Environment, Different Strategy, Different Results

Operating in foreign markets is essential to the long-term health of most companies. Both the decision of when to go international and the specific approach are strategically important. Comparing the internationalization of the two French cement producers, Lafarge and Ciments Français, presents an interesting example of how corporations can be successful when their internationalization strategy fits the environment. The story also suggests that some adaptations have to unfold in small steps over long periods of time.

Lafarge already possessed some international experience when it established subsidiaries in northern Africa at the beginning of the 20th century. Generating capital at the stock exchange, it increased foreign operations after World War II, particularly after the first oil crisis in 1973–1974. Since then, Lafarge has kept up efforts, making many acquisitions in the 1990s and at the beginning of the 21st century. Ciments Français, on the other hand, did not attempt to internationalize before the 1970s despite being a larger company than Lafarge at times. Its strategy focused on being the strongest competitor in France. This approach backfired during the oil crisis, however, and Ciments Français fell prey to a takeover by Paribas, a French bank, which acquired a controlling stake. Ironically, Paribas eventually sold out to Italcementi, making Ciments Français a victim of another firm's internationalization strategy.

Lafarge originally was a family-controlled cement producer in the south of France.[25] In the 18th and early 19th centuries, business relied heavily on regional contacts, and the Lafarge family was well positioned to succeed. As the environment changed, Lafarge had to adapt. A large contract to deliver 110,000 tonnes of lime for the construction of the Suez Canal in 1864 marked the beginning of a new era. Lafarge had to become more international and eventually turn from a family-run company into a publicly traded firm. The change was incremental and took several steps. Key executives came from outside the family, while the business morphed into a partnership and then into a public corporation. "Société anonyme des Chaux et Ciments de Lafarge et du Teil" was first listed at the Paris stock exchange in 1923. The final steps were taken under the leadership of Jean de Waubert, who moved the headquarters to Paris and established a functional structure in the 1930s. In a recessionary business environment he was able to make important acquisitions and establish Lafarge as the biggest cement producer in France.

After the Second World War, Lafarge's evolution tracked closely with France's development as a whole. The rebuilding of a war-ravaged country was followed by a period of internationalization and finally diversification into related industries, like aggregates and ready-mix concrete. Lafarge supported these strategic changes by evolving first into a more centralized, functional organization and then into separate divisions reflecting both geography and lines of business. Meanwhile, a French family-centered culture evolved into a more dynamic international one that rewarded values such as hard work and collaboration.

Lafarge's internationalization proved considerably more successful than that of Ciments Français because it started much earlier and had the time to adapt to different local environments. Lafarge first moved into countries with close ties to France. This step-by-step process allowed it to grow without overstretching its budgets. Of particular importance was the Lafarge family's willingness to reduce its own influence by continuously selling parts of the firm at the stock exchange and thereby generating the capital needed to finance continuing expansion. Other than working on specific contracts like the Suez Canal, Lafarge had limited presence abroad before the end of World War II. During the rebuilding of the nation after the war, Lafarge's leaders understood that the company faced a great opportunity to expand abroad. French influence around the world was still significant, while growth at home generated handsome returns. At the same time, it was unlikely that demand for cement would stay at such a high level after the rebuilding. Lafarge established subsidiaries in North Africa and Canada before the end of the 1950s. This paid off when the oil crisis hit Europe in the 1970s. Lafarge had activities in 15 countries by then and could offset some of the slowdown in France with healthy operations elsewhere. As the developing world was set to be one of the most promising markets of the future, internationalization was further enhanced by merger with Coppée in 1980, market entry in China in 1994, and the takeovers of Redland and Blue Circle in 1997 and 2001, respectively. Each of the new subsidiaries was permitted to operate independently, and a localized structure was established that works well in an industry where local market preferences differ and high transport costs make location a major factor. In sum, Lafarge's history illustrates how the best response to global competition is the strategic decision to go international earlier than the competition, taking one step after the other.

Ciments Français was still essentially a domestic company before the 1970s, although it had a small presence in Morocco. The company built on its local position through a number of smaller acquisitions and finally a merger with Poliet et Chausson in 1971, which made the combined company the largest cement producer in France.[26] Unfortunately, the merger proved untimely. During the first oil crisis, demand for cement in France tumbled, and between 1974 and 1979 Ciments Français' main markets—the Paris region—contracted by 40 percent.[27]

The cement giant had failed to come up with a strategy to prepare it for a potential change in the business environment. While it was impossible to predict the oil crisis, a slowdown of the market after the rebuilding of the nation could have been expected—as Lafarge had perceived. Ciment Français could have prepared for tough times either by diversifying into new markets or into new products. Unlike Lafarge, it did neither. Only in the late 1970s, when management had been under pressure for several years, did the company begin to adjust its strategy. By then, however, it was late in the game and the company had difficulty raising funds. The equity market was down, so the company had to approach the banks for loans. For a few years Ciments Français performed quite well, expanding particularly in the Mediterranean region; in 1990 it was the world's fourth-largest cement producer. It operated through a decentralized structure similar to that of Lafarge. Headquarters of some businesses were relocated outside of France. Ultimately, however, this was not enough to withstand the need for long-term restructuring of the cement industry in the years after the oil shocks.

The merger with the cement division of Poliet et Chausson did not help either. The company now had a larger share of a declining market. But the most damaging mistake was to provide Paribas with a controlling stake in the new company. The price paid for becoming number one in France was the eventual loss of independence. In 1992 Paribas decided that its investment had reached maturity, and it sold a 40 percent stake in Ciments Français to Italcementi. Italcementi initially allowed Ciments Français to operate independently, but over time it increased its ownership stake while also integrating operations.

Lafarge followed a simple recipe for enduring success: it formulated a strategy that enabled it to generate returns in a given business environment while at the same time preparing the company for inevitable change in the business environment. Ciments Français lost its touch when it failed to internationalize in the 1950s, preferring to be a strong local player. When the environment changed, the company was ill prepared and entered into a merger that cost it its independence.

Summary: Aligning Strategy, Organization, and Environment

Companies can be successful only if they manage to align their strategy and organization with the environment they operate in. As the environment is constantly changing, this means that enduring success depends on a company's ability constantly to adapt its strategy and organization.

HSBC performed considerably better than its main competitor in Southeast Asia, Chartered Bank, due to an organizational setup that fit perfectly with the immediate business environment. It was the only British overseas bank that set up its headquarters in the region, and it gained both a better understanding of the market and a closer connection to customers. When the London market increased in importance, HSBC set up a secondary board, allowing itself to be present there as well. Chartered Bank, on the other hand, took a centralized approach and forfeited important business when products were changed in a way that did not suit the business needs of its customers in Asia.

The founding period of Shell and BP shows us that a similar strategy and organization can have very different results in different environments. Both companies relied on independent managing agents to conduct their sales operations. In Shell's case, 19th-century Southeast Asia fit that approach. In BP's case, the same approach did not work in the different circumstances of Persia. In fact, by the time BP introduced a system modeled on Shell's, Shell had already organized its own sales operations avoiding permanent conflicts of interest

The international strategies of the French cement producers Lafarge and Ciments Français affirm that companies need to find strategies that prepare them for a changing environment. In the 1970s the two firms were about the same size, but they chose radically different growth strategies. Lafarge pursued a strategy of internationalization, while Ciments Français focused on France. When the oil crisis slowed demand for cement in France, Lafarge was active in 15 international markets, while Ciments Français had only minor operations in Morocco. The former was able to offset losses. The latter could not.

In Chapter 3 I will explain some of the steps that the outstanding firms took to ensure that their strategy and organization were aligned with the environment in which they did business. This moves us from the question of WHAT they did to a consideration of HOW they did it.

3   HOW — STRATEGIES TO
IMPLEMENT THE FRAMEWORK

On November 9, 1989, Günther Schabowski, the East German minister of propaganda, returned to Berlin after his vacation. Little did he know that a routine press conference he was slated to give that evening would make him a footnote in one of the greatest events of the 20th century. Under the mounting pressure to open up the border, the East German government had passed a law that very day to lift visa restrictions for its citizens traveling to West Germany. Just before Schabowski started his news conference he was handed a note reminding him that the new legislation was to take effect the following day. Schabowski missed this detail, however. After his description of the new legislation, an Italian reporter asked him when the law was supposed to take effect. Schabowski answered, "As far as I know effective immediately, right now." Thousands of stunned East Germans had tuned in live on the state television station. Hardly able to believe their own ears, they rushed to the crossings to West Berlin, where overwhelmed border guards eventually let them through. The fall of the Berlin Wall had started!

While nearby pubs provided free beer, the powerful symbol of East German communist tyranny came tumbling down.[1] The terrifying years of the Cold War were coming to an end.

The capitalist system of the West had prevailed over the communist system of the East. But was it really a victory of ideology? Had Adam Smith dealt Karl Marx a fatal blow? Judging by the popularity of the latter, who was elected the "greatest philosopher of all times" by BBC radio listeners in 2005,[2] this can hardly be the case. Even hard-nosed businessmen will admit that the idea of sharing rewards equally among all citizens, although not appealing to them, enjoys considerable support among those who are less fortunate. The businessmen argued that a communist system was inherently flawed and unworkable. In their view, when people are not rewarded according to their contribution, it is hard to see why anyone would make an effort. Thus society will stagnate, as happened in the Soviet Union and its satellites.

In other words, communism did not fail because leaders in the East did not know *what* they wanted. Their aim to provide prosperity and distribute the gains fairly was not all that different from what Western statesmen wanted to achieve (although the interpretation of "fairly" would be much disputed). The real difference was *how* prosperity and equity would be achieved. One choice was a state-run system lacking individual rewards and resorting to repression as an alternative tool on one side of the Wall; the other was a market-based system generating phenomenal growth and prosperity on the other side. We all know which came out on top.

What is true of communism is also true of companies that fail to achieve long-term success. In most cases they know about the importance of keeping business environment, strategy, and organization aligned. Their failure is not primarily a failure of understanding *what* they need to achieve but *how* they should do so. The companies that achieve enduring success mas-

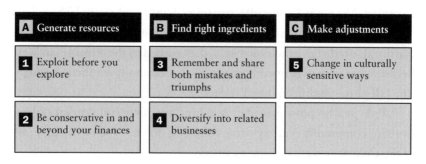

FIGURE 3.1. Strategies to Implement Framework for Enduring Success

ter the task of change and adaptation over time. They develop approaches that allow them to find the right recipes for competing today while getting ready to compete tomorrow. To gain the breathing space required to take the necessary actions—also when unexpected events unfold and threaten them—they do not forget the mundane task of making money and building up reserves despite constant temptation to push in new directions.

If companies are to succeed in keeping strategy and organization aligned with the environment in which they operate, they must excel in three areas:

A. Make money

B. Find the right ingredients

C. Manage the required change

In order to make money, companies need to go beyond exploration. In fact, some outstanding companies like Glaxo or Nokia do not stand out as great innovators. They have been able to compensate for this by being brilliant exploiters. Exploration, however, does not compensate for lack of exploitation, as we can see from Glaxo's and Nokia's respective comparison companies, Wellcome and Ericsson (originally Telefonaktiebolaget LM Ericsson), which failed to exploit their exploration successes. Besides making money, firms also need to ensure that their hard-earned assets stay with them. Taking a conservative approach in finances helps them to survive during difficult times. At the same time, conservatism spreads beyond finances. The simple rule is that firms should never put all of their eggs in one basket. BP consistently failed to acknowledge that the oil business is so risky that it is dangerous to be heavily dependent on operations in a single country. BP lost almost 70 percent of its total assets when oil fields were nationalized in Iran. Thereafter, the company focused heavily on Alaska and the North Sea, but once again found itself in trouble when these assets did not perform. In more recent years, Russia has taken a dominant role for BP. Shell, on the other hand, was able to rely on other oil fields when those in Mexico, Venezuela, or Russia were nationalized.

Besides making money, a company also needs to find the right ingredients to succeed over time. A first step to longevity is a proper system to enable the flow of knowledge and the preservation of experience. Successful companies do this through their corporate culture and powerful stories.

They also use their planning system as a learning opportunity and have training sessions in place. Above all, though, their leaders acknowledge that one of their main tasks is to learn and teach. While these mechanisms combined with internal growth go a long way, companies will eventually have to diversify if they want to succeed in a changing environment. Siemens would hardly generate the handsome returns its investors are accustomed to if it had continued to build telegraph lines as it originally did in 1848. Taking a step at a time, the company slowly evolved, spreading into related businesses and divesting itself of businesses that were not related were divested. In some cases—the consumer products business, for example—Siemens remained a joint venture partner, benefiting from the generated returns without losing valuable management time in a field in which the company had less expertise. AEG, Siemens's comparison company, was less decisive. It kept a flourishing consumer products division, unfortunately resulting in successive top managers' being unable to fully understand either consumer products or other parts of the company. A recipe for disaster!

Internal growth as well as acquisitions and divestments are necessary to continuously align a firm's strategy with a changing environment. At the same time, the organization needs to enable the implementation of new strategies. The change processes are most effective when they are performed in a culturally sensitive way. Should leaders decide to press forward without concern for traditions, structures, and processes, they will quickly learn that none of their bright ideas are able to flourish.

In the following chapters we discuss the challenge of achieving enduring greatness in more detail and describe how outstanding companies met that challenge. While it is important to know *what* to do, it is more important to know *how* to do it.

Exploit before You Explore

Corporations need to perform both in the short term and in the long term; they need to explore for new possibilities to prepare for the future, and they need to exploit the existing certainties to generate the funds to survive today.[3] They also need to search, take risks, experiment, play, be flexible, discover, and innovate. *Exploitation* points them in the direction of refinement, choice, production, efficiency, selection, execution, and implementation,[4] while *exploration* requires innovation, searching, taking risks. In an ideal world, corporations would not have to trade off exploitation and exploration. They would combine the ability to run smooth operations and effective marketing campaigns with the ability to develop fantastic new products and innovative processes with the capabilities required. In the real world, unfortunately, balancing the refinement of an existing technology and the exploration for a new one represents a constant challenge.[5] Exploring new alternatives reduces the time and resources available to improve existing skills and vice versa.[6] Nonetheless, some of our outstanding corporations are indeed able to strike an effective balance. Two broad measures provide us with a first impression of how our sample of outstanding companies does in relation to the sample of comparison companies: patents per sale and return on equity.

While the general impression from these two sets of data is that outstanding companies are better in terms of both exploration and exploitation, the picture becomes patchier once we start digging deeper. As scholars interested in innovation commonly do, we used patents per sale as a variable to measure exploration success. This choice of variable

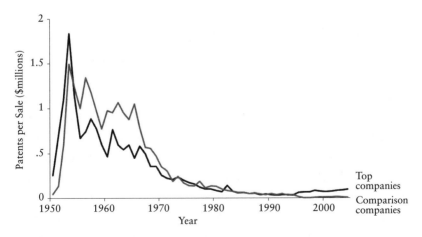

FIGURE 3.2. Top and Comparison Companies' Patents per Sale
SOURCE: Data from annual reports and European Patent Office.

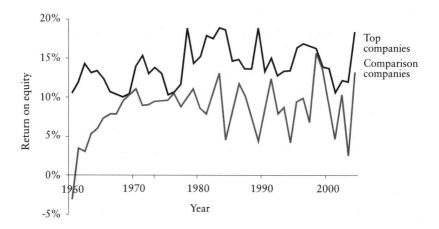

FIGURE 3.3. Top and Comparison Companies' Return on Equity
SOURCE: Data from annual reports.

limits the measurement to the five manufacturing firms in our sample and therefore presents only a partial view of the entire sample. In a way the measurement is also crude as it does not weigh the importance of an invention. Consider, for example, the case of Siemens and AEG around 1900. The data does not reflect AEG's lead in power current at that time. Siemens, as the incumbent corporation dominating the German market, initially missed the opportunity to throw itself fully into the new technology. The absence of Siemens provided AEG, led by Emil Rathenau, with an opportunity to make an impressive entry. The new market for power stations required previously unprecedented capital, which AEG was able to raise through a listing of its shares and the strong support of German banks. Siemens, however, was reluctant to offer banks more of a say in its affairs, as the founder, Werner von Siemens, wanted to keep the family in full control. Even the fact that his cousin Georg von Siemens was in charge of the Deutsche Bank did not change this situation. It took the succession of the next generation to move the company ahead. Werner von Siemens's sons were able to understand that the corporation's success depended on their ability to master the new technology. They took the necessary steps and listed the corporation to raise funds. Thus they had access to the capital they needed to gain a competitive position in high-voltage current. The later takeover of Schuckert, another big player in the new field, allowed Siemens to catch up and eventually overtake AEG once again. While Siemens was partly an innovator in the new technology, it had clearly been outmaneuvered by AEG in the early phase. Siemens's strategy and structure were not in harmony with the pace of technology change at the time. While the decision to list the corporation was a crucial move, it was clearly a reaction, as was the acquisition of Schuckert. Still, we know that Siemens has been considerably more successful in the long run. But as the story shows, exploration capability by itself certainly does not explain Siemens's dominance over time.

What is true for Siemens and AEG is true for most of the corporations we studied. Unfortunately there is no single metric that describes the balance between exploration and exploitation across many industries and decades. We therefore decided to combine different data. To measure exploration, we use patents per sale and R&D spending per sale. To measure exploitation, we use return on equity, profit per sale, and return on investment. Due to the limitations of the data, our main source of information was the historical analysis of the companies in our sample. A detailed analysis of each company reveals a picture that is slightly different and surprising from the original impression gained when looking at the companies in combination: top companies are more efficient but not necessarily more innovative than their comparison companies. They emphasize the former at the expense of the latter, though they do not neglect exploration. Bearing in mind that the comparison companies in most cases also have a track record of more than 100 years, we learn that incremental innovation is certainly important for success in business environments, but top performance can be guaranteed only by being efficient. In other words, firms are able to compensate for a lack of exploration capabilities by being more efficient exploiters, but they are not able to make up for deficiencies in exploitation capabilities through exploration.

Figure 3.4 presents an overview of the entire history of the firms we studied. The Siemens story already made it clear that the top companies do not necessarily outperform their comparison companies every year. In the long run, however, they are more efficient. More surprising is the failure of top companies to outperform competitors in terms of exploration.

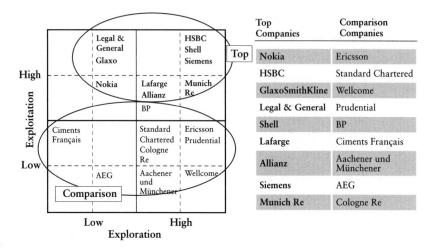

FIGURE 3.4. Exploration and Exploitation Performance of Top and Comparison Companies

As Legal & General's former CEO Sir David Prosser put it in an interview with us: "In Legal & General we took the view that we were not necessarily very good at inventing new things but we were able to profit from new things very fast."[7] Most management scholars and practitioners, on the other hand, put great emphasis on exploration. Hardly a speech goes by that a CEO does not mention ongoing efforts and investment to generate innovation. Is all of this investment necessary? Or is a new era erupting at the moment, an era in which exploration is taking the lead? Will some of these shining examples of corporate success possibly stumble as a result of their failure to invest in exploration?

The answers to the three questions are relatively simple. That corporations do not generate many breakthrough innovations does not mean that they do not invest in exploration. The top companies all do. Most of them also think that they are very innovative. And in absolute terms they often are. But so are their peers. The top companies are also more likely to produce incremental innovation rather than new breakthroughs. This is not necessarily a great problem if companies can buy exploration capabilities. But buying exploration capabilities is possible only if a company generates the funds to pay for it, which can be done successfully over time only if the company is more efficient than its competitors. This has been true in the past and will continue to be true in the future. Building tomorrow's business at the expense of today's is not a successful strategy.

BUYING EXPLORATION CAPABILITIES —
GLAXO AND WELLCOME

If the superiority of our top companies is not the result of exploration capabilities, how is it that they are so efficient? A comparison of the development of Glaxo and Wellcome provides important insights. From the point of view of R&D achievements measured in patents per sale, Wellcome beat Glaxo decisively until the 1970s and has continued to stay slightly ahead in the following decades.

Quite clearly Glaxo's triumph over Wellcome cannot be attributed to a superior ability to explore. On the contrary, Wellcome is often referred to as a bustling innovation machine. Its research focus led outsiders to refer to the firm as the "only listed University in Britain." So why is Glaxo more successful? How did it manage to develop new business and secure its own future? The answer is twofold: First, it was a master of exploiting existing assets through clever marketing. Second, it was honest enough to admit its research limitations and it used acquisitions to gain access to important innovations.

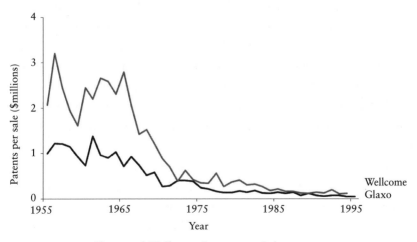

FIGURE 3.5. Glaxo and Wellcome Patents per Sale
SOURCE: Data from annual reports.

Glaxo's exploitation strength first became evident when the corporation moved into the dried milk business early in the 20th century.[8] The young company had recently started to manufacture butter and was left with skim milk as a by-product. No one was quite sure what to do with the skim milk, until Maurice Nathan—a member of the founding family—stumbled across a package of skim milk powder at Debenhams, a wholesale warehouse in New Zealand. Joseph Nathan & Co. (as Glaxo was called at the time) got in touch with James Robinson Hatmaker, an American who owned the foreign patent rights to the powdered milk process. Nathan eventually set up a corporation to exploit the patent together with Debenhams, then took control in 1905 and secured the full patent rights several years later. The original plan to get rich did not materialize quickly. When Nathan purchased the patent, he was convinced that dried milk would replace fresh milk as a more convenient product. Although the first dried milk put on the New Zealand market was readily received, it became clear that customers had purchased it out of curiosity but were not necessarily planning to buy again.

This early setback prompted Nathan to develop a new and efficient marketing campaign. Rather than trying to come up with innovative products to succeed, he decided to rely on the existing assets and put them to better use. The first important insight was that the most promising market for dried milk was the baby market. The medical press at the time aired widespread concern that the raw cow's milk sold to the public was not fit for infants, who needed healthier food. So Nathan switched his existing product to this new market. The second important insight concerned the appropriate sales channel. Rather than setting up an expensive force of sales representatives to sell the product to pharmacies, Nathan & Co. identified doctors and nurses as the appropriate "representatives" for the product. The company realized that it had to win the trust of doctors and nurses in order to reach the mothers. In order to do this, the company arranged feeding trials at the Finsbury Health Centre in London and Lewisham Infirmary to test the responses of both babies and physicians to the dried milk. The tests showed that the product was free from infectious components and contained important nutrients.

Meanwhile Alec Nathan—who had moved from New Zealand to

England to promote the product—contacted physicians who treated small children and initiated the composition of the first "Glaxo Baby Book" (Glaxo was the name the firm chose for its dried milk at the first relaunch) in 1908. (The book was later revised by Margaret Kennedy, a qualified nurse, and by 1922 more than a million copies had been printed.) Also in 1908, an entire front page of the *Daily Mail* was booked to inform the general public of the virtue of the new product. The real masterstroke of the firm was the final step of its marketing campaign, when Alec Nathan personally wrote to doctors and potential customers. As he later explained,

For five long years I depended almost entirely upon the post, and I can pretty well claim that Glaxo is the only baby food in the country that has been built on the principle of a mail order campaign. . . . Every letter delivered at the Glaxo offices received individual attention and each and every reply emphasized the vital message of service to the mother, the baby and to the trade.

The quote highlights how carefully the campaign was conducted. Each reply was followed up, and Alec Nathan ensured that even little vanities of customers were taken care of. Rather than spending on glamorous new products, he saw to it that the emphasis was put on efficiently using what the company already had. Getting the most out of dried milk forced Glaxo to pay attention to every detail. For example, pharmacists were referred to as "druggists" rather than "chemists" to accommmodate their preference. In 1913 the company spent £4,270 on a second campaign and was able to increase net profits to £3,311. By 1914 Glaxo was the established brand leader in Britain, stocking 9,000 pharmacists and 189 municipal health departments. The original direct mail campaign was still going strong, with 50,000 letters being sent out each month. Glaxo had clearly shown its mastery in exploiting a process developed by someone else.

While Glaxo's growth was a product of its ability to efficiently use a product that it did not even develop itself, Wellcome's rise came about through exploration. To what extent this was the result of the founder's biography is open to speculation. Nonetheless, the comparison between Alec Nathan, who grew up in a commercial environment and had his first job as a merchant, and Henry Wellcome,[9] who first came in contact with the medical world at the age of 13, is striking. Young Henry helped in the family pharmacy in Garden City, Minnesota. His interest in science and medicine was inspired by his uncle Dr. Jacob Wellcome and a British pharmacist named H. J. Barton. Starting work at Pool and Geisinger, a pharmaceutical company in nearby Rochester, Henry Wellcome wanted an academic qualification and studied pharmacy first at a college in Chicago and later in Philadelphia. Wellcome's partner, Silas Burroughs, had a similar biography, gaining experience in a pharmacy during his youth and returning to a pharmaceutical firm after his studies.

In 1880 Wellcome and Burroughs started to sell medicine in the form of tablets in Great Britain. At the time, pharmacies were selling medicines in the form of powders, and the new compressed medicines presented a considerable innovation already being applied in the United States. The new firm was able to exploit the American knowledge. At the same time, the company started to show great interest in exploring new ideas. In 1894 the partnership set up its famed Wellcome Physiological Research Laboratories, the first in-house research facility within a pharmaceutical company.[10]

Henry Wellcome's drive to gain a place in the history of medicine as a pioneer is best shown by his enthusiasm for expeditions and tropical medicine. He put much effort into the development of lightweight cases containing medicine that could function in different climates. The organization took great care to create a research-friendly environment. Researchers working on tropical medicines were the first to be allowed to publish. While today it is routine for companies to provide room for creativity and publishing among scientists is common practice, this practice was revolutionary at the beginning of the 20th century.

Another pioneering move was the introduction of a swimming laboratory, which was first used on the river Nile in 1907. This allowed scientists to collect and analyze components at the same place. The medical classic *Protozoology* by Dr. C. M. Wenyon[11] was based primarily on the research conducted on this boat. In terms of exploring for innovative new medicines, the conditions were perfect.

Under the inspiring leadership of Sir Henry, the firm was also commercially successful. This changed, however, when he handed over operational control to George Pearson after the consolidation of the different research and business activities in 1924. The commercial success of earlier years began to subside, while the scientific excellence remained. Scientists in the research labs did not seem to mind if their findings were used for commercial ends, but that was apparently not a primary concern. The earlier consolidation of research activities in the new Wellcome Bureau of Scientific Research, established in 1913, did not help either, since the field of tropical medicines had limited commercial potential.

After Wellcome's death in 1936, the trend continued. In his will he made it clear that research was his main interest. He ordered the entire income of the commercial activities to be used to fight disease and to support medical sciences. A trust fund was set up as the owner of the pharmaceutical company. The Wellcome Trust supported basic research and the documentation of medical history through the funding of universities, museums, and laboratories. At the same time, the board of trustees functioned as a supervisory board for Wellcome, the pharmaceutical corporation. True to its own mission, the board looked favorably on research, and the motivation to pursue groundbreaking innovation filtered down through the organization. Structures and procedures were set up to create an ideal environment for scientists, while commercial people had less power. Exploitation clearly took the backseat.

At Glaxo the story was very different. Exploitation became a part of Glaxo's DNA as exploration became part of Wellcome's. Glaxo had learned the lesson that efficient use of an existing asset provides handsome returns.

Dried milk remained an important income generator for a while, but eventually lost its appeal. The ability to exploit ideas efficiently, on the other hand, was there to stay. While Alec Nathan's leadership was crucial in this campaign, the later history indicates that Glaxo relied on its operational excellence again and again to ensure that strategy and organization fit market needs. The company understood that each time it became more competent in a certain activity the rewards for engaging in that activity increased and in turn the likelihood of becoming more competent once again increased.[12] In fact, the subsequent history of the corporation illustrates continuing exploitation success.

Of course, Glaxo also engaged in important research efforts—particularly in the more recent past—but exploitation was Glaxo's main strength in comparison to Wellcome. After World War II, for example, under the leadership of Harry Jephcott (who initially joined the company in quality control when Alec Nathan was in charge), the firm engaged in a number of takeovers, including Murphy Chemical, Allen & Hanburys, and Evans Medical, which added to the chemical and pharmaceutical base. The corporation also licensed technology and processes, such as the deep fermentation process for the production of penicillin, and did good business applying the exploration successes of others. In fact, Jephcott was reluctant to search for novel drugs, and the company rarely developed any new medicine during this period.[13]

Glaxo's most impressive and dramatic success, though, was Zantac, a treatment for ulcers.[14] As the *Economist* wrote in 1997, "Zantac was a triumph not of research but of marketing."[15] It was a classic example of Glaxo being better than their competitors in using assets efficiently. In the 1970s Glaxo put a number of successful products (e.g., for fighting asthma) on the market, but it remained a respected British corporation doing business primarily in former colonies and Italy. Zantac changed all of this. Within a few years Glaxo became a global force to be reckoned with.

In the drugs business—as it was known then—the natural assumption would be that such success could only stem from a novel product. This is only partly true for Zantac. In the 1970s stomach ulcers caused by gastric acid secretion were common conditions and none of the treatments were particularly effective. Eventually many patients had to endure surgery. When Glaxo started its own research in 1970, it was aware of the work done by Smith, Kline & French (later SmithKline Beecham), Pfizer, and Eli Lilly to inhibit the stimulant action of histamine as a potential cure. Zantac was ready to be launched in 1981, but SmithKline had already launched Tagamet in 1976, solving the problem of ulcers and greatly reducing the need for surgery. In a short time Tagamet was the highest-selling prescription drug of all time. Compared to Tagamet, Zantac had the advantage of a simpler dosing regimen and possibly limited side effects (though this had not been proven at market entry).

According to the conventional wisdom, "me-too products" would never gain more than 50 percent of market share. Glaxo, or more precisely Paul Girolami, the new CEO, was not ready to accept conventional wisdom, however. Girolami was convinced that the new drug had more potential.

For starters, the apparent disadvantage of being a second entry into the ulcer market could also be viewed as an opportunity. Doctors were already familiar with the benefits of Tagamet. Market research indicated that they viewed Zantac as "another Tagamet." The medical press argued along the same lines. Consequently Glaxo had to do little education on the mode of action of H2 blockers. SmithKline had done their work for them and Glaxo's salespeople were able to concentrate on promoting the benefits of Zantac versus Tagamet.

While there was wide agreement among Glaxo's top management on this approach, there was no consensus on pricing. At the beginning of 1981 three different scenarios were considered: high volume—low price, high price—low volume, medium price—medium volume. This fit the commonsense view of second entries into novel therapeutic fields. These three options were put on the table when Girolami met with his senior management team. He rejected all three. He thought that with projected sales of £6 million by 1986 and gross profits of 43.7 percent Zantac would be a commercial failure. He put forward a very different strategy: launch Zantac at a premium to stress its superiority over Tagamet. His colleagues felt that this might put Zantac in a "special treatment" market, seriously endangering volume. They argued that there was firm evidence that SmithKline was planning to reduce its daily dosage of six tablets to two in order to match Glaxo's dosage and consequently take away the main advantage of Zantac. What's more, physicians regarded Zantac merely as a monopoly breaker conveniently being used to attack Tagamet, which they viewed as having only one major fault: a high price. But Girolami did not falter. He threatened to bring in a rival pharmaceutical company to co-market Zantac if his strategy was rejected. While Farmer and Baker, two Glaxo executives who were involved in the pricing decision, suggested a wholesale price of £15 for a 60-tablet pack, Girolami wanted to charge £24. The latter represented a substantial premium over Tagamet's £13.50.

In September John Reece, who was responsible for marketing Zantac, presented the findings of the July meeting to the Group Management Committee. The company's leadership team decided to back Girolami and market Zantac not as a monopoly breaker but as a major evolutionary advance in the treatment of ulcers. The dosage and better safety profile were to support this argument and wholesale prices between £23 and £28 drove home the message. Zantac was introduced in the same month in Italy and in the UK at the beginning of October. Sales reached £42.5 million in Italy and £6.5 in the UK. By 1985 Zantac held more than 50 percent of the UK market, with annual sales of £46 million and global revenues of £432 million. As Girolami had suggested, the sales force stressed the incremental gains and made much of the simpler dose regime and the limited side effects that became more apparent over time. Glaxo once again succeeded with a product that was not noble by concentrating on efficient marketing. Its sales exceeded SmithKline's return considerably despite SmithKline's continued R&D efforts. During the period of observation, SmithKline spent more on R&D per sales and generated more patents but failed to put the innovations to efficient use the same way Glaxo did.

One additional aspect enhanced the success of Zantac: the co-promotion of the product in the United States by Glaxo and Roche. Glaxo formed a subsidiary in the United States in 1972 but remained relatively inactive at first, seriously arriving only after the 1977 takeover of Meyer Laboratories. When Zantac was ready for the U.S. launch, the leadership was aware that

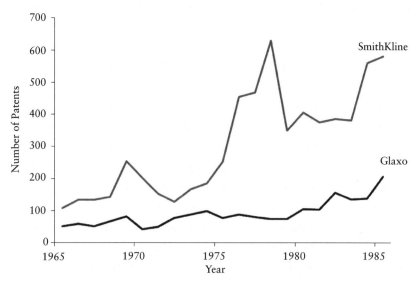

FIGURE 3.6. Glaxo and SmithKline Cumulative Number of Patents
SOURCE: Data from European Patent Office.

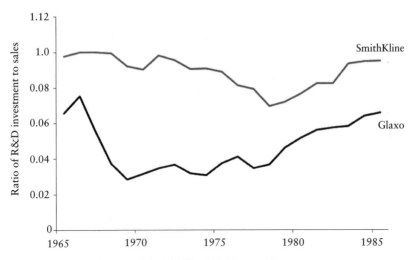

FIGURE 3.7. Glaxo and SmithKline R&D Intensity
SOURCE: Data from annual reports.

a sales force of about 300 would not be sufficient to beat the 800 Smith-Kline salespeople.[16] Further expansion of the sales force was not really an option, since the organic growth would be too slow. Licensing Zantac was one of the options on the table and a strategy that the group had followed in America before. At the same time the leadership was aware of the unique opportunity provided by Zantac: Glaxo could become a force in its own right in the U.S. market. Licensing was not really a promising approach. An alternative idea was to find a partner to co-promote the product. This relatively uncommon approach was first discussed with Bristol-Myers, but nothing came of it. The head of the U.S. subsidiary suggested talking to Hoffmann–La Roche instead. The Swiss company had a large U.S. sales force and a problem: the patents on Valium and Librium were about to expire. Glaxo approached the head of Roche in the United States and suggested "renting his sales force."[17] While this idea seemed outrageous at first, negotiations quickly moved ahead, and within six weeks a deal was finalized. Zantac would be promoted and sold by Glaxo and Roche under the Glaxo name. To motivate Roche sufficiently, sales reps were granted a 40 percent return of sales revenues on a rising scale.[18] Together Roche and Glaxo were able to muster a sales force of more than 1,000 representatives. The critical mass combined with the marketing strategy described above helped Zantac to take off in America. While the commercial success allowed Glaxo to become a serious player in the United States, it provides us with an understanding of how the company was prepared to make pragmatic decisions to guarantee maximum success. Understanding that they had not enough salespeople themselves, they swallowed their pride and found a partner.

Glaxo dealt with exploration challenges in a similar way. At certain crucial points in the company's history, it recognized the need to acquire exploration strengths. The solution was "simple": buy a strong innovator. It did so with the acquisition of Allen & Hanburys in 1969 to help Glaxo change from a producer of milk powder to a proper pharmaceutical firm. Having a limited research tradition itself, Glaxo left Allen & Hanburys intact. This proved to be a crucial decision, as this laboratory, under the gifted leadership of Dr. David Jackson, turned out to be exceptionally inventive. In fact, Zantac was discovered in these laboratories, as was Ventolin, another successful product launched in the late 1960s. Once Zantac was facing patent expiration, another acquisition was able to guarantee continuous success. Sir Richard Sykes had four years to find a substitute when he took over the leadership of the company in 1993. In 1994, 43 percent of Glaxo's revenue was still generated by Zantac,[19] and there was no obvious substitute in the pipeline.

As Sir Richard Sykes told us in an interview, "Zantac was bringing in sales at that time of about 2.5 billion pounds a year. A lot of that would be profit. Now the patent expiry was going to come in a few years and patent expiry means you lost almost immediately 60 percent of the sales, which is very dramatic. So, how do you cope with that? We cannot cope with it organically. So an acquisition was an obvious thing to do."[20]

The obvious candidate to fill the gap was Wellcome. The innovation machine had several promising products in the pipeline, but could not boast commercial success. In the science-dominated environment, marketing often seemed more of an afterthought. This was primarily a governance problem. The Wellcome Trust, which was the principal owner of Wellcome Ltd., the pharmaceutical firm, had to carry out Sir Henry Wellcome's will and therefore supported primary medical research. Wellcome Ltd. was a vehicle to fulfill this mission. On the one hand the company had to produce a steady income, but on the other hand it was also used to engage in research unlimited by market interests. This arrangement makes for great exploration but not necessarily for great exploitation.

The tricky bit for Sir Richard Sykes started when he had to negotiate with the Wellcome Trust to sell the drug company to Glaxo. Having a background in research himself, he found it easier to convince the board of the trust that research would play a major role in the combined company too. Eventually they reached an agreement, and the merger took effect in March 1995. Wellcome's product portfolio broadened the therapeutic field of Glaxo. The impact of Zantac's decline was easily compensated for. The merger allowed Glaxo to apply its marketing power and revitalized several Wellcome products, such as Retrovir, or AZT, for HIV infection, and Wellbutrin, an antidepressant.[21] Structural changes were implemented to shift away from individual products to disease management and to enable the organization to work more closely with customers and partners.[22] Successful drugs are the product of a three-stage development process. First, basic research turns genetic information into physical entities. This is a pretty straightforward process, and size matters. Likewise, in the final stage of late clinical development, when patients test the new drug, size matters. Between those two stages, the creative types have to take the floor. In Glaxo's new structure, scientists have the freedom to play with complicated computer models, set up clever pre-clinical experimentation, and hopefully turn an unassuming compound into a promising new medicine. This structure strengthened Glaxo's own exploration capabilities. At the same time, management was keenly aware that their main strength was efficient operations and clever marketing. Consequently, the new structure was implemented with an eye on cooperation with other firms, particularly biotech firms such as Nobex, Exelixis, and Adolor.[23] As Jean-Pierre Garnier, Glaxo's CEO from 2000 to 2008, explains, "You have a bunch of core skill sets, but then there are many others you have no access to . . . and you can buy your way to them. Companies of course realize that you can't rely exclusively on your own research. We have to try and select the best programs and I think an important element when you outsource some of your discovery and you count on somebody else to do it is the ability to pick and choose these programs carefully and well. So the actual ability of the company to find top-notch programs depends on having top-notch scientists. . . . It's like helping your odds in finding oil with good geologists."[24] In other words, Glaxo builds R&D capabilities only partly to explore itself. More important, strong R&D capabilities help the firm to identify suitable partners. The resulting cooperation benefits both sides. Small biotech firms often struggle to convert their wizardry into products. Glaxo, on the other hand, makes products and uses science primarily as a means to serve that end.

AVOIDING EXPLORATION OVERKILL —
NOKIA AND ERICSSON

Exploration is exciting. Tackling a new problem, searching for unknown ideas, and finding revolutionary methodologies are rewarding. Discovering the unexplored is inspiring. We admire great scientists like Albert Einstein and adore explorers like Christopher Columbus. They made their mark on history, unlike those who merely followed. Nonetheless, Einstein and Columbus would probably not be the celebrated figures they are if others had not brought their ideas to fruition. What if every scientific paper dealt with a previously unknown idea? What if no idea would be fully thought through? We would simply end up in chaos. There can be too much of a good thing. There can be too much exploration. Ericsson is a prime example of a corporation putting too much effort into exploration at the expense of existing business.[25] As a proud leader of technology development for mobile phones, it wanted to stay ahead. As one of the first firms to build an analog mobile system, it also wanted to lead the industry in the development of a global digital system for mobile communication. In terms of technology, the decision to employ more than 30,000 people in R&D in approximately 100 technology centers paid off. The company pioneered general packet radio system (GPRS) and third-generation mobile technology standards. Unfortunately, all of this came at a high price: lots of duplication, big expenditures, and a substantial bet on the future growth of mobile technology. When the telecom industry entered recession after 2000, Ericsson was hit hard. It had to lay off around 60,000 people and close many of its technology centers. Eventually it decided to combine its mobile business with that of Sony.

Ericsson got carried away by enthusiasm for new technologies, and Nokia[26] certainly faced the same danger. The company was traditionally not strong on exploration, and the decision to put its entire R&D budget into the exploration of digital technology in the 1980s marked a turning point. Nokia became a successful explorer. The number of patents per sale compared to Ericsson increased.

The major innovations and the crucial insight that mobile phones were first and foremost consumer goods helped Nokia to generate fantastic growth at the beginning of the 1990s. Nokia was part of the mobile phone craze as much as Ericsson, if not more, but it soon realized that this was not simply a game of exploration but one of operations as well.

Jorma Ollila, Nokia's famed CEO, had set up a highly decentralized organization to create the perfect environment for exploration. The emphasis was on motivation and growth. A full third of the employees worked in 50 research labs around the world. Like Ericsson, Nokia invested heavily in exploration. The R&D efforts did, however, include an element of exploitation, as most research teams focused on incremental rather than fundamental exploration. They worked closely with marketing and production people and kept in close contact with the operational

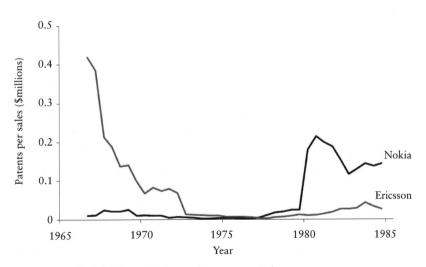

FIGURE 3.8. Nokia and Ericsson Patents per Sale
SOURCE: Data from annual reports and European Patent Office.

side of the business as well. Nevertheless, a system geared almost entirely toward exploration was bound to stumble at some point.

At the end of 1995, it became evident that the mobile phone division was going to fall short of its budget. Operations and logistics had not been able to keep pace with the phenomenal growth. Chaos had not quite taken hold of the organization, but serious shortcomings worried Ollila and his team. Inexperienced personnel failed to bring new products to market on time. Purchasing managers often went to the spot markets to buy overpriced components and at the same time were lenient with suppliers. Cost and quality control had not been a priority. Group margins fell from 14 percent to 6 percent[27] as a result of slowing demand in the U.S. market, Nokia's overestimation of the rate of conversion from analog to digital technology, and the failure of purchasing managers to benefit from falling parts prices. Unlike Ericsson, Nokia acted decisively. Management understood that future success could not be generated at the cost of current business. Exploitation had to be taken seriously. In a quick initial troubleshooting effort, teams were formed to cut inventories, renegotiate component prices, and order chip suppliers to deliver in 12 rather than 8 weeks. A new information management system was installed to track excess parts and reroute them. The celebrated "Nokia Way"—a set of values stressing openness, innovation, and collaboration—was kept alive by the decision not to fire people.

These measures helped Nokia to get back on track, but eventually a more structured approach was required. The old system, which tolerated chaos in the name of entrepreneurship, had to be overhauled. A more centralized approach was slowly introduced in the following years. Headquarters grew, setting clear targets and holding managers accountable. Business processes received more attention than in the past. In hindsight, an early decision to list Nokia in the United States probably helped the corporation to make a timely shift from exploration toward exploitation. The financial markets put great pressure on Nokia to sort out its operations and generate the returns it had promised. As Jorma Ollila put it, "Everybody was saying, okay, these guys made it in handsets, but they couldn't scale, they couldn't make it globally. Interesting start-up . . . , but it didn't work."[28] Ericsson lacked the same pressure. One move of Ollila was also of particular significance

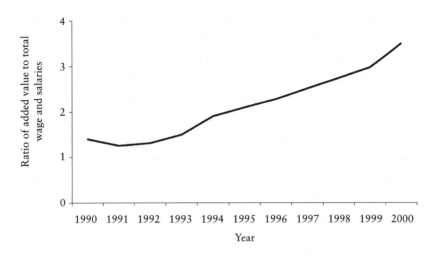

FIGURE 3.9. Nokia Added Value/Total Wages and Salaries Yearly
SOURCE: Data from annual reports.

TABLE 3.1. Exploitation at Nokia Mobile Phones

Changes achieved in 1996

- Smaller inventories released $570 million
- Inventory cycle reduced from 154 days to 68 days
- Raw material cycle reduced from 86 days to 26 days
- Cash flow increased from –$690 million to $980 million
- Inventory costs halved from $42 per handset

New production goals

- Number of parts down from 900 to 400 for one mobile phone model and below 200 for another
- Production time down from 40 to 4 minutes
- Production start-up time and efficiency down from 6 months (early 1990s) to 1 month
- Improvement of production yield from 30% (early 1990s) to 90% with latest products
- Improvement of line efficiency from 35% to 92%
- Hourly performance of SMD pick-and-place machine from 15,000 to 40,000
- Line capacity from 35,000 units in 1992 to 110,000 units in 1997
- New production test equipment, reducing testing time by 30% to 50%
- Reduction of mechanical parts by 20% to 30%

SOURCE: Data from Häikiö, *Nokia: The Inside Story*, p. 182.

in gaining operational excellence: the introduction of the simple operating performance measure added value/total wages and salaries. To generate the figure, all external purchases (components, goods, and services) were subtracted from total sales. Then the figure was divided by salaries and wages, including pension and Social Security contributions. The higher the number, the better. If it was 1, personnel had managed to add value equaling their salaries and wages. Anything above this was a sign of improving productivity. Ollila preferred this measure to the more widely used measurement of sales/employees because it was more difficult to manipulate the number—for example, by outsourcing production.[29]

The crisis helped Nokia to regain momentum. Exploitation capabilities improved tremendously. While Ericsson lost market share in the coming years and eventually had to team up with Sony, Nokia grew to become the market leader in mobile phones, beating the then unchallenged Motorola.

SUMMARY: EXPLOITATION TAKES PRIORITY OVER EXPLORATION

In an ideal world companies would manage both to explore and to exploit. The bad news is that innovation and efficiency call for radically different approaches. The good news is that outstanding companies develop an ability to move beyond exploration. While they know that innovation is important, their first priority is exploitation, the efficient use of existing assets. In some cases this means that companies buy exploration capabilities.

Siemens clearly outperformed AEG over time. AEG's technology lead around 1900 demonstrates that exploration capabilities are not sufficient.

The story of Glaxo and Wellcome shows why exploitation takes priority over exploration. Wellcome was often referred to as the only "quoted University" in the UK, due to its strong research focus and the ability to generate breakthrough innovation. Glaxo, on the other hand, had limited innovation capabilities. Its main strength was the exploitation of existing assets and products. This expertise goes back to the origins of the corporation, when Alec Nathan was able to become the main player in powdered milk through relentless marketing campaigns. The same trick was pulled again with Zantac, an ulcer treatment. Although SmithKline had won the innovation game by putting Tagamet on the market several years earlier, Glaxo's marketing machine won the exploitation game. A dedicated sales force promoted the me-too product as a major innovation and made Zantac the best-selling drug of all time. The profit from Zantac also allowed Glaxo to compensate for its lack in exploration success. It simply bought an innovation machine to compensate for the expiring Zantac patent: Wellcome.

The recent history of Nokia and Ericsson shows us the danger of exploration overkill. Ericsson as a proud leader of technology development for mobile phones employed more than 30,000 people in 100 R&D centers. It pioneered the general packet radio system (GPRS) and third-generation mobile technology standards but was hit hard by the telecom recession after 2000. Nokia was able to avoid the same blow by putting more emphasis on logistics and efficiency in production.

Be Conservative in and beyond Your Finances

Today, the Fuggers, a banking family in Germany, are remembered only by historians. In the 16th century, though, they bankrolled Europe's greatest empire. In those days the Habsburg king Charles V famously claimed to rule an "Empire on which the sun never sets." After the death of his grandfather Ferdinand, the king of Spain who had commissioned the voyages of Christopher Columbus, in 1516, Charles inherited Spain and the recently discovered territories in America. In 1519 his other grandfather, the emperor Maximilian I, passed away, and the Habsburg lands in Austria were added to his rule. Nonetheless, the powerful king faced a final obstacle before he could assume the title "Emperor of the Holy Roman Reich." As tradition demanded, the German electors[30] first had to choose him as king of Germany. France's Francis I and England's Henry VIII both thought themselves better suited for the position of emperor. While it was unlikely that they would succeed, they managed to substantially increase the "price" paid to the electors.

Charles, unable to bankroll his own election campaign, turned to the most successful merchant family of his time, the Fuggers.[31] The Fuggers had first dealt with the Habsburgs in 1473 as merchants of fine costumes. Slowly expanding their traditional line of business, they started to provide financial services for merchants and kings across Europe. Keeping Charles V's grandfather, the ungifted administrator Maximilian I, afloat,[32] they were able to increase their influence significantly as Maximilian provided them with land and mining rights in return for their money. At the beginning of the 16th century, Jacob Fugger II was able to hold a virtual monopoly in the mining and trading of silver, copper, and mercury in Europe. Allegedly the political influence of the Fuggers was comparable to that of the Medici in Italy, and it took several centuries before another family, the Rothschilds, once again amassed similar wealth.[33]

The story of this German merchant family is colorful and their subtle influence on European affairs is fascinating. More than anything else, though, their story is a reminder of how fast an economic powerhouse can lose its position if it forgets to accumulate reserves for times of hardship. A careful and prudent approach to growth might be slow and tedious at times, but it is rarely counterproductive. While this does not mean that you should not take risks, it does stress the need to be smart about taking risks. In fact, the early history of the Fuggers provides an enlightening example.

The foundation of the family wealth was laid by Hans Fugger, who moved to Augsburg and set up shop as a weaver and trader. His two sons, Andreas and Jacob, inherited 3,000 florins, a respectable fortune then. Andreas, the richer of the two, led an aggressive and fast-growing trading house. He established connections with the Netherlands, Leipzig, and possibly even Denmark. To mark his success he married the daughter of an aristocrat. Unfortunately he forgot to stash enough money to fund some of his riskier activities. When a number of high-risk loans were not repaid, his family's fortune declined rapidly. The situation worsened under his sons. When Lucas, his last-born son, passed away, he left more debts than wealth behind.

Their descendants were forced to work as craftsmen and servants. Some of them, in fact, started to work for the Fuggers of Lily, the descendants of the humble and modest Jacob Fugger, whom Andreas had looked down upon. Jacob did not engineer the fantastic success of his brother, but neither did he emulate his brother's spectacular fall. He understood that there would be future generations to worry about and he devoted himself to the careful nurturing of existing resources. His own personality and his traditional German merchant's approach led him to put money aside in prosperous times. The lesson we can draw from his approach is simple:

1. Do not spend beyond your means
2. Build up your fortune (reserves)

The second generation of the Fuggers was able to build an unmatched business empire. While Jacob II—who was originally meant to become a priest—was no doubt a gifted businessman, he was able to succeed spectacularly by building on the resources his father had accumulated step by step. Taking the same approach, he created the golden era for his family.

The eventual decline of the family would not have happened had the later generations of the Fuggers thought and acted the same way as their forebears. In 1546, the firm Anton Fugger and Sons had a working capital of 5 million guilders—the highest in the firm's history.[34] While this could have been exactly the sort of cushion that the family could rely on, a fatal decision was made. Anton Fugger came to the conclusion that none of his nephews had the necessary qualities to lead the business empire in the future, and he started to withdraw substantial amounts of the capital to distribute among his heirs. The intention was to wind down the activities over time. Yet, this intention was reflected only in the reduction of capital. Meanwhile, the Antwerp office, led by Mathias Oertel, continued to write large loans. To a certain extent, the long connection with some powerful customers such as Charles V made it difficult to manage a smooth exit. Still, there were other deals that the firm was not required to make, such as an engagement with the British crown. When Charles V started a new war against France, the Fuggers were fully back in business, providing large funds from 1553 onward. Similar deals in the past gave them the confidence that they could handle such business successfully. But while the track record was certainly there, this time the capital base was too small. The reduction of capital a few years earlier had substantially increased the risk of such dealings. Sure enough, an unexpected financial crisis in Antwerp dealt the Fuggers a hard blow. Meanwhile, some of their customers, like King Philip of Spain, were no longer able or willing to repay their loans. The Fuggers accumulated substantial losses. For a while the reputation of the firm allowed them to borrow on favorable terms to meet other obligations, but soon their difficulties became known and interest charges began to climb.

The Spanish episode was a sign of things to come. Frequent financial crises and the deterioration of the power of the Habsburg family brought such fundamental changes to the business environment that only a highly capable management could have weathered the storm. Anton Fugger's successors were not up to the challenge, however. Indeed, they were quite unwilling to take family matters into their hands. Sound financial grounding could have helped the family to take a more prominent role up to the Thirty Years' War in the 17th century. While the Fuggers actually continued to finance kings and merchants into the 17th century, they did so in a much less prominent way than before. The capital and property that Anton had distributed among his heirs was missing during the bumpy ride at the time. Leaving the reserves in place could have changed the family's fate.

FROM THE RENAISSANCE INTO THE 21ST CENTURY

It turns out that the lessons of Jacob Fugger, while lost on his descendants, are relevant to the great corporations of later Europe. The enduring companies that fared the best put money aside in prosperous times in anticipation of meeting challenges in the future. This practice may seem obvious. In our personal lives we try to save money, build up pensions, and prepare for the future. We take great pains to save enough not only for our retirement but also for the education of our children and perhaps grandchildren. Why do corporations fail to automatically do the same? Why would well-educated and intelligent managers not ensure that their corporation accumulates money in the same way they do for their own personal needs? A number of reasons come to mind. First of all, they can use their profits to generate growth. They are under pressure from investors to put the money to good use. They might want to invest the money for tax reasons. Finally, a company that stashes large amounts of cash is an attractive target for corporate raiders, who would be happy to recover the costs of their purchase. Despite these plausible reasons for spending money, a conservative approach pays off in times of trouble. The insurance company Munich Re, for example, built up its reserves right from the start. Paying out low dividends with the agreement of its main shareholders, the company had reserves that were almost 100 percent higher than those of its competitors by 1910. This paid off in 1906, when the earthquake in San Francisco resulted in the most expensive catastrophe for insurance companies to date. Munich Re's CEO, Carl Thieme, was able to reimburse customers without much fuss. The reserves were large enough to cover this expensive but farsighted decision. In fact, Munich Re made the largest payout of its history—equivalent to 11 percent of its premiums—and was still able to report a profit. Americans recognized the reliable support of Munich Re when they talked about "Thieme is money." The company's subsequent growth in the United States is no surprise; customers understood that they could trust Munich Re to be there for them in troubled times.[35]

The virtue of a conservative approach is true not only for finances. While finances might provide easily accessible proof of the top companies' conservatism, they apply the same diligence in other areas as well. They simply refuse to put all their eggs in one basket. Their history has taught them that the only certain thing is uncertainty. When an unpredicted event unfolds, they are prepared. They have assets to fall back on and alternatives up their sleeves.

To gain a first impression of the financial conservatism of outstanding companies, we can refer to Standard & Poor's credit risk rating, which shows the current opinion of the creditworthiness of an entity with a financial obligation. It takes into consideration the creditworthiness of guarantors, insurers, or other forms of credit enhancement on the obligation. Standard & Poor's obtains information from both the particular corporation and other sources that it considers reliable. The top rating is AAA, reflecting a corporation's unquestionable ability and willingness to repay an obligation when it is due.[36] Consequently, a rare AAA rating indicates the financial strength of a firm. It also suggests that a corporation has the required reserves to meet its obligations regardless of the economic environment. Not all corporations have a credit rating—as not all of them deem it necessary to purchase such a rating from Standard & Poor's—but in general those top companies from our sample that are rated achieve a slightly higher score than their comparison companies.

We are also reluctant to rely exclusively on such ratings in our quest to determine how conservative a company is. After all, ratings have not always been exactly spot on when it came to investment products in the recent past. So in order to confirm the impression from the Standard and Poor's rating—which dates back to the mid-1990s—we consulted additional data published in annual reports. Common sense would suggest that data on reserves could be helpful. This source of data is misleading, however, as corporations define reserves in many different ways, thus making a comparison virtually impossible. In addition, corporations do not publish hidden reserves, which are often more important than the published data on reserves. A ratio that is more robust and informative is profits divided by revenues.

The data shows that outstanding corporations do not grow at the expense of their profits. They do not invest to an extent that makes it impossible to declare a profit year after year. They take the same approach that

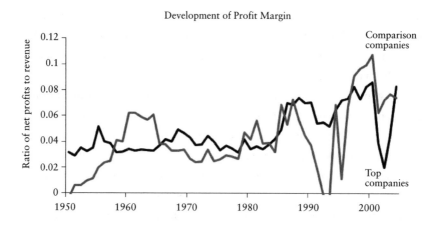

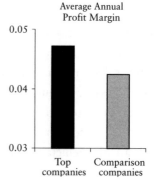

FIGURE 3.10. Profit Margin of Top and Comparison Companies
SOURCE: Data from annual reports.

Jacob Fugger took in the 16th century to build the most powerful business empire of its time: growing step by step and not beyond the financial means available. This might not generate spectacular growth at all times, but a solid climb is assured.

A second ratio, leverage (total liabilities divided by stockholder equity), highlights the fact that enduring success cannot be achieved without a conservative business approach. A lower and more stable run of the curve indicates a more conservative approach, as firms borrow less money compared to what they can afford.

Considering the compelling logic of this argument and the decision by outstanding corporations to take a conservative approach toward finances, it seems curious that not all companies would follow this path. But then again, there is the lure of growth. Managers are locked into a

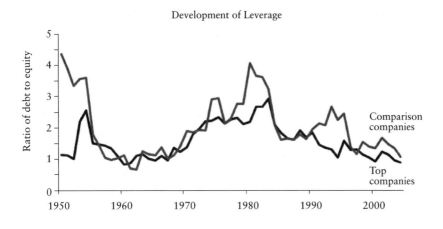

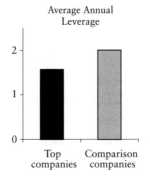

FIGURE 3.11. Leverage of
Top and Comparison Companies
SOURCE: Data from annual reports.

system where most incentives are tied to growth. Expectations of both employees and shareholders put pressure on management to leap forward. To slow the firm down amid such demands for prosperity requires extraordinary discipline. In some cases, this course may threaten a CEO's survival. Ironically, it may be precisely at those times that leaders should grow reserves instead of focusing on growth alone. Rather than relying on cheap credits to gain theoretically unlimited freedom to act, a CEO should think ahead to times of trouble. Expansion is spectacular and rewarding in the short run. Carefully and diligently planned expansion is also the right thing to do. What should not be forgotten is the uncertainty of the future. Any business environment can change overnight, no matter how stable it seems today. If the firm is forced to meet obligations and faces fierce competition at the same time, the CEO might remember in vain that he or she should have taken more time before making a speedy acquisition or orchestrating a spectacular new market entry. The key is timing. If the firm can afford an acquisition or a new market entry and if it fits the company's strategy and organizational capabilities, fine. If not, why try to fool anybody?

In the long run it is precisely the decision to be careful and build up reserves that enables a firm to make a move when others cannot. While Jacob Fugger II was able to grow an unmatched merchant empire because of his father's careful preparation, his cousins were knocking on his door to find work. During both recession and boom a company's reserves create freedom of action that is not available to competitors. In good days a firm is able to pursue opportunities without lengthy negotiations with banks, and in bad days the reserves are able to protect the corporation from going under.

SIEMENS VERSUS AEG — THE LURE OF GROWTH AND THE VIRTUE OF CONSERVATISM

Comparing the development of Siemens[37] and AEG[38] after World War II allows us to see the virtues of both conservatism in finances and hedging against political risk. On the surface, both corporations were in a similar position in 1944. Both had around 200,000 employees heavily engaged in the war. Both faced production constraints because of continuous Allied bombing. Both were headquartered in Berlin. And still there was a vital difference. The seed of AEG's misfortune that eventually led to corporate death was planted in the final period of the Third Reich. At the same time the seed for the growth of Siemens in the second half of the 20th century was also planted. While Siemens moved substantial parts of the corporation to the west and south of Germany before the end of the war, AEG made no such move. In autumn 1944, Siemens learned from sources in Sweden about the Allied plan to split Germany into zones. Since the corporation's headquarters and substantial production sites were in the Berlin area, this division threatened the sheer survival of the firm. Siemens's leadership acted decisively, reorganizing the group in a way that would allow them to function in the event that communication between Berlin and the rest of the country ceased. The firm was split into four groups: Berlin, Group West, Group South, and Group South-East. Machines and tools were transferred to Group West. Each group was able to function independently. Foreign subsidiaries were told to build up inventories and to stop transferring capital to Berlin. Important technical documents were sent to Switzerland, and Ernst von Siemens was instructed to lead the firm if Hermann von Siemens, the chairman at the time, became no longer able to do so. The wisdom of this decision became clear after the war, when Russia stripped factories under its control and transferred equipment to the east. Siemens's employees in Berlin were forced to help with this process. Siemens & Halske (telecommunication) lost 98 percent of its substance in Berlin that way, and Siemens Schuckert (high-power current) lost 85 percent.[39] AEG faced similar losses in Berlin. The vital difference, though, was the concentration of AEG in Berlin. In Germany's capital city, 90 percent of the company's production facilities generated 70 percent of the firm's revenue. Consequently, AEG lost 74.5 percent of its assets after the war.[40]

One way to interpret these events would be to attribute the outcomes to sheer luck: Siemens knew about the plan to split Germany into zones while AEG did not. Unfortunately archival sources do not allow us to fully understand the thinking at the time, since official communications had to take the requirements of the Nazi Party into account. There is no indication that AEG knew about the occupation plan and failed to act accordingly.

Nonetheless, it is hard to imagine that AEG failed to understand that the end of Nazi Germany was near. Likewise, it was anybody's guess that Russia would most likely occupy territories in the East. What was up for speculation, though, was the behavior of Russia. Nobody could foresee its policy of taking equipment and machinery to Russia. Siemens did not anticipate that either, as some of its actions showed. For example, just before the end of the war, the head of finance in Berlin refused to split the group's capital equally between East and West. As a result, most funds were confiscated shortly afterward. Siemens could also have moved more equipment to the West. In short, Siemens might have expected that after the war the business environment would be friendlier in the West, but the company did not *know* that. In addition, management did not agree about Berlin's future after the war. An influential group continued to push for greater concentration in Berlin and started activities there, only to lose them when the split between East and West was finalized. What distinguished Siemens from AEG was its refusal to put all its eggs in one basket. Siemens hedged its bets and decided to act conservatively. This strategy had its roots in Siemens tradition just as the more aggressive growth strategy was in keeping with AEG tradition.

Twelve years earlier, both firms had faced the Great Depression. AEG felt a heavy blow, while Siemens was able to weather the storm much better. Prior to the economic crisis, Siemens had taken a conservative approach in its finances and investment policy. The Siemens balance sheet listed equipment, machines, and tools but did not include the value of these assets, while AEG used such assets to inflate its balance sheet. In 1926–1927 AEG was booked with 22.7 million Reichsmarks (RM), equivalent to 10 times the company's profit, or about 5 percent of revenue.[41] The difference between Siemens and AEG was even more pronounced when the appraisal of property was taken into account. AEG valued its property much higher. The same creativity was used in the valuation of bonds. On its 1932–1933 balance sheet, AEG booked $6.17 million bonds using the current exchange rate rather than the exchange rate at the time of purchase. In effect this meant that an accounting profit was reported that was not realized at the time. AEG also suffered from underperforming investments. The aggressive expansion policy of previous years took its toll. Unlike AEG, Siemens was able to cover losses during the Great Depression by relying on its reserves. The fully amortized equipment helped too. Essentially, Siemens had taken an approach that was similar to that of Jacob Fugger. The company invested only when it could afford to do so and took great care to put money aside for rainy days.

After World War II these instincts continued to be at work. Despite its heavy losses, AEG set out to grow. Crafty deals and fast expansion were intended to put the company on a par with Siemens once again. The focus was on revenue growth rather than steady profit generation. Management fell for the lure of growth and "forgot" to earn the capital necessary to finance its adventures. Raising capital was not a problem during the Wirtschaftswunder—the German "Economic Miracle." Rather than trying to beat Siemens in terms of revenue, AEG should have taken the time to build a strong and stable corporation step by step. Comparing Siemens and AEG in terms of both profit/revenue and gearing ratio puts the spotlight on the issue of a "growth trap." Siemens stayed at a stable level over time, while AEG experienced much more volatility.

AEG's growth was breathtaking. Revenue in 1945–1946 was at RM 87 million, well below the RM 541 million in 1938–1939. In 1948–1949 the revenue of DM 213 million was already moving toward the 1938–1939 level. By 1950–1951 revenue had grown to DM 432 million and continued to climb. The same was true for employees. In 1945, the firm

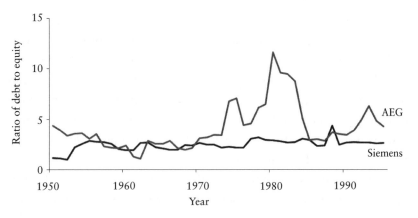

FIGURE 3.12. Siemens and AEG Leverage
SOURCE: Data from annual reports.

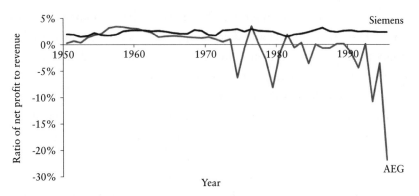

FIGURE 3.13. Siemens and AEG Profit Margin
SOURCE: Data from annual reports.

had 9,600 employees; in 1949 there were 23,900; and in 1951 more than 32,000. As spectacular as this growth was, profits were not able to keep pace. Capital was provided primarily through debt. In 1955 the firm had liabilities of 157 million DM, compared to profits of 14.8 million DM. AEG's CEO, Friedrich Spennrath, decided in 1952 that a consolidation would be necessary, but the required actions were not taken. Instead the corporation decided to continue growth. The unofficial strategy was to be as big as Siemens. By 1959 the new CEO, Hans Boden, was very worried about the corporation's development and started structural reforms to get a grip on the situation. But AEG was already facing serious problems. The structural reforms fell short of a real turnaround, and the following decades marked the slow decline of an established institution. Boden's successors tried various new approaches, and at times it looked as if AEG was gaining momentum. Nonetheless, growth remained important, with fiscal discipline of secondary concern. AEG never managed to make a full turnaround. Its broad diversification made it even more difficult for the leadership to find a winning strategy and a fitting organizational structure. Bankruptcy and takeover marked the end of a proud firm that ran out of funds to fulfill its mission.

Siemens had taken a different path. Throughout its history the firm was careful to grow in a responsible way. Management made a conscious decision not to jump at every possible expansion opportunity. In order to ensure liquidity they used the available shareholder fund as a guideline for acquisition activities. In addition, they had always kept dividends low and increased the company's inner strength instead. Siemens never forgot that solid finances and patience are required to increase market power and influence. AEG acted more opportunistically, relying heavily on banks and external finances. Siemens prevailed; AEG did not. A clear and compelling lesson!

NEVER PUT ALL YOUR EGGS IN ONE BASKET

The story of Siemens and AEG underlines the virtue of conservatism in finances but also indicates that being smart about how to choose your risks in other fields is equally important. Companies that perform outstandingly well over time act cautiously on many levels. They know that the future is uncertain and that they should never make assumptions that potentially threaten their existence. In other words, they need to ensure that their core business is resilient enough to hold up against unexpected disasters. They refuse to put all their eggs in one basket. While it is impossible to predict where disaster will strike, there are three conditions that put corporations in a position of particular vulnerability:

dependency on banks or outside investors other than the founding family;

dependency on a single supplier for vital components of the production process; and

dependency on a single country if vital parts of the corporation cannot be relocated.

A conservative approach toward finances provides a corporation with the means to avoid becoming dependent on other stakeholders. To ensure independence, a company also needs to build a certain level of flexibility into the structure and strategy of the organization. While varying degrees of dependency with other entities will exist, a firm is much more likely to be struck by disaster if it is locked into a system in which no alternatives are available.

One corporation that experienced major setbacks due to a failure to think the unthinkable was Ericsson.[42] At two decisive points in its history, the firm found itself in a difficult position, having almost completely lost control over its destiny. In the 1930s, Ericsson's failure to ensure its independence led to a takeover by its main competitor, and in the 1990s the company's reliance on a single supplier for vital parts of its mobile business cost it the leading position in the mobile phone sector when a disruption occurred in the supply chain. Both incidents draw attention to the need to act conservatively—and not only in financial terms. Corporations always need to have backup plans, as the unthinkable is bound to happen at some point. If it does happen, decisive action is required. So how exactly did Ericsson fare? When did management go awry? What should they have done differently?

Ericsson's first misfortune—the point at which an outsider began to dominate the firm—was rooted in the rise of Ivar Kreuger, who became a major force in the world's match trade in the 1920s and eventually controlled almost 75 percent of the world market. The "Match King," as he became known, developed a taste for deals outside his original industry. Ericsson caught his eye and he started to secretly buy shares in 1925, first through a firm called Ängsvik and later on the open market. In 1930 he had a large enough stake in the company to control the board. While in principle a controlling shareholder is not a reason to worry, that holds true only when the dominant owner has the good of the company in mind. Research on family businesses supports that claim in the sense that family-owned companies perform particularly well.[43] Ivar Kreuger did not fall into this category. His interest was not the success of Ericsson but his personal gain. He used his position to milk the firm and used the company as security against which to borrow more. Eventually, in 1931, he decided to sell out to ITT, Ericsson's main competitor at the time. ITT was prevented from taking over by Swedish law, which did not allow non-Swedish ownership to exceed 20 percent. Kreuger and ITT were aware of this clause and agreed that the company that Krueger ran, Kreuger & Toll AB, would keep the shares and vote as instructed by ITT. A later transfer to a nominee holder—for example, a bank—might have been contemplated. This course of action never materialized after ITT's management took a look into Ericsson's books. They were not impressed and canceled the deal. Kreuger had to repay $11 million—which he did not have. Other creditors started to pull the rug out from under him, and Kreuger committed suicide. "I have made such a mess of things that I believe this to be the most satisfactory solution for everybody concerned,"[44] he wrote in his farewell letter.

Preventing an outside investor from taking control is admittedly a very difficult task. Ericsson's options to fight off Kreuger and ITT were pretty limited. Still, Ericsson should have made it clear from the beginning that it would fight to the death. Ericsson should have brought the Swedish government in from the start to prove to ITT that the attempt to swallow the company would end in vain. Ericsson could also have employed various financial maneuvers. In fact, it was not the only company to face corporate raiders during the Great Depression. Other companies were able to fight them off by acting decisively. Ericsson, however, seemed happy to sit back and resign itself to being in the hands of a crafty investor. In 1931, for example, several months had passed before the managing director even became aware of the details of the Kreuger-ITT deal. Ericsson's experience shows that acting conservatively does not mean acting slowly. Fighting fiercely for independence and survival is as conservative a value as there is.

After Kreuger's suicide the situation remained unsatisfactory for Ericsson. It could not repay ITT for the shares the firm held as security for the $11 million. Under the skillful leadership of Marcus Wallenberg, the president of Stockholms Enskilda Bank, an agreement was reached in 1932. The Articles of Association were changed and approved by the King in Council to allow ITT to own 35 percent of the corporation, while the rest was received by Svenska Handelsbanken and Stockholms Enskilda Bank. Wallenberg also succeeded in securing the right to operate without restrictions in foreign markets. The unfortunate Kreuger episode had cost the shareholders dearly: they did not receive a regular dividend until 1941. It took the firm until 1960 to gain full independence once again.

The second misfortune, which Ericsson encountered 70 years later, once again illustrates the importance of remaining in charge of one's destiny by avoiding dependency on outside entities. While Nokia had several suppliers for vital parts in its mobile phone business, Ericsson had put all its eggs in one basket. The company was not smart about which risks to take in the name of cost cutting, and it paid the price when disaster struck.

On March 17, 1999, a fire in a Philips factory in Albuquerque, New Mexico, disrupted the supply chain of Nokia and Ericsson.[45] Lightning from a thunderstorm in New Mexico struck an electric line, causing power fluctuations throughout the state. In the Philips semiconductor plant in Albuquerque, either the drop or the surge in power started a small fire. Workers were able to extinguish the flames even before the fire brigade arrived, but unfortunately everything that could have gone wrong did go wrong during this brief disaster. Water sprinklers went off, causing extensive damage. Eight trays of silicon wafers that were to be used in the production of thousands of chips were destroyed. Most damaging, though, was the smoke. Particles of smoke had entered the sterile room that contained the entire stock of millions of the chips that were vital for mobile phones. They were all destroyed.

Nokia and Ericsson, both facing the same disruption to their supply chain, could not have responded more differently. In fact, the two companies' approaches had been different even before this event. Ericsson had failed ever to contemplate disastrous contingencies. To cut costs, it had streamlined its supply chain and had no alternative chip suppliers. Nokia, on the other hand, had kept several suppliers despite the potential cost disadvantage. This strategy gave Nokia a competitive edge in the struggle to keep production going at a time when mobile phone sales were booming. Nokia's logistics team was much more adept in many ways. Within days Nokia noticed that the numbers were not adding up. On March 20—three days after the fire—Tapio Markki, Nokia's chief component-purchasing manager, received a phone call from Philips and learned why. He was also told that production should be up again within a week. Not terribly worried, he reported to his superior, Pertti Korhonen, anyway, who later commented in an interview with the *Wall Street Journal*: "We encourage bad news to travel fast."[46] At the time, Mr. Korhonen also expected no major disruptions. Still, he put the five components made at the Philips plant on a monitoring list, used regularly to keep track of potential troublemakers. An offer by Nokia to send its own engineers to New Mexico was declined by Philips, as the company thought this might add to the confusion on the site. In the following days Nokia became more concerned. Instead of the weekly call, Nokia personnel started to contact Philips every day. Matti Alahuhta, Nokia's mobile phone division president, met with Philips officials and made it very clear that he expected a fast solution. Two weeks after the fire in New Mexico, Philips called Nokia to say that it would take weeks before production could start again. This development threatened the production of 4 million handsets, or the equivalent of 5 percent of total sales. Now Nokia took action on two fronts. Two components that were produced in Albuquerque were indispensable, and one of them was produced only by Philips. Nokia's CEO, Jorma Ollila, personally met with Philips's CEO, Cor Boonstra, to put pressure on him to find a quick solution. As a major customer, Ollila was taken seriously and the two firms feverishly worked on a solution together. Two Philips factories, in Eindhoven in the Netherlands and in Shanghai, were freed for the production of the vital component. At the same time, Nokia's logistics people asked some of their other suppliers in Japan and the United States to jump in and produce the other missing components on short notice. As a result of Nokia's action and its ability to fall back on other suppliers, the company was able to meet production targets despite the fire.

While Nokia reorganized its supply chain, senior officials at Ericsson were still unaware of the immediate danger. Like Nokia, Ericsson had first heard about the fire three days after it struck. Unlike Nokia, the technician who received this news did not communicate it up the hierarchical ladder. Two weeks later, when Nokia's mobile phone president met with Philips officials, Ericsson's middle management became aware of the seriousness of the situation. It was not until early April that the head of Ericsson's mobile division started to find out what was going on. By the time Ericsson approached Philips it was too late. Nokia already had a deal. Ericsson could not rely on other suppliers, as it had none. Customer orders could not be met and Ericsson lost market share to Nokia. After the incident, Ericsson assigned a second supplier for key parts, but the lesson had been learned too late.

The danger of a firm's losing control over its own destiny is particularly high if it is a company that depends on natural resources and concentrates its activities in a single country. Naturally, when that country is in an unstable region, the situation is even more precarious. The industry most used to the pains of nationalization is the oil industry. When BP, then called Anglo-Persian, started operations in Persia in 1909, the firm should have been aware of this potential risk. In fact, management did try to diversify into other regions and countries, but without success. Unfortunately, the British government played a dominant part in this corporation in two ways: the government was the largest shareholder, and the Royal Navy was the largest customer. For strategic reasons, the British government preferred that BP concentrate on operations in Persia to ensure cheap and reliable oil supply for the navy. Various attempts by BP's management to build up operations outside Persia found little government support. When Mohammad Mosaddegh became Persia's famously anti-colonial prime minister in 1951, he set about nationalizing the country's oil industry and BP lost almost 70 percent of its assets. Lengthy negotiations followed, and the company received partial compensation for its losses. Still, the Persian nationalization was painful, and it took years for BP to make up for the losses, to build up a new supply base. A comparison of BP's experience with that of Shell, the corporation that fared better over the past century, underlines the virtue of spreading risk. Shell also experienced nationalizations, losing vital operations in Mexico in 1938, in Russia when the Bolshevists came into power, and later on in Venezuela in 1975. Each time, the corporation experienced painful losses. But unlike BP, Shell always had alternative production sites. In an industry where success depends so heavily on the ability to find reliable reserves, Shell understood the virtue of hedging its bets.

SUMMARY: CONSERVATISM AS A WAY OF LIFE

When we initially floated the idea that companies need to be conservative, not everyone was convinced. Our gold medalists had similar experiences. Lehman Brothers, for example, reminded Shell as late as 2008 that the oil company was not bold enough. Today, we all know where Lehman Brothers ended up with all its bold investments! Companies need to be smart about taking risks. To achieve enduring success, companies have to hedge their bets. When the unavoidable surprise strikes, a firm needs to have a plan B. In the case of our gold medalists, this was most obvious in their conservative approach toward finances, but they also addressed other areas equally well. Outstanding companies need to avoid dependency on a single owner other than the founding family, exclusive relations with a single supplier for vital components, and concentration of operations in a single country. To have money in their pockets in times of need, companies need to consider the following.

Conservative Finances   AEG lost 74.5 percent of its assets because it failed to spread those assets across Germany before the end of World War II. Siemens had done so before the Soviet occupation and thus avoided the same fate. The decades following the war were marked by growth. Siemens combined that with a conservative approach toward its finances, while AEG borrowed heavily. Eventually AEG was no longer able to meet its obligations. One failed turnaround followed the next, until Daimler eventually bought the firm.

Danger of Outside Owner   Ivar Kreuger, a corporate raider, was able to take control of Ericsson in 1930. He sold his stake to Ericsson's main competitor, ITT. Although Swedish law prohibited the American firm from taking formal control, it was nevertheless able to wield great influence. Had Ericsson used its political clout, the unsatisfactory situation could have been avoided.

Danger of Single Supplier   When a thunderstorm in Albuquerque caused a fire in a Philips plant and wiped out the supply of important components for Ericsson's and Nokia's mobile phone production, the two companies responded quite differently. Nokia got Philips to move production to another factory and called two of its other suppliers to produce some of the components. Ericsson had no system in place that alerted its management about the shortage of vital components, and as a result of an earlier cost-cutting exercise, it had no alternative suppliers. Nokia's production did not fall for the year. Ericsson was hit so hard that it lost its strong position in the mobile phone business.

Danger of Single Country   Nationalization is a common danger in the oil business. Shell was nationalized in Mexico, Russia, and Venezuela. While this development was certainly unwelcome, Shell had alternative production sites each time it was hit. BP found itself in quite a different mess when the oil business was nationalized in Persia. The result was that almost 70 percent of BP's assets were wiped out overnight.

Remember and Share Both Mistakes and Triumphs

After 7.4 million years of calculation, the second-greatest computer in all of time and space, Deep Thought, provided the *Ultimate Answer to Life, the Universe, and Everything*. A seemingly excited crowd had shown up, only to be deeply disappointed by the forthcoming answer: 42. "I checked it very thoroughly," said the computer, "and that quite definitely is the answer. I think the problem, to be quite honest with you, is that you've never actually known what the question is." To find the Ultimate Question, an even greater computer called Earth was designed. Unfortunately the question was lost, five minutes before it was to be produced. The Vogons, one of the galaxy's most unpleasant races, destroyed Earth to build a hyperspace bypass. As futuristic and bizarre as Douglas Adams's story in *The Hitchhiker's Guide to the Galaxy*[47] might sound, it has the ring of truth for managers in large multinational corporations. They know that the accumulated wisdom of thousands of well-educated employees spread over dozens of countries is bound to provide both the right questions and the right answers for their corporation to thrive. But how should they possibly go about tapping into that wisdom? Too often they learn about the right questions and answers when it is too late. Is there a way they could have possibly known? Are there mechanisms, instruments, approaches that could help them ensure that the right piece of knowledge is at the right place at the right time? Heinrich von Pierer, the CEO of Siemens from 1992 to 2005, articulates this challenge as follows: "If Siemens knew what Siemens knows . . ." And Siemens certainly does know a lot, with 400,000 employees in 190 countries and experiences gained over more than 150 years. In a recent study,[48] some colleagues and I have shown that Siemens is not alone in its search for how to share knowledge. While everyone is aware of the importance of knowledge sharing, the challenge is to find the right tools. Unfortunately, many of the available tools are technology-based systems that are not well equipped to transfer experiences. In particular, tacit knowledge that is often based in experience does not travel well over the Internet. The good news for von Pierer is that despite his distress, his firm and the other gold medalists were doing relatively well in terms of knowledge sharing. They had developed a number of different ways to capture important experiences and make them available to their peers and future generations. Not surprisingly, the leaders themselves were in a key position to ensure the flow of ideas. We also found corporate culture to be a great "knowledge storage device," in the sense that successful behavior patterns became part of the way things were done in a corporation. Experiences that carried a particularly defining message sometimes took on a life of their own beyond becoming part of the corporate culture. Some of the messages became powerful stories that influenced strategy and structures for decades. A more formal instrument was the corporate planning system. Successful firms used the planning cycle not simply as a target-setting device or as an unavoidable annual practice but as a way to learn and prepare for the future. A final instrument that we identified was the widespread use of training sessions. Once again, the gold medalists were different in the sense that they introduced corporate universities and formal training long before their comparison companies did. While not all of the successful companies use the various means of knowledge sharing to the same extent, all apply some of them. An additional insight from our research is that the different measures are used to achieve different goals. While corporate culture had—in the successful companies, that is—a very lasting effect, the immediate relevance to the task of an individual might not always be obvious. In comparison, the endurance of

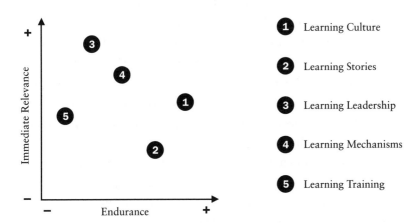

FIGURE 3.14. Learning across Time and Space

knowledge sharing guided by a specific leader is limited by the eventual departure of that leader. People, however, strongly feel the impact of this leader while he or she is around. Every one of us knows how much our workday depends on our boss.

In an effort to gain a better understanding of how these different aspects of learning were part of the corporate environment and how they helped a corporation to succeed, the development of the outstanding companies and the comparison companies provides significant insights. The following discussion will focus on Shell and BP, but additional examples from other companies will show that the same pattern emerges in other corporations.

LEARNING CULTURE

Culture does not transmit hard knowledge in the sense of factual data. Nonetheless, it has a very real and powerful influence on how employees learn and behave. When people join a new company, they learn from the first day on which types of behavior are appreciated and which are not. As a result, new employees start to behave according to the lessons the organization has learned and incorporated into its culture over many years. Culture is an ideal, though often undetected, transmitter of knowledge, and it causes people to do things in a certain way. While the original context for a certain behavior may change, the successful behavior nonetheless continues to be passed on—in some cases over many generations.

One way to look at culture is through an analysis of a company's core values. Shell's core values are integrity, trust, and respect for people. The statement of these values is nothing remarkable in itself. In fact, many companies have similar statements. BP—Shell's comparison company—for example, states: "In all our activities we seek to display some unchanging, fundamental qualities—integrity, honest dealing, treating everyone with respect and dignity, striving for mutual advantage and contributing to human progress." Where Shell distinguishes itself is in how deeply these values are rooted in its history and how much effort is put into bringing them to life.

Shell first stated its core values in the 1970s, long before this practice became fashionable in management. What is even more interesting, though, are the circumstances under which this was done. At the time, the British public blamed Shell for literally fueling a civil war, during a time of internal conflict in Rhodesia—today's Zimbabwe. Shell South Africa sold oil products to Total and other intermediaries, which then moved those products farther, to Rhodesia via Mozambique. This was a serious political issue, as Rhodesia was under an international trade embargo at the time.[49] Particularly embarrassing was the fact that Shell had just managed to overcome another scandal in Italy, where the local subsidiary had been generous in handing over money—defined as marketing expenses—to political parties. Although such a practice was not uncommon in Italy at the time, it proved embarrassing for the head of Shell, Gerrit Wagner, who had a hard time explaining it to the media.[50]

Following these events, Shell decided to codify its General Business Principles. While these principles were intended to express the company's core values, they put particular emphasis on eliminating bribery and corruption. The document made it quite clear that senior management would not tolerate such practices, no matter the norms and expectations in a particular country. For managers on the ground, the General Business Principles document provided something concrete that they could show other parties when asked to "grease the system." Senior management backed up the document by firing individuals who did not comply. Over many years the General Business Principles helped drive home a simple but important message across the organization: Shell does not make such payments.

The codification of Shell's General Business Principles demonstrates how great companies turn major embarrassments into long-term opportunities. Management at the time understood that situations similar to Rhodesia and Italy might arise again in a highly political industry such as the oil business. To avoid making the same mistakes again, the combination of a statement of core values and the memory of recent painful experiences is certainly helpful. When memory began to fade in the 1990s, Shell introduced a number of mechanisms to ensure continuous implementation of the principles. It installed a process requiring the chairman of each country organization to commit in writing at the beginning of every year to act according to the principles. At the end of the year each country chairman would discuss the year's events with the Committee of Managing Directors (CMD). In a decentralized organization where the country chairmen enjoyed great operational freedom, implementation of these steps meant that Shell's most senior executives took responsibility for ensuring behaviors consistent with the company's values. The pressure was further increased by publishing an annual report on the General Business Principles.

Another initiative built around the company's core values was a company-wide employee survey, first conducted in 1999. While the organizers were struggling to create interest among line management for the first survey in some parts of the world, a response rate of around 70 percent (pushed up to 80 percent in 2002) gained the attention of top managers. Some parts of the organization now use the survey when setting personal development tasks and targets, though most employ it as a communication tool to facilitate dialogue between employees and their managers.

The Shell story shows how a company can use its core values to influence its culture in a way that allows fundamental messages to prevail over time. It is not the statement itself but the continuous engagement of employees through a combination of mechanisms that makes this possible. At Shell this goal was certainly fostered by a more general culture that stimulated learning and discussion. Rather than being told by their bosses how to behave, employees engage in decision-making processes. For example, when Shell's return on average capital employed dipped below 7 percent in 1994, Cor Herkströter, the chairman of Shell's Committee of Managing Directors, started a major transformation process. He understood that he had neither the knowledge nor the power to undertake this journey on his own. Instead of unleashing a number of initiatives straightaway, he and his fellow board members compiled a list of themes to be addressed. Using these themes, they engaged with a wider community of managers in the following months. They met, they listened, and, on the basis of what they learned, they were prepared to modify their plans. Herkströter said, "Management became much more visible, management became much more part of the organization, management was prepared to be vulnerable, saying we are not the ones who know everything. Yes, we are indeed in charge of this organization, but we are prepared to demonstrate our weaknesses and share them with you. At the same time this is not simply to be open and honest without development but to show that together we have to learn a lot."[51] Shell's transformation unfolded over seven years.

Continuing to embrace and foster a culture that stimulated learning, Shell managed to make the adjustments. By 2000 the return on average capital employed exceeded 19 percent.

At BP, Shell's comparison company, the corporate culture did not nourish learning until comparatively recent times. For many years, BP operated as a slow-moving bureaucracy. Under the leadership of John Browne in the 1990s, however, a new culture based on knowledge exchange began to emerge. To put this change in perspective and understand the differences between BP and Shell, we need to go back to BP's early days.

Starting in the 1920s, BP's close relation to the government of the United Kingdom was visible not only on the board but throughout the organization. In many ways the company resembled a government department. Robert Horton, CEO from 1990 to 1992, describes his perception of BP's culture upon his return to London after a long stint in the United States with a subsidiary: "When I returned from Cleveland to London, I spent six months in deep culture shock because until I had been away for a couple of years, I hadn't realized how deeply embedded the bureaucracy, the distrust, the second-guessing, had become. We want a more flexible organization that works on trust and openness and teamwork rather than on hierarchy."[52]

At the time, the firm had 80 standing committees, 11 layers of management separated Horton and a first-line supervisor, and stringent budget caps suffocated managers at lower levels. To receive authorization for spending, a manager was typically required to secure 12 to 13 signatures.[53]

Teamwork, a given at Shell, was much harder to organize at BP. Although employees did work in formal teams, fruitful exchange of knowledge across geographies and functions is difficult in a bureaucratic organization. In the late 1980s, BP faced serious problems, including an annual production decline of 10 percent in Prudhoe Bay, Alaska, and in the Forties Oil Field in the North Sea, where 42 percent of the company's operating profit was generated. Earlier diversification into unrelated areas and a weak position in the downstream market caused additional problems, and in 1992 the company narrowly avoided bankruptcy.[54] While the strategic positioning was the main reason for this trouble, a different type of culture might have nurtured an organization that would have been able to learn, develop, and make better strategic decisions in the first place. Changes at BP after this brush with disaster support this line of thinking.

Horton initiated some serious reforms, though his abrasive style did not play well and he left after only two years. His successor, David Simon, held on for only one additional year before John Browne was handed the top job. BP embarked on a bold strategy of elephant hunting, a drive to go after risky big projects. The two most successful initiatives were a commitment to deepwater exploration in the Gulf of Mexico and formation of a joint venture with TNK in Russia. In both cases BP was able to succeed because it transferred knowledge that had accumulated over several decades.

In the Gulf of Mexico, BP started to acquire leaseholds in the 1980s. By then it had already accumulated more than 10 years of substantial offshore experience in the North Sea. This was certainly useful expertise. At the same time, the company had to face new challenges. The climate was harsher in the North Sea, but tropical storms and unprecedented levels of deepwater called for new generations of technology. BP invested heavily and became one of the pioneers in the region. The Atlantis, Thunder Horse, Holstein, and Mad Dog oil fields—which are among the largest discoveries—each cost in excess of $1 billion. Although BP has received a lot of bad press as a result of the Deepwater Horizon disaster in the Gulf of Mexico, the company continues be on the forefront of deepwater technology, working in water that is close to 10,000 feet deep and drilling more than 20,000 feet into the sea floor. New advanced drilling rigs, for example, allow the company to conduct drilling and completion activities at the same time.

The TNK success is even more closely related to the expertise that BP accumulated previously, during the company's long presence in Alaska. The development of Alaska's Prudhoe Bay posed huge, unprecedented challenges. BP had to learn how to operate in an arctic climate, a physical environment that, according to one geologist, was "a mean, nasty, unforgiving place to work."[55] Yet over several decades BP succeeded under these conditions. The company's record clearly influenced the Russian government's decision to approve a 50/50 joint venture between TNK and BP. Typically, national oil companies such as TNK or companies that own large reserves choose their partners in order to gain access to new markets and to knowledge that they do not themselves possess. From TNK's perspective, BP had deep knowledge of how to operate in arctic environments.

In the "new" BP under Browne, it became easier to transfer knowledge accumulated in Alaska to Russia. The most effective way remains the old-fashioned approach of transferring people. Despite modern communication technology, sharing experience depended on the ability of geologists and engineers from Alaska to work in close physical proximity to colleagues in Russia. In addition to transferring employees for long-term assignments, BP sent experts from London to help with particular tasks, such as the on-going effort to integrate information technology systems. Having common IT platforms and systems facilitated communications among geologists, geophysicists, and engineers. It became possible, for example, for personnel in Russia to get timely advice from colleagues in Alaska.

The principal enabler for this new spirit of knowledge sharing was a change in culture at BP. The old bureaucratic mind-set was laid to rest in favor of a new can-do spirit, while peer groups, formed around common expertise and problems,[56] proliferated across the company. The common goal to move forward, combined with a few group-wide systems (primarily financial reporting), formed the glue that held the company together. From a cultural perspective, BP managed to turn around and catch up with Shell. Not coincidentally, its financial performance also improved dramatically in the 1990s.

LEARNING STORIES

Powerful experiences often develop into stories. Some of these stories are nurtured by the corporations and passed on from generation to generation. Naturally, corporations love to tell heroic stories, stories in which the firm has fared very well. Such stories help to motivate people and inspire them to act in a certain way that ensured success in the past. While some of the comparison companies do that as well, the top companies are particularly skillful at this task. Glaxo, for example, loves the story of Alec Nathan's successful marketing campaign of dried milk. When Girolami started his breathtaking Zantac experience, he was able to follow the same tide as Nathan had almost 80 years earlier. He was able to stress the force of personality applied by Nathan when concentrating on the marketing of his product. Girolami's successor Sir Richard Sykes was equally taken by this story. He often recited it and also kept a picture of Alec Nathan in his office, reflecting his enthusiasm for the man. At Siemens many of the stories told over the past 150 years include its founder, Werner von Siemens. His drive to explore and participate in all fields of electrical engineering inspired technical staff for generations. It also had lasting implications for the strategic positioning of the firm, as Siemens held true to Werner von Siemens's paradigm to engage in all fields touched by electricity up to the 1960s and continues with a broader approach than most competitors do.

Besides these heroic stories, firms can also learn from negative experiences. This task is, of course, much more difficult and painful, for the natural desire is to leave such stories behind. With time, it becomes even harder to reap benefits from negative outcomes, since the original pain is no longer felt and there seems to be no obvious reason to keep reminding staff about things that they are bound to feel less proud about. Still, those companies that managed to generate outstanding performance over time went to great lengths also to pass on the knowledge that they gained during times of difficulty. As Nokia's celebrated Jorma Ollila puts it:

In my experience, looking at the long term, looking at Nokia over a 20-year period, it's difficult to see how you can learn without learning from mistakes, which often develop into a mini crisis, or even a crisis. Which then is a very useful vehicle in sending the right messages to the organization. They are much more powerful than any management textbook, or a burning speech by an eloquent CEO as a speaker.[57]

With such an approach, companies like Nokia manage to avoid similar troubles in the future. The initial setback turns into a learning investment. Once again, the comparison between Shell and BP highlights the difference between a good company and an outstanding company particularly well. At Shell, one of the most significant stories relates to Henry Deterding. In 1900 Henri Deterding arrived at the top of Royal Dutch Petroleum Company. Right from the start he had a brilliant touch for business. As he had proven in his earlier appointments in the Far East, he had an immediate grasp for financial details and a gift for organization building. Eventually he became the architect of the merger with Shell Transport and Trading in

1907 to form the Royal Dutch/Shell Group of Companies, which is commonly known as Shell. Under his firm control the oil major prospered and became one of the main challengers of the great American Oil companies that came out of the Standard Oil Trust.

Deterding's success put him in a position of unchallenged power. He was the strong CEO we are so familiar with from the American model today. This should not have been a great worry considering Deterding's golden touch. Unfortunately, certain political events almost brought Shell into a compromising situation. After the communists took over in Russia and nationalized the oil industry, Deterding became strongly anti-communist. He felt that no measure was too drastic to counter the enemies of capitalism. When Adolf Hitler came to power in Germany, Deterding felt that this might be the man to oppose the Russians. He started to travel to Germany more frequently and eventually married a German. Deterding's favorable judgment of Nazi Germany might have easily positioned Shell as an important supplier to the Third Reich. Fortunately for the company, however, Henri Deterding retired in 1936, before he established any links between Shell and the Nazis,[58] and the company thus narrowly escaped disaster. The incident shaped Shell's thinking in the decades to come. In 1961 the collective approach—meant to avoid such catastrophes—was formalized. The Committee of Managing Directors (CMD), headed by a chairman who is slightly more equal[59] than his three to seven peers, has guided the conglomerate since these reforms were initiated by John Loudon. Such a structure was clearly against the advice of McKinsey & Company, the consultancy firm. McKinsey suggested an American model, with clear accountability and a strong CEO. Because of the always fresh memories of the Deterding story, however, Shell declined to follow McKinsey's recommendation.

These arrangements stayed in place for decades, and only recently— following a crisis triggered by the company's overstatement of its proven oil and gas reserves—has Shell moved to a classic CEO leadership model. Even now, though, the company has remained remarkably careful to avoid placing an authoritarian leader at the top. "On the one side, we have our chief executive with more power to drive speed or to put his foot down about the things he wants to achieve, and at the same time we thought how we can put checks and balances around that person,"[60] says Jeroen van der Veer, Shell's recently retired CEO, in describing the transformation of the governance structure.

BP did not muster the same courage to learn from its most dramatic experience, the nationalization of its assets in Persia. Following his election to the post of prime minister in Persia, the well-spoken populist Mossadegh forced BP to leave his country. Overnight the oil major lost almost 70 percent of its oil supply. In the years leading up to the crisis, the firm had failed to diversify into other countries. Although it successfully managed to develop new assets in Alaska and the North Sea, it once again was heavily dependent on a small number of sites. The simple lesson of spreading the eggs to more than one—or in this case more than two—baskets was not passed on. Possibly the successful expansion into the new regions had prevented the development of a powerful story to this end. But then again, Shell had escaped the potential Deterding disaster without actual damage and nevertheless learned from the incident.

At the end of the 1990s, BP once again came close to disaster. One reason was its concentration on a few declining assets. Again BP failed to learn the lessons. Instead, the company embarked on a new elephant-hunting policy, being now heavily dependent on Russia. In an industry where nationalization is always a possibility, it remains a threat that is not fully appreciated by either BP or analysts. The spectacular performance resulting from high oil prices and the relatively healthy reserve replacement rate tend to push such hypothetical threats to the background. Although BP has already suffered dramatically from its failure to observe the principle of diversification, it is clear that the company has not taken the lesson to heart. It is striking how easily CEO John Browne brushed off concerns about taxes and the role of the Russian state. "The temperature always keeps changing—from cold to medium," he said in a 2005 interview in the *Guardian*,[61] "but the back taxes were sorted out for 2001, and I expect there will be further large claims for 2002 and so on, but equally these are not unusual. There are many other places in the world where large claims are made. Discussions usually take place, and a settlement is reached." Our comparison of good companies with great companies suggests that Browne is expressing a rather shortsighted view. Indeed, the

Russian government's 2008 denial of visas for a number of BP staff is a sign of things to come. BP was punished before. Why does the firm fail to keep the story alive and thereby prevent the same mistake from happening again? Shell avoided the repetition of a Deterding-like incident because it kept the story alive.

The failure to learn from mistakes is something we observed in our comparison companies again and again. AEG, for example, was hit in the 1930s when it forgot the virtue of conservative finances. Forgetting to keep this story alive, the company undertook massive growth after World War II and found itself in serious trouble once again in the 1970s. Gold medalist Siemens, on the other hand, took painful experiences to heart. It was temporarily outperformed by the then newly established AEG when Werner from Siemens refused to dilute the family ownership. As a consequence, the financial means necessary to compete in the power-generation business were not available. Werner von Siemens's sons changed the course of the firm when they took it public. Siemens did not make the same mistake twice. It never again failed to dilute the shareholding when that was required to increase the firm's capital base.

Gold medalist HSBC also recalls the lessons of its past mistakes. The Hongkong and Shanghai Banking Corporation (later HSBC) was set up in 1865 by the merchant community in Hong Kong to finance international trade. A close relationship with the bank's main customers guaranteed a strong start, but there were also drawbacks. Financing investments in fixed assets in China turned out to be riskier than anticipated, and access to London capital was more complicated for HSBC than it was for its UK-based competitors. This hit HSBC doubly hard when a severe recession struck in 1873. In response, the bank decided to adopt a more balanced management approach, which continues to dominate its strategy to this day. In 1876, it established a second executive board in London, creating a balance of power between the trade finance business in the East and the capital allocation center in London. The bank also increased its efforts to build up reserves and made sure that senior managers no longer had business interests outside the bank.

Silver medalist Standard Chartered (the Chartered Bank of India, Australia, and China at its founding in 1853), in contrast, did not learn from its biggest mistake, which was creating a centralized London-based management system that had a limited understanding of the China market. It lost major business to HSBC on numerous occasions—in the mid-1860s, for instance, it lost out because repayment periods for trade bills were shortened by London, against the advice of local managers. Nonetheless, the company stuck to the old system. In the following decades, the firm survived despite—not because of—its centralized management. Local branch managers simply ignored orders from London, which they viewed as unfit.

LEARNING LEADERSHIP

Leaders play an important role in creating a learning organization. The real challenge, though, is not for a single leader to foster learning at his time; it is to install a system that ensures a replication of leaders nurturing knowledge exchange as well as keeping important stories from the past alive. To that end, it is not a coincidence that Shell's CEO from 2004 to 2009, Jeroen van der Veer, is a strong team player who himself is keen to learn, to pass on his knowledge, and to encourage others to do the same. Shell has a system in place that fosters the development of leaders who see themselves more as trainers and teachers[62] than as charismatic overachievers who want to call the shots. The system developed gradually, beginning in 1966. At the time, the firm engaged Professor David van Lennep, an industrial psychologist at the University of Utrecht, to help it identify what distinguished those people who made it to the top of the organization from others.[63] On the basis of these results, the company started to establish a sophisticated HR system that continues to work in a similar manner today. The difference between Shell and the average large firm is that Shell has had such a system in place for decades and in fact uses the system to evaluate potential employees. During the recruitment process, applicants are ranked on three different characteristics: *capacity* (analytical ability to place problems in a wide but relevant perspective), *achievement* (ability to get things done), and *relationships* (ability to work efficiently with others on a team).[64] To test their abilities they submit a detailed application form, back up their claims in an interview, and finally spend one day at an assessment center. At this assessment center they will do a case study, hold a group discussion, and hopefully master an interview scenario. The recruiters, including at least one senior manager, on this final day then decide if the company wants to offer the candidate a position or not. So far, this process is far from unusual and would no doubt be similar to that of many large multinational corporations. But Shell takes one additional step in assessing a candidate. It provides each future employee with what is called a CEP (current employee potential). What this means is that the firm estimates at what level the future employee will most likely end up in the Shell hierarchy. The CEP helps HR and line management to enable leadership development from day one. It provides a basis for determining the best form of training and, even more important, the specific job that will best allow staff members to develop their skills. Before 1995, this was a fairly harsh system, in the sense that staff members had little choice when it came to assignments. A personnel planner in cooperation with line management would decide which positions were most suitable. Since the company had an expatriate force of more than 5,000 (or 5 percent of total staff), placement often required a change in continent. Although this was not easy from a personal point of view, it presented a great learning opportunity in terms of both gaining technical knowledge and, even more importantly, creating a multinational network rooted in different cultures. In 1995 the system was modernized, giving employees a greater say in their own future. An internal online job market was created to facilitate the process. What remains is the principle that the firm needs to develop its people right from the start if its goal is to create a large group of potential top managers.

The emphasis on training and development is no doubt one of the main reasons why Shell creates leaders at the top who see their role as similar to that of a soccer coach.[65] As Cor Herkströter, Shell's leader from 1993 to 1998, put it, "Managing an organization is much more coaching an organization rather than directing an organization or saying that is what we want you to do."[66] Soccer coaches or leaders are hardly the ones that score the goals themselves. Their responsibility lies elsewhere; they must create a winning team. They set guidelines for the players, provide them with more training, and perhaps look on the transfer market for additional players. They also change incentives and substitute players who do not perform too well. Occasionally a coach may shout from the sidelines or try to interfere in operations. But this should not happen too often, as the result is chaos, not the superior performance that is the goal. Direct action—such as the substitution of a player—is important, but it must be selective and limited! The action that the leader—coach or CEO—should be strongest at is training the team, creating learning opportunities.

Shell's leadership is not alone in the effort to learn and teach. Leaders of other outstanding corporations do exactly the same. Harry Jephcott, Austin Bide, Paul Girolami, and Richard Sykes from Glaxo were all very keen on learning from their experts. Harry Jephcott, for example, took extensive annual trips to the various subsidiaries, accompanied by his wife, who kept a diary including details about the personal lives of staff they met. This record enabled Jephcott on subsequent visits to be more personal and create an atmosphere of trust, which is absolutely vital to stimulate learning. Creating personal trust as a condition of sharing insights was something that leaders at Lafarge also understood most intimately. For example, Léon Pavin de Lafarge, who took over from his father, Auguste, in 1833, was a very down-to-earth person despite his education at the elite École Polytechnique. He spent considerable time at the plant chatting with workers, and no doubt he benefited from their ideas, as they did from his thoughts. More than 100 years later Alfred François Lafarge managed the transition from a family-dominated corporation to a truly public corporation. Despite the changes of the time, management continued to understand that personal relationships and trust matter. As François put it, "The legitimacy of a leader is based on his ability to serve."[67]

In the comparison companies the leadership's ambition to foster learning is less pronounced. There is, of course, the occasional exception, but overall, other aspects seem to carry greater importance for these CEOs. What is most striking, though, is the missing continuity. At BP, for example, CEO John Browne managed to foster learning through his peer group system. But he seems to have been an exception. None of his predecessors was able to install a system similar to Shell's structure, which fostered leadership development that emphasized learning and survived for several generations. The first managing director of the Anglo-Persian Oil Company (later BP), Charles Greenway, for example, concentrated his energies on building an integrated oil company while engaging in tedious infighting with government officials. The tension became much worse in the 1940s when William Fraser was in charge. Ministers and senior civil servants at Whitehall described him as secretive and autocratic[68]—certainly not qualities that inspire the flow of ideas. In more recent times, we have already mentioned Robert Horton and David Simon, who were able to hold on to their positions as CEO for only a year or two. Horton, in particular, was known for his abrasive style.

LEARNING MECHANISMS

A more formal way to foster learning in an organization is through established processes. This does not necessarily mean that an entire corporation runs through an annual learning exercise. In fact, such a prescribed process would seem rather artificial and would be difficult to integrate into regular business processes. None of the outstanding companies took such an approach. A much more effective strategy is to take an already well-established procedure at the firm and transform it into a learning experience. One obvious choice is the planning process. On the surface, planning seems to be primarily about setting targets and allocating budgets that help firms to achieve those targets. In fact, most corporations understand the planning process exactly this way and thus miss a great opportunity to stimulate knowledge exchange. They more or less remain stuck in the 1960s, an era when leaders decided on budgets for the next few years but saw no need to develop a sophisticated and integrated approach to strategic planning.[69] At the other extreme are corporations that view strategy as an "elite" academic subject. A few specialists conduct complicated economic analysis that goes almost unnoticed by the majority of the staff. No doubt the specialists learn a lot, but the benefit for the wider corporation is limited. The companies that we identified as great performers over time certainly moved beyond this paradigm. According to Arie de Geus, the former head of Shell's strategic planning unit, his firm interprets planning primarily as a learning opportunity.[70] Going through the annual process means that managers have an opportunity to collectively think about the future. They are able to exchange ideas and to learn from their colleagues.[71]

A technique that Shell found to be particularly helpful in its ambition to transform the planning process into a learning exercise was scenario planning.[72] Being aware of the limits of a linear planning effort, Shell was inspired by Herman Kahn and Anthony Wiener[73] from the Hudson Institute and started to develop an alternative planning process in the 1970s. While the traditional way to create forecasts worked in a stable environment, it failed when most needed, namely "in anticipating major shifts in the business environment that make whole strategies obsolete."[74] In other words, Shell admitted that it was simply not possible to predict the future. Therefore the best the company could do was to develop a number of equally valid scenarios instead of forecasts. The real value of such an approach was captured in the following step, during which managers throughout the company discussed what actions they would take if one or the other scenario were to unfold. (A key to the success of this exercise was that they avoided engaging in heated debates about the likelihood that a scenario would occur.) They developed a "memory of the future," which allowed them to act fast if they needed to. Shell borrowed this term from the neurobiologist David Ingvar,[75] who uses it to describe our preparation for an unpredictable future. He argues that we instinctively create action plans for the future at every moment of our lives. They are time paths into an anticipated future that combine a future hypothetical condition of the environment with an option for action, but they are not predictions. Our brains store these time paths and assign relevance to incoming images and sensations. Ingvar says that signals from the outside world are not perceived unless they are relevant to an option for the future that we have already worked out in our imaginations. This means that we are more open and receptive to signals from the outside world if we increase the number of memories of the future that we develop.[76]

This is exactly what Shell tried to do for the corporation as a whole by imagining different options and contemplating how the firm would react under the different circumstances. The scenario planning team was able to book a number of great successes, which certainly helped to establish the new tool. Namely, they anticipated the first oil crisis in 1974—the impact of higher oil prices on economic growth in the 1970s and the subsequent fall in oil prices in the mid-1980s, the collapse of the Soviet Union and the European integration. At the same time, they missed some major developments, including the importance of China and the backlash against globalization in the 1990s.[77] The real value of the scenario planning approach was much more than the ability to correctly predict events. What mattered was the mind-set of leaders. They became aware that the world around them is primarily unstable and that predictions are problematic. Instead they could discuss potential actions with their colleagues and learn from their experiences. Shell's top management in the 1990s grew up in this system, and they were accustomed to having to defend their annual budgets against several scenarios. They were familiar with Ingvar's "memory of the future" and were deeply convinced that the future is plural. They knew that events do not unfold with average regularity and that adjustments rarely produce the desired effect. They also knew that a company is not reinvented overnight and that it always has to prepare for the unthinkable. As Cor Herkströter, Shell's leader from 1993 to 1998, puts it, "Shell has always been known for scenario planning . . . but the operating companies were told not to simply follow the scenarios presented by the center but—if necessary—indicate why they couldn't precisely follow the scenarios . . . and what they took . . . as an alternative. So that already gave the organization almost a silent possibility of taking into account developments in the different environments and to gradually change if necessary."[78] Bearing that in mind, Shell's application of planning as a learning exercise has been a very successful approach. In the case of the first oil crisis, it is viewed as the main reason that Shell was able to respond to the new situation much faster than its competitors could. Refinery capacities were shifted and production areas outside OPEC were able to cover for immediate losses, enabling Shell to pull ahead of the other oil majors.

LEARNING TRAINING

Companies spend a lot of money on the recruitment process. When they finally get their selected candidates, they are eager to put them to work and show that they got their money's worth. Not so at Shell. When engineers and geologists show up for their first day of work at the exploration and production division, they are taken to a training facility, where they spend the next six weeks getting accustomed to Shell and their future responsibilities. The content of the course hopefully provides them with important knowledge. More importantly, though, they start building a network before they even start working! The course creates an opportunity for people to meet. When they face problems later on in their jobs it will be easy for them to pick up the phone or send an e-mail message to somebody they met at the training course.

Shell is not alone in its emphasis on training. All the companies in our sample—including the comparison companies—organize formal training opportunities of some sort. This does not diminish the importance of training as such but highlights the fact that training is merely one of the building blocks necessary to create a learning organization. The crucial issue is that it fits the other elements mentioned above. We also noticed that outstanding corporations started to organize training courses earlier on in their history than most of their comparison companies. Nokia, for example, started a school for employees in 1891.[79] It also took a more inclusive approach than Ericsson, which had a very engineer-based culture where people with other backgrounds found it harder to prevail. Shell decided to set up three training centers in Holland in 1947, accommodating a total of 200 trainees and replacing the more informal approach of the past. In 1952 the Lensbury Club near London opened to provide executive courses for a maximum of 100 participants a year. BP had no comparable courses at the time. Particularly noteworthy about Shell's approach is the focus on personal development rather than technical knowledge at all levels. By 1972 Shell had 75 expatriates working as trainers in 42 centers in 30 countries.[80] Lafarge put a similar emphasis on leadership training at an early stage when it formed its École de Contes in 1950. At this training center staff received technical training, but future managers also invested several months in training. The ability of the latter to form networks was enhanced through the institutionalization of the Groupe des Cadres, a body that organized the participation of middle management in important decisions made by the company, in 1964. The comparison companies BP and Ciments Français, respectively, did not display the same passion for learning at the time.

In more recent years an emphasis on personal development has become as universal as technical training has been for many years. The comparison companies also acknowledge this, and those that have been transformed into successful enterprises have adopted the strategy with great passion.

BP, for example, has a *first-level leadership program*, bringing together people who lead a group for the first time in their career. What is impressive about this particular program is its scale. Every first-level leader across the entire group goes through the program. This means that more than 10,000 people become part of a network.

SUMMARY

In a changing world companies need to develop the ability to learn constantly. While bright individuals are able to provide the important ingredient of new ideas, the trickiest part is the transfer of this knowledge, the transformation from individual insights to organizational capabilities and resources. Outstanding companies use different approaches to ensure such a transformation. Five of them are particularly useful and common:

Learning Culture: Culture is a main driver of our behavior and therefore an ideal vehicle to transport knowledge across time. At Shell, for example, the core values—trust, integrity, and respect for people—capture the insight that in the long run the firm will prevail in a highly political industry only if it sticks to these rules.

Learning Stories: The greatest mistakes are also the greatest learning opportunities. Unfortunately many companies fail to use them as such. BP lost almost 70 percent of its assets when they were nationalized in 1951. Instead of learning the lesson, the company became heavily dependent on the North Sea and Alaska in the following decades. Once again, it was hit hard when these oil fields started to decline at the end of the 1980s and once again it has particularly large exposure to one region today: Russia.

Learning Leadership: Leaders who know everything simply do not exist. Outstanding leaders prevail primarily because they are ready to learn from members of their organization and they teach others the lessons. This is possible only if they succeed in creating personal trust. Léon Pavin de Lafarge, who took over the firm from his father, Auguste, in 1833, for example, was a very down-to-earth person despite his education at the elite École Polytechnique. He listened to his workers, and they in turn were happy to listen to him.

Learning Mechanisms: Maybe sometime in the future corporations will run through an annual learning exercise. At the moment such a procedure remains an illusion. Nonetheless, companies can use established processes to transfer knowledge. One of the most impressive exercises of this kind is the planning cycle of Shell. The company uses a scenario planning technique, not in order to predict the future but to help its managers to create an open mind-set and prepare for the unexpected.

Learning Training: There is probably not a single large company that does not engage in some form of learning today. What distinguishes outstanding companies from their competitors is their ability to use such opportunities as network creation exercises. In addition, outstanding companies started to organize training for their employees early in their history. Nokia, for example, established its first school for employees in 1891.

Diversify into Related Businesses

One of the great success stories of 20th-century universities was the growth of the business school. From modest beginnings as small departments or faculties in the early 1900s, business schools have experienced commercial success that provides them with much clout and independence today. Part of their success was, of course, a result of the undiminishing demand for graduates with commercial knowledge. But there is more to it. The most prestigious schools have long branched out into new but related areas. Take Harvard Business School, for example. Founded in 1908, the school gained its first experience in publishing when the *Harvard Business Review* was released in 1922. Two decades later, the executive education program began, with 60 executives and veterans returning from World War II in 1945. By 1993 the publishing enterprise had become so large that it was spun off into a separate subsidiary. Staying within its expertise of management sciences, the school has diversified from graduate studies into executive education and publishing. In 2009 it collected revenues of $84 million from its MBA degree program, while executive education brought in $107 million and publishing $137 million. New opportunities are currently being tested, with offices opening in California, Latin America, Asia Pacific, Japan, Europe, and India. The logic to which HBS and other business schools adhere is actually quite simple: a strategy of diversification that combines related businesses to exploit economies of scope is most likely to succeed, while diversification into unrelated businesses is less likely to succeed. It seems indeed unlikely that HBS will move beyond its sale of HBS merchandise in the local bookshops to become a national clothing retailer. What is true for business schools also holds true in the world of business. The history of business in Europe and elsewhere is full of examples illustrating the point. Related diversification tends to work, as Lafarge's move from cement into aggregates or the branching out of German chemical companies into the new pharmaceutical industry at the end of the 19th century shows. Meanwhile, history has many stories to tell about misguided and expensive unrelated diversification: BP's experiment with fish farming, Daimler-Benz's adventure in aerospace, GE's purchase of Utah International and Kidder, Peabody, AOL's merger with Time Warner, and many others.

Diversification is an emotional subject. One reason is that owners and managers hold divergent perspectives. In 1932 Adolph Berle and Gardiner Means[81] pointed out that ownership and control are separate in many large corporations. Decisions that are supposed to guarantee a company's profits are made by managers who do not bear the full costs if things turn sour.

From the owner's perspective, diversification seems sensible only if it increases a company's long-term potential for growth and profitability. Managers might have additional motives. The economist Michael Jensen, for example, argues that managers may simply enjoy running a large company for its own sake: "Corporate growth enhances the social prominence, public prestige, and political power of senior executives. Rare is the CEO who wants to be remembered as presiding over an enterprise that makes fewer products in fewer plants in fewer countries than when he or she took office."[82] Other motives might be appointments to the boards of other companies[83] or the diversification of their own portfolio. For example, AOL's acquisition of Time Warner in 2000 allowed AOL CEO Steve Case to diversify his personal investment portfolio. Before the merger he held nearly 1 percent of AOL's shares, worth $1 billion. Through the purchase of Time

Warner, he was able to reduce his exposure to the Internet business and acquire interest in the potentially more stable broadcasting and media business. Selling AOL shares on the market and buying Time Warner shares instead was not really an option. Such a step could have raised questions about whether Case knew about impending bad news before it became public.[84]

Needless to say, great companies do not pursue diversification simply for the benefit of managers. So the question remains as to how diversification can be of value to shareholders and also to other stakeholders, including management. Before we explore this question for our sample of outstanding and comparison companies, it will be helpful to consider an overview of diversification in Europe.

One way to approach the subject is through a classification similar to the one developed by Richard Rumelt when he did his Ph.D. dissertation at Harvard in the 1960s and early 1970s.[85] Rumelt introduced the notion of "relatedness" and built eight categories. Three of his fellow doctoral students—Heinz Thanheiser, Gareth Dyas,[86] and Derek Channon[87]—adapted these categories slightly for a study of diversification in Europe: single, dominant, related, and unrelated businesses.

In a single-business company, 95 percent or more of the revenues are generated by a single activity or line of business. A classic example would be De Beers diamond production or Hugo Boss in fashion. In a dominant-business company, between 70 percent and 95 percent of revenues are generated by a single activity or line of business. This would include companies like Essilor, which in most years realized a little over 90 percent of its revenues from the sale of corrective lenses and the remaining from the sale of related instruments. Another example is SAB-Miller, a British company that generates 89 percent of its revenues from beer and the remainder from non-alcoholic beverages and hotels. The third category contains companies in related businesses. Such companies derive less than 70 percent of their revenues from a single activity or line of business but have other businesses in related areas. Examples include Shell, Siemens, Henkel, Nestlé, and Alcatel. Finally, companies in unrelated businesses derive less than 70 percent of their revenues from a single activity, while at least 5 percent of revenues are generated in businesses not related to the principal activity. LVMH, for example, produces fashion items, wine, and spirits. RAG in Germany is in real estate, coal, chemicals, utilities, and power generation.

Using Rumelt's methodology and building on subsequent research done primarily at Harvard[88] and more recently at Glasgow and Oxford,[89] it is possible to track diversification in Germany, France, and the United Kingdom in the past 50 years. A look at the top 100 manufacturing companies in these countries provides information about what percentage of them were single, dominant, related, or unrelated businesses.

In 1950 single-business companies accounted for 37 percent of all European companies. In subsequent decades the number of single businesses started to decline. Only in more recent years have they begun to gain prominence again. This is particularly due to the reduction of the number of diversified companies in France and Germany, where single businesses now form the largest group, accounting for 26 and 29 percent, respectively, of large companies. One possible explanation is a shift in management thinking, perhaps epitomized by Gary Hamel and C. K. Prahalad's popular book *Competing for the Future*.[90] Whereas in the 1960s and 1970s, conglomerates—unrelated diversified companies—were regarded as effective vehicles for spreading risks across business cycles, it has since become conventional wisdom that companies need to concentrate on their

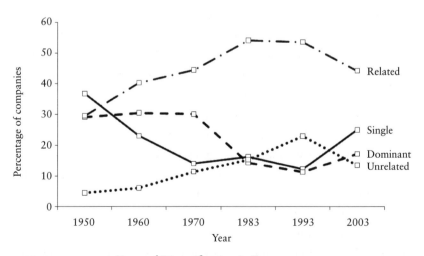

FIGURE 3.15. 50 Years of Diversification in Europe
SOURCE: Data from Channon 1971; Dyas and Thanheiser 1976; Whittington and Mayer 2000.

core competencies. The verdict of the stock markets bears this out: high price-to-earnings ratios for conglomerates in the 1960s and 1970s have been replaced by "conglomerate discounts."[91] Meanwhile, globalization in general and European integration in particular opened up previously protected markets and increased competition in Europe. As a result, many companies started to divest non-core businesses. Not only did these divestments create more single businesses, but the spin-offs themselves often were large single businesses. Infineon, a chip maker, and EPCOS, an electronic component manufacturer, for example, were both divested from Siemens.

The second category, dominant business companies, accounted for a 30 percent share of large businesses in Germany, France, and the United Kingdom until the 1970s and then slipped down to around 15 percent. In the same period, substantial growth of both related and unrelated diversified businesses can be observed. While the spotlight has often focused on conglomerates, related diversified companies clearly outperformed them. Since the 1960s these companies have accounted for 40 percent to 50 percent of all large corporations in Europe.

This is hardly a coincidence. An examination of the relationship between performance and diversification helps to clarify why related diversified companies account for such a high percentage of the total. Rumelt argues that moderately diversified firms have higher capital productivity while moderately to highly unrelated diversified firms have moderate to poor productivity. Later studies confirm this conclusion.[92] Notably, Leslie Palich, Laura Cardinal, and Chet Miller do so in a synthesis of 55 studies conducted over the past 30 years. Neither narrower nor broader strategies are a match for companies pursuing related diversification.[93]

In the short run, single businesses also perform very well—often better than related diversified firms. This fits with the notion of core competencies. For those investors who look for a quick buck, this certainly adds to the attractiveness of single businesses. For those investors who look for long-term returns, the story is different. While single businesses perform well in the short run, they are less likely to sustain high performance. The diversification study of European firms showed that between 1953 and 2003 a number of them dropped out of the sample of the 100 largest manufacturing companies. Business cycles and unexpected events are more likely to hit single businesses hard. To ensure performance over time, the formula for success is diversification into businesses where current capabilities can best be applied. As Sayan Chatterjee and Birger Wernerfeld discovered in a comprehensive study of stock prices and diversification, companies with highly specialized resources and capabilities engage in more related diversification strategies and achieve results superior to those achieved by companies that use unspecialized resources, such as cash, to diversify.[94]

Our enduring success study affirms the same conclusion. Related diversified companies are disproportionately represented among both the gold and the silver medalists. Top companies know that today's business might no longer be profitable tomorrow. They prepare. They start new businesses internally and through alliances and mergers. At the same time they know that this can be done well only in areas where they have resources and capabilities. In general they do not attempt to compete in unrelated businesses.

Analysis of our top and comparison companies also makes obvious that shifts in the business environment tend to force companies more and more to position themselves in the related diversified category. While protected national markets allowed some companies, like Nokia, to compete successfully as an unrelated diversified company in the 1960s and 1970s, the downfall of the Soviet Union—which provided stable business—forced the company

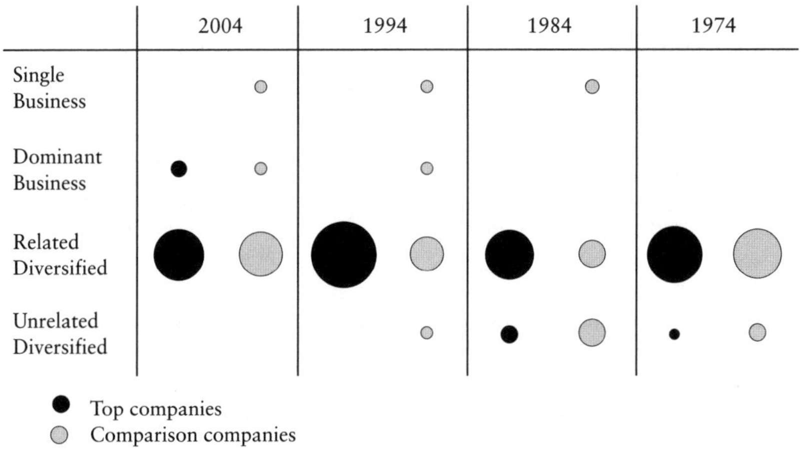

	2004	1994	1984	1974
Single Business	○	○	○	
Dominant Business	● ○		○	
Related Diversified	● ◯	● ○	● ○	● ◯
Unrelated Diversified		○	● ◯	• ○

● Top companies
◯ Comparison companies

FIGURE 3.16. Diversification of Top and Comparison Companies

TABLE 3.2. Diversification of Top and Comparison Companies

Top Companies		Comparison Companies	
Nokia		**Ericsson**	
Related, then Unrelated, and now Related	The only top company that remained unrelated diversified in its early history. When the Finnish market started to open up, the company began to focus on mobile phones and networks.	Related and more recently Dominant	A pioneer in telephones, the company diversified into related areas. An adventure in military equipment turned out to be less successful. In recent years the firm has concentrated on networks.
HSBC		**Standard Chartered**	
Related	Set up to finance British trade in China, the company was quick to diversify into related areas such as large government loans in China. After World War II the firm successfully took direct investments and moved into retail banking in Britain when the opportunity arose.	Between Single and Dominant	Also set up to finance British trade in Asia, the Chartered Bank was too slow to diversify in government loans originally. The attempt to diversify into retail banking in Britain in the 1970s and 1980s failed.
Glaxo[1]		**Wellcome**	
Related	Selling milk powder in its early days, the company first diversified into over-the-counter medicine. It used World War I as an opportunity to begin penicillin production. This was the start of a growing prescription drug business. The company remains the broadest-based Big Pharma company.	Originally Related and later Dominant and Single	A pioneer in research-based drugs, the company originally focused on building a broad base. As history moved on, the company narrowed its focus to become a single-business firm.
Legal & General		**Prudential**	
Related and recently Dominant	Starting with insurance products that targeted the legal profession, the company diversified as new businesses emerged in the industry. It became particularly strong in pensions.	Related	Clearly a related diversified insurance company building a broad base. One of the few areas where the company was left behind was in the development of the pension business after World War II.
Shell		**BP**	
Related	An integrated oil company with a particularly strong marketing arm. The industry trend to diversify into unrelated areas in the 1970s and 1980s was broadly resisted, although the company made a major investment in BHP Billiton, a coal and mining firm.	Originally Single, then, Unrelated, and now Related	Although BP also attempted to become an integrated oil company when it started business in the early 20th century, it is much more narrowly focused on the upstream business. The 1970s and 1980s brought ill-founded ventures into nutrition, fish farming, and metals.

TABLE 3.2. *(continued)*

Top Companies		Comparison Companies	
Lafarge		**Ciments Français**	
Related	A classic example of successful related diversification. From its beginnings in lime production, the company later moved into cement, then aggregates, and more recently roofing.	Single	The firm has remained a single-business company solely focused on cement and less ready to pursue new opportunities.
Allianz		**Aachener und Münchener**	
Related	Allianz started off in transport insurance when that was a niche market. As new insurance areas have developed, the company has always been ready to build up a substantial position in them, using a number of opportunities to buy troubled competitors. In recent years the firm purchased Dresdner Bank to diversify into financial services.	Originally Single and later Dominant	A big player in fire insurance, the company missed opportunities to branch out in new areas such as transport insurance. Its dependence on farming insurance turned out to be a problem when that sector in the economy was declining.
Siemens		**AEG**	
Related	The company's founder had the vision to play in all areas of electrical engineering, and that has guided Siemens throughout its history. At the same time, areas too far removed from the core were usually kept at arm's length and often sent into joint ventures or spun off..	Originally Related and then Unrelated	Starting with a more narrow focus than Siemens, the firm quickly began to diversify. When the consumer products business became a distinctly different market, the firm failed to decide whether to be a big player in this area or in the more traditional line of electrical engineering. The resulting conglomerate missed a focus, compared to Siemens.
Munich Re		**Cologne Re**	
Related	A pioneer in many reinsurance areas, the company was always ready to diversify into related fields. A cross-shareholding since 1914 with Allianz—which had the same founder—guaranteed closeness to primary insurance. In recent years this has been enhanced through the formation of its own primary insurance, ERGO.	Related	The oldest reinsurance company in the world remained more focused than Munich RE throughout its history, concentrating on accidents and liabilities and keeping its positions in life insurance small.

[1] Today GlaxoSmithKline

to rid itself of unrelated businesses. Interestingly, some comparison companies have not been willing or able to make this adjustment. Overall, the comparison companies are more likely to follow management trends like conglomeration. More of them diversified into unrelated areas when it was fashionable, and more of them have since become single businesses.

In the following pages a more detailed analysis of the development of companies in our sample will shed light on how the most successful ones managed continuously to diversify into related areas. We start with a comparison of two German insurance companies: Allianz and Aachner und Münchener.

ALLIANZ AND AACHNER UND MÜNCHENER

If there ever was an impressive career, it was that of Carl Thieme. Born in 1844 in Erfurt, he followed in his father's footsteps into the insurance industry. By the age of 27, he was already in charge of the Munich office of Thuringia Versicherungs AG, a large German company. Two years later he headed the company in Bavaria and grew his region to become the largest in the firm. By 1880, Thieme seemed to be ready to take on new challenges when he founded Munich Re, the second-largest reinsurance company today. His entrepreneurial drive continued, and in 1890 he and his partner Wilhelm von Finck founded Allianz. Backed by the established Munich Re, the new company experienced phenomenal growth. By 1914 the Allianz was the largest German non-life insurer, and today it is among the giants of its industry.

Allianz's development is a powerful example of a company that constantly reaches out into related areas. Step by step, Allianz has experimented with new types and forms of insurance. Occasionally a takeover of a troubled competitor or company in an adjacent market generated faster growth, but none of these moves seemed sensational at the time. On the contrary, being careful to avoid overstretching its resources and capabilities when starting new activities and integrating new companies proved to be a vital ingredient of Allianz's success. In reaching out into new areas, the company always seemed prepared when the market changed. It had an almost perfect portfolio mix of stable, growing, and declining units long before the Boston Consulting Group designed its famous matrix.

Right from the start in 1890 the company united diverse businesses under one roof. In the late 19th century fire insurance was the most commonly sold type of policy. Although it accounted for the most premiums, fire insurance was nonetheless a declining business.[95] Allianz steered clear of this market and concentrated on a new type of policy with better prospects: transport insurance. At the time, foreign companies were the primary source of transport policies. Thieme and his colleagues made a good bet, however. In the course of industrialization, a rising volume of goods was transported across Germany. In addition to the establishment of a new cash cow, Allianz also set the direction for future growth in a related area, casualty insurance. Although it did not generate big premiums at the outset, this type of insurance would soon grow dramatically.

Meanwhile, Allianz used cash generated by transport insurance to branch out into industrial insurances. In 1900 the company sold its first equipment policies. Building on the growing expertise in this area, in 1911 it introduced a policy covering production losses when a machine needed to be repaired.[96] While experiments like this did not generate income to start with, the experience and knowledge that the company accumulated helped it to win later on.

The next important diversification occurred after World War I. The Treaty of Versailles prohibited German companies from expanding in international markets, and thus Allianz was forced to focus on Germany. In 1918 the company formed Kraft-Versicherungs AG to unite car insurance activities in a single organization. Four years later, it cofounded Allianz Life. After merger talks with a potential partner broke down, Kurt Schmitt, the top executive at the time, contacted Friedrich Wilhelm Lebensversicherungs AG. The parties agreed initially to cooperate, but again negotiations stalled. Schmitt was prepared, however, and had already written to the head of Munich Re, Wilhelm Kisskalt, suggesting the formation of Allianz Life. Munich Re and Allianz would each hold a 25 percent stake, with German banks supplying the remainder.

The new venture opened for business early in 1922. Allianz's know-how from the earlier partnership with Karlsruher Lebensversicherung came in handy. The acquisition of Lebensversicherungsbank Arminia a few months later also added momentum. Within a few years the new company became the largest life insurer on the continent.[97] Allianz now was a major player in both life and non-life insurance.

At Aachner und Münchener Versicherung the story unfolded quite differently. To begin with, Aachner und Münchener had less ambition to become a broadly based insurance company. "Schuster bleib bei deinen Leisten" (loosely translated as "stick to the knitting") was an old German principle that Aachner und Münchener interpreted too literally.

In August 1824, 13 local investors had signed a contract to form the Aachener Feuerversicherungs-Aktiengesellschaft, which started business the following month after receiving permission from King Friedrich Wilhelm III. The inspiration and leadership of the new company came primarily from David Hansemann, who had started his career in textiles and had been an investor in another fire insurance company.[98] Hansemann certainly was a visionary. At the time, the insurance industry was very fragmented. Insurance companies and their customers hardly trusted each other, and it was far from uncommon for one to decide against honoring an agreement. Hansemann wanted to establish trust with the general public by committing 50 percent of profits to charity.[99] It took nine years after the foundation of the company, however, before enough profits were generated to dedicate any money to charity. Still, this was five years before the first dividend would be paid out.

Hansemann's concept worked. People started to trust the company, feelings that were reinforced after 1842, when the company paid out 320,000 taler after a great fire in Hamburg. The move nearly bankrupted the company, but premiums grew quickly in the following years. The engagement of the able Friedrich Adolph Brüggemann in 1845 also helped. He built up a powerful distribution network.

In 1848 Hansemann left the firm to become Prussian finance minister. Aachener und Münchener (originally Aachener Feuerversicherungs-Aktiengesellschaft and then Aachener und Münchener Versicherung after its expansion into Bavaria) continued to grow and seemed destined for greatness. Between 1860 and 1870, however, the tide started to turn. Competition in fire insurance picked up considerably. Revenue growth slowed, while profits declined.[100] For the first time, Aachener und Münchener considered diversifying into new businesses. While Allianz had thought about tomorrow's business right from the start, it took Aachener und Münchener four decades to do so. Allianz had started diversification before growth had slowed in its main business, but Aachener und Münchener did so only when the need was all too obvious. Better late than never, of course, but Aachener und Münchener's diversification was also less pronounced and less successful. Forming a reinsurance branch and insurance against hail kept the company focused on the same customer segment, farmers. The firm's charity foundation had a close relationship with various farmer associations. Its agents were not prepared to approach factories and plants, a fast-growing and promising customer segment that arose during the second half of the 19th century.[101] Even fire insurance products were focused on rural areas, though competitors were signing up industrial customers.

With growth prospects declining, Aachener und Münchener's owners became impatient. At the 50th anniversary in 1875, shareholders demanded a reduction of charitable actions. Some were not satisfied with that step and established a competitor, Aachen-Leipziger Versicherungs AG.[102] In 1892 the decision was made to support charity only after a minimum profit was reached.[103]

In the end, these measures had little impact. The essential problem was that Aachener und Münchener was overinvested in a declining segment. The leadership failed to pay appropriate attention to this issue. The company failed to diversify into products tailored for the industrial society that emerged. Fritz Schröder, who took over the top position in 1896, started an international expansion instead. This move was initially successful but had no impact on the fundamental portfolio. World War I wiped out most of these initiatives.

Only in 1924, 99 years after its founding, did Aachner und Münchener undertake more serious diversification. Brüggemann, who led the company in the 1890s, had first brought up the idea to start a life insurance business, but he was not able to make it happen. A quarter of a century later, Wilhelm Spans relaunched the idea and managed to acquire the Aachen-Potsdamer-Lebensversicherungs-Gesellschaft. Another step to broaden the customer base was the formation of the Rheinische Gruppe, a loose cooperation of 15 insurance companies with Aachener und Münchener, Colonia Versicherungs AG, and Vaterländische Feuerversicherung at the core.

Both diversification attempts amounted to moves in the right direction. However, they came too late to make a significant impact on Aachener und Münchener's fortunes. The life insurance business remained relatively small, while the Rheinische Gruppe proved difficult to manage and grow. The strong dependence on rural areas remained. Failure to adapt to the structural shift from an agricultural to an industrial economy continued to haunt the company. When the Soviet Union dominated East Germany after World War II, an agricultural region served by Aachener und Münchener was lost. Forty percent of its fire insurance business had originated there.

In contrast, after World War II, Allianz's diversification strategy continued to pay dividends. When industrial customers moved abroad, they brought Allianz with them. A 1927 merger with Stuttgarter Verein Versicherungs AG also had proved a great success. The acquisition of the leading liabilities insurer guaranteed a strong position in this market. Allianz also became an active investor, accumulating large stakes in Beiersdorf, Linde, BASF, RWE, VEBA, Leifheit, Schering, Bayer, Thyssen, Siemens, Daimler-Benz, Bayerische Hypo- und Vereinsbank, and Dresdner Bank, among other leading German companies.[104]

After World War II, Aachener und Münchener finally succeeded in diversification, growing significant customer bases in both car and life insurance. When the Rheinische Gruppe was dissolved in 1968, Volks-hilfe Lebensversicherung was acquired from Colonia and integrated with Aachener und Münchener's existing life insurance business. Minority stakes in liabilities insurance of Gladbacher and Schlesischen were divested, while the company took a 25 percent stake in Cologne Re. In the past, Allianz's close relationship with Munich Re had been beneficial when launching new ventures. The reinsurance company, for example, had supported Allianz's diversification efforts in such areas as life insurance. However, Aachener und Münchener did not enjoy a similar supportive relationship with Cologne Re.

In 1970 Aachener und Münchener bought Badenia Bausparkasse, a home loan bank and Central Krankenversicherung, a health insurance company. These acquisitions marked a trend that became evident in the insurance industry in Germany in subsequent years: the transformation of insurance companies into financial services companies, often referred to as *Allfinanz*. Before the 1970s, mergers between banks and insurance companies were not permitted under German law. This sharp line between industries began to erode, however. In theory, insurance companies appeared to face huge new business opportunities. They would now be able to serve a broad range of their customers' financial needs. Unfortunately, the implementation of this idea proved difficult.

Aachener und Münchener's first attempt to diversify into banking is a classic example of how not to implement such a strategy. In 1987 it bought the troubled BfG Bank in hopes of using it as a direct distribution channel for a broad range of products. When this idea failed dismally, tough reforms followed. Half of the bank's staff were fired.[105] Unfortunately, however, no lasting turnaround was achieved. Meanwhile, the bank committed a fundamental mistake by targeting affluent customers. This segment did not fit the bank's image. Traditionally it had served the working class and it was the house bank of many German unions. It had little experience in dealing with wealthy customers. Losses piled up, and in 1993 Aachener und Münchener decided to sell the bank to Crédit Lyonnais.[106] While Aachener und Münchener's strategy to become a financial services company made sense from a diversification perspective, the BfG Bank acquisition was a poor first step. Subsequently, the company proved more successful through a cooperative agreement with Commerzbank.[107] Failing to initiate the growth that management had hoped to generate through becoming a financial services firm, Aachener und Münchener eventually fell prey to the largest players in Europe. Allianz and Generali, an Italian insurance giant, both were interested in AGF, a French insurance company. AGF in turn held 25 percent plus one share in Aachener und Münchener. In 1998 Allianz and Generali agreed that the latter would sell its stake in AGF to Allianz and would buy both Allianz's and AGF's Aachener und Münchener holdings, providing Allianz with a new foothold in France and Generali with a majority stake in Aachener und Münchener.

The ambition to become a broad-based provider of financial services also proved difficult for Allianz to realize. On the asset management side, the development was relatively smooth, but diversification into banking turned out to be tricky. In 2001 Allianz acquired Dresdner Bank, but the integration proved difficult and expensive. Millions of euros were invested, while thousands of Dresdner Bank employees were let go. In 2008 Allianz finally pulled the plug, selling the bank, and Commerzbank became the largest shareholder of the new institution. Nonetheless, the story differs from Aachener und Münchener's BfG Bank acquisition. In contrast to BfG Bank, Dresdner Bank was not focused on a specific customer segment; it was a broadly diversified banking institution. Allianz's and Dresdner Bank's customer bases were compatible. Another factor was Allianz's great financial strength. The diversification never presented a substantial risk. Allianz would have been able to take the time required to make the diversification work. In fact, the company had previously displayed such patience when it had started out in transport insurance. Essentially Allianz decided that the payoff was too low. In the first five years profits were less than 20 percent of what the firm generated in casualty and liability insurance.

The divestment of Dresdner Bank did not mean that Allianz stopped diversifying. In France, Italy, and Eastern Europe, for example, Allianz continues to grow banking services organically, and in Germany it owns the Oldenburgische Landesbank. In China Allianz made major investments in ICBC, the country's largest bank. In other words, Allianz was not overly dependent on the success of the Dresdner Bank deal. Aachner und Münchener, in contrast, relied too much on BfG Bank to deliver what it could not do.

This review of the histories of Allianz and Aachener und Münchener shows how important it is to diversify into related areas to hedge against the risks of fundamental changes in markets and economies. The first important shift in the insurance industry was the emerging industrialization in the 20th century, and the second big wave of change is ongoing integration of financial services as well as globalization of financial markets. In addition to constant preparation to embark on new opportunities and the right timing, the way diversification actually unfolds is crucial. Buying BfG Bank was not helpful for Aachener und Münchener's diversification strategy because of the poor fit between the company's goals and the market actually served by the bank.

We turn now to the story of Nokia to gain additional perspective on diversification. Is it possible for outstanding companies to appear in the unrelated diversified category? At first glance, Nokia seems to indicate yes. There is an important caveat, though. The company long enjoyed serving a relatively protected market in the Soviet bloc. When the Soviet Union collapsed, Nokia initially found itself in trouble. At the same time, competition in Finland picked up. Nokia excelled after it divested unrelated businesses. The conclusion thus seems clear and reaffirms the lessons of the Allianz and Aachner und Münchener stories: in a competitive environment unrelated diversification is unlikely to succeed for long.

NOKIA

Today Nokia is a highly successful related diversified corporation. This standing is the result of a transformation that started in the 1980s. Before then, Nokia was a classic conglomerate, an unrelated diversified business. The pattern of Nokia's development might be highly unusual in most countries, but Finland is a special case.

Nokia emerged out of three different businesses: paper and power, rubber, and cable works.[108] The oldest of these is the first, paper and power. In 1865 Fredrik Idestam established a stone-ground wood pulp plant on the banks of the Tammerkoski River in Finland. The production method that Idestam had imported from Germany kept costs relatively low and allowed the young company to expand. Originally 80 percent of the company's revenues were generated by brown wrapping paper, with the remainder by colored wallpaper. At the end of the 1880s white paper production began.

Nokia's first diversification occurred up the supply chain in 1902. Nokia started its own power generation to meet the large energy demand of the paper production. In 1925 the Turun Voima electricity company was acquired to grow this business. Over the next few decades, the company's focus shifted between paper and power, depending on the situation and the priorities of a particular administration.

One of Nokia's main customers was Finnish Rubber Works, which had been founded in 1898 by a group of investors under the leadership of Eduard Polón. The company produced shoes, boots, overshoes, and hoses and belts for industrial use. In its early days it struggled to compete against dominant Russian companies. Its fortunes changed with the outbreak of World War I, which curtailed Russian imports. Russia's withdrawal from world markets after the war allowed Finnish Rubber Works to grow further and become the market leader in Finland. In fact, the company's financial position grew so strong that it was able to acquire controlling stakes in Nokia Ab in 1918 and Finnish Cable Works in 1922. The logic of the alliance was in fact to unite related businesses. Nokia Ab's power was important to ensure a stable supply for the Rubber Works. Meanwhile, one of the Cable Works' most important raw materials was rubber.

Finnish Cable Works, the last component of what later became Nokia, was founded in 1912. Due to introduction of electricity and the growing number of telephones and telegraphs in Finland in the early 20th century, the demand for wires soared. Arvid Wikström, the founder of the company, decided to start his own cable production to benefit from this development. Supplying electrical wires and cables for industrial customers, the young company started off well. Unfortunately World War I greatly increased the cost of raw materials. Finnish Rubber Works was able to charge a premium for rubber, and copper had to be imported from Sweden at high cost. Nonetheless, Finnish Cable Works was able to expand

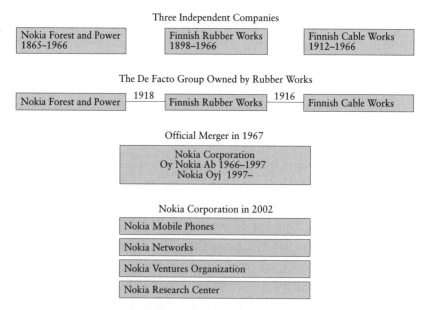

FIGURE 3.17. The Evolution of Nokia
SOURCE: Data from Häikiö, *Nokia: The Inside Story.*

when one of its main shareholders, Strömberg Ab, a large electro technical company, had to sell its cable division in 1917. Several years later, in 1922, Strömberg Ab faced financial difficulties once again and sold its stake in Finnish Cable Works to Eduard Polón's Finnish Rubber Works.

Under Polón, the three different businesses continued to operate independently. The same decentralized approach was followed after the formal merger in 1967. By then, the originally related businesses had experienced significant changes in technology. In fact, they had become unrelated. The most important division was the cable business, which generated roughly the same revenue as the other businesses together. Meanwhile, paper, rubber, and electronics were managed in separate business segments. Rather than focusing on any one of them, the company management encouraged the various divisions to grow further apart, and several started to diversify into new areas. The power generation business, for example, moved into nuclear technology, while the electronics business migrated from components into consumer goods such as television sets.

Nokia managed to prosper as an unrelated diversified business for several reasons. The main one is the protected business environment in which it operated. Competition in Finland was limited, and each of Nokia's separate divisions was a major player in its respective market. Of particular importance was Finland's position as a mediator between the Soviet Union and Western Europe. This unique position allowed Nokia to supply superior Western technology to the Soviet market. Most obviously, these circumstances helped the cable business to thrive. Another factor important to Nokia's success was the historical pattern of decentralized growth. The century-long evolution allowed Nokia's management and staff to accumulate resources and develop capabilities to manage a complex institution.

When the geopolitical and economic environment shifted in the 1980s, Nokia had to adapt. The old conglomerate was no longer able to compete in a global economy in which Soviet demand dried up and the pace of technological change accelerated. Nokia had to shed unrelated businesses and focus on its most successful operations. The Nokia "fairy tale," as it became known, started to unfold.[109]

When Jorma Ollila became president and CEO of Nokia in 1992, the company was in serious trouble. His predecessor had started to focus the conglomerate by divesting some businesses such as flooring, paper, and rubber. The well-meant and necessary move did not result in the hoped-for business improvement, however, as Finland was hit by the worst recession in its history after the collapse of the Soviet Union. Ollila was given 18 months to get the company back on track. Uniting the corporation behind the bold vision of becoming a telecom company, he was able to achieve just that. Though Nokia incurred heavy losses at the outset, it was able to break even before the end of 1992 due to a 73 percent surge in telecommunications, particularly in mobile phones.[110] Nokia had been a pioneer in mobile phone technology. Unable to provide a complete network system based on analog technology, in the 1980s the company decided to put its entire R&D budget into the exploration of digital technology. The gamble paid off when digital GSM emerged as the common European standard and Nokia was able to deliver the first operational network nine months before its competitors were ready. By selling off the non-telecom business—including profitable divisions such as cable—Nokia generated the capital necessary to fund its exploration efforts.

Nokia's approach was revolutionary in two respects. First, the company understood that mobile phones were consumer goods. Success therefore was heavily dependent on design and user friendliness. Hiring the Los Angeles designer Frank Nuovo led to a hot product: the smooth, rounded-looking Nokia 2100. The large screen included features such as switchable covers, different ring tones, and a battery indicator.[111] Second, the Nokia 2100 was the first mobile phone that shared platforms across the different standards in Europe, the United States, and Japan and looked the same in all markets. The original goal of selling 400,000 Nokia 2100s was quickly and spectacularly surpassed.[112] Eventually 20 million customers became proud owners of the new phone.

Nokia thus managed to change from a faltering conglomerate into a thriving related diversified company. It became the world's number one mobile phone producer and a strong player in wireless networks. The establishment of Nokia Ventures Organization enhances the openness for future steps into related areas, preparing the company for the day after tomorrow.

Nokia's history is highly unusual among the outstanding companies we analyzed. It was the only company in our sample that spread across many different businesses. Although these businesses were originally related, they developed into unrelated categories. As long as its business environment was protected, Nokia could prosper. Once competitive pressure increased, Nokia—after feeling the heat—was forced to focus. It became the type of related diversified business we observed to be most likely both to generate considerable returns and to survive when the business environment starts to change again.

JOINT VENTURES AND ALLIANCES — ORGANIZATIONAL SOLUTIONS TO BENEFIT FROM HEALTHY BUSINESSES NOT RELATED TO THE CORE

Joint ventures and alliances are often regarded as vehicles for acquiring new skills and gaining access to new technologies. In the oil industry, for example, many governments consider technology capabilities of oil companies when awarding exploration and development contracts. Foreign producers get the work, but they may be required to partner with a local company. Consequently, it is not surprising that different companies are invited to join projects in neighboring development blocks. Thus local companies can boost their capabilities rapidly. Malaysia's Petronas or Brazil's Petrobras are two national oil companies that have gained considerable know-how in just this way. Both are respected international players today, and Petrobras has become a leader in deepwater technology—an area with great potential in the Gulf of Mexico and elsewhere.

Joint ventures and alliances can also be used as an organizational solution to a different challenge that receives less attention. In the course of a long history large multinationals develop a number of new businesses. Some of them start out as related businesses, but as technology evolves, this relationship becomes less and less apparent. The Nokia story presented above is a good example of how an alliance can evolve. In the 1920s the company was related diversified. Over time the technology development in the different businesses moved them further and further apart. By the time the company merged in the late 1960s, it had evolved into a conglomerate of unrelated businesses.

One way to avoid unrelated diversification obviously could involve divestiture of units that do not fit. Many companies, however, find this difficult to do. Strong growth prospects, established expertise, stable income generated by these units, or simply the fact that the units have been around for a long time may make leaders reluctant to divest them. A potential solution involves two steps: the formation of a subsidiary, followed by the formation of a joint venture. Under such arrangements, an unrelated unit is kept at arm's length, treated more like an investment and less like an operating unit. The corporate parent can concentrate resources and capabilities on areas it is most familiar with, but still benefit from the positive development of the unrelated business.

Siemens has taken this approach several times in the past 50 years. The company had a long tradition of home appliances, going back to 1906, when the first vacuum cleaner was produced. After World War II, it realized that consumer products require a totally different business approach that did not fit well with the rest of the company, which was focused on industrial markets. Siemens initially established a subsidiary to manage the consumer products business and eventually in 1967 decided to form a joint venture with Bosch, BSH Bosch und Siemens Hausgeräte.[113] Siemens's comparison company, AEG, failed to take a similar step. It grew a successful home appliance business that also unfortunately did not fit with the rest of the company. Over time, both AEG's home appliance business and its core electrical and electronic businesses ran into trouble, in part because management's attention was divided between them and neither received the support it needed.

A more recent example of a joint venture involving two outstanding corporations was Nokia's and Siemens's decision to merge their network businesses in 2007. In this case Nokia takes the operational lead, as the business is closely related to its mobile phone activities. Siemens, on the other hand, sees it more as an investment while it concentrates on the markets for power and telecommunications infrastructure and medical technology.

SUMMARY

In the 1960s and 1970s conglomerates were fashionable. In recent years, the pendulum has swung to the opposite side, as analysts praise highly focused corporations. The fact is that neither extreme will guarantee success over time. As illustrated by the outstanding companies in our sample, the right thing to do is to constantly diversify into related areas. While a protected market may not punish a failure to do so, the competitive environment of recent years has been less forgiving. AEG, the once powerful electrical conglomerate, slipped into bankruptcy. Its main competitor, Siemens, prevailed as it pursued a strategy of outsourcing products and technologies that did not fit its core. In financial services, where products are harder to understand, the lesson is essentially the same. From its first day on, Allianz was ready to branch out into nearby markets. Starting in machine insurance, the company was able to benefit from the dynamic industrialization of Germany at the end of the 19th century. The cash generated along the way was used to build up first transport insurance, then car insurance, and finally a life insurance business. Allianz's comparison company, the older Aachener und Münchener, was much more narrowly focused, with its premium income derived primarily from fire insurance. It introduced new products but focused them on a dwindling number of agricultural customers. Thus the company lost out when Germany shifted to an industrial economy. Once Aachener und Münchener tried to widen its scope in earnest, in the 1970s, it was too late. The lack of experience with mergers finally led to an ill-advised merger, creating financial constraints that eventually prompted the takeover of the company.

Change in Culturally Sensitive Ways

Schumpeterian logic tells us that creative destruction is the fundamental dynamic in modern capitalism. Change is inevitable and it's better to lead change than to follow it—at least, that's the conventional wisdom. Great companies beg to differ. They go through radical change only at very selective moments in their history, and they take great care in doing it. They do not jump into every new management fad. Rather, they have learned through experience that a certain level of conservatism and caution is more beneficial.

This conservative outlook toward change might be related to long traditions and subsequently clearly developed cultures. The great companies have strong cultures that can be traced all the way back to their origins. In 1865, when Thomas Sutherland from the Peninsular and Oriental Steam

Navigation Company inspired the Hong Kong merchant community to start the Hongkong and Shanghai Banking Corporation (later HSBC), they felt strongly about being an Asian- rather than a London-based institution. The new bank succeeded because it understood the needs of business on the ground better than the boards of competitors in faraway European offices did. Being "the local bank" has been central to HSBC ever since—it is at the core of HSBC's culture. At the same time, this does not mean that the behavior resulting from a company's core values necessarily remains the same today as 100 years ago. HSBC no longer has a three-tiered system of international officers managing the endeavor and dealing with the large trading houses, Europeans who were raised in the East doing clerical work, or Chinese compradors serving the non-European customers. Neither do international officers routinely gather in the legendary gentlemen's clubs of the Far East. But the principle of being a decentralized, locally responsive bank remains.

The challenge for great companies is to distinguish between principles and capabilities that are enduring and should be preserved and those that emerge to suit particular times and places and should be changed or abandoned as the context changes. There is danger when the latter, masquerading as core beliefs, turn into core rigidities.[114] A good example is customer focus at Siemens. Prior to a 1989 reorganization and transformation, Siemens's telecommunications units were highly bureaucratic. While this does not now seem a desirable structure, it suited the company's customers at the time. Siemens dealt mainly with state-run telecom monopolies. Organizing to reflect the structure and style of major customers was a good idea, and it worked well for a long time. Once the market changed and national telecom giants no longer dealt exclusively with suppliers from their own country, however, Siemens responded rapidly, changing both its structure and its personnel. The efficient, rapidly moving organization that we see today is as much the result of customer focus as was the slow, bureaucratic one that existed before 1989. While the new approach toward customers simply reflects the new challenges that arose after deregulation of the telecom industry, the point is that Siemens had developed a focus on customers in the middle of the 19th century but changed the interpretation of that focus, adapting when it became necessary.

This story illustrates that although the great companies occasionally decide to adjust their business according to shifts in the marketplace, they do so without changing their basic values. Their apparent conservatism does not prevent them from adapting their strategy and structure in line with the environment in which they operate. Contrary to popular belief, however, successful changes undertaken are not necessarily the results of proactive steps to keep ahead of the competition. That does happen sometimes. Large corporations like Nokia, HSBC, Shell, Siemens, or Lafarge might indeed launch a transformation because their leaders recognize an opportunity or a looming threat. Enduring greatness, however, is only partly the result of such transformations. Rather, more often the great companies change along with their changing environment. As Loo van Wachem, Shell's leader from 1985 to 1992 and the head of Royal Dutch's supervisory board until 2002, puts it: "Every company is continuously adapting itself, transforming itself. It may occasionally have a somewhat higher speed of change than at other times."[115] This is a natural process that the great companies understand better than their competitors.

Effective organizational change typically emerges quietly, without fanfare, and proceeds in an orderly, systematic fashion. Large and dramatic change exercises are successful only if employees understand the need and are prepared to pitch in to help. Consequently, a leader's first and foremost duty is to pay attention to signals from the marketplace and to listen to employees in order to understand when to accelerate change. If a leader is not careful, he or she runs the risk of unleashing too many change initiatives and too much unproductive change.

The best way to approach change is in a culturally sensitive manner.[116] There is no one-size-fits-all approach. Each transformation process happens in a particular organizational and environmental context. This rather simple insight has profound implications that are often underestimated. It affects the role of leaders. Taking context seriously means that even the most celebrated visionary leader is restricted in his options. Any change process has to fit with the market needs on the one hand and the organizational culture and capabilities on the other.

Path dependency and organizational cognition are major variables in leading and managing change. Take Glaxo's workforce in the early 1990s, for example. While some employees were keenly aware of the implications of the fast-approaching expiration of the Zantac patent—the company's major revenue source—many hoped that the company leadership would easily find a replacement source of income. However, the ongoing success of Zantac prevented them from understanding that they had to change their way of doing things, that certain structures, policies, and routines would no longer be effective in the highly competitive UK pharmaceutical marketplace. Still, Glaxo's leaders understood that dramatic organizational changes could endanger ongoing operations. Employees had to be prepared slowly for the new environment. In a first step, a cultural change program called RATIO (role clarity, acceptance of change, teamwork, innovation, output orientation) was initiated.[117] A large part of the sales organization participated in this program, creating a context in which more fundamental changes became possible. Two separate internal sales forces—a legacy from the Allen & Hanburys and Glaxo merger in 1958—were integrated. Second, the newly acquired Wellcome sales force was also integrated after the 1995 merger. The old product focus was replaced by a new organization structured around therapeutic areas. The company supported this change with heavy investments in communications and training: workshops, seminars, announcements, and numerous meetings helped to inform employees and guide them through the change.

Meanwhile, key members of the staff were empowered with increased responsibility and budgets. Instead of looking to their bosses for direction, these staff were handed real responsibilities and were held accountable for their performance. To support employees in this process, personal development received much attention. Course-based training was replaced by personal coaching and counseling—once again putting the focus on personal responsibility and teamwork. The reward system was also modified accordingly, replacing the old hierarchical grading system with a new one emphasizing job families and individual development. Eventually the different steps added up. The sales force transformed from a product-based hierarchical group into a fast-moving, well-trained force fit to face the new challenges of the 1990s.

The change process at Glaxo illustrates three steps that together ensure a culturally sensitive approach to organizational transformation:

(1) the ability of leaders to understand when major change is required; (2) their subsequent interaction with the organization to prepare employees for fundamental change; and finally, (3) an implementation phase taking culture and capabilities into account without overstretching the organization. A vital aspect in this process is time. Despite the pressure from analysts and shareholders, it makes little sense to reinvent a large and established company overnight. The risk of failure in such dramatic interventions is high. It is better to change carefully and consistently over time.

In this context the leader is primarily a coach, someone who helps people reach their full potential, who encourages them to use their creativity. Like any good teacher, he or she is aware of his or her limitations and understands that he or she is also a student of the organization. Leaders have to be aware of the mental models and core values of the company they lead. In companies with strong values they have to act in a culturally sensitive way. That this remains true over time becomes evident by comparing the histories of Siemens and AEG. While the former took a culturally sensitive approach toward change, AEG sometimes acted more forcefully—and less successfully.

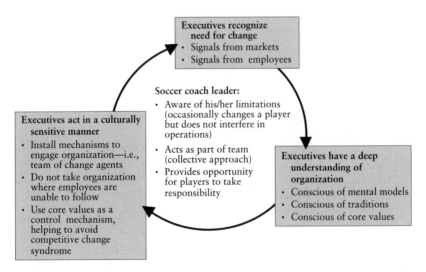

FIGURE 3.18. Culturally Sensitive Change and the Soccer Coach Leader

CHANGING SIEMENS AND AEG

In the 1960s Siemens and AEG were operating in the same business environment: a postwar Germany that enjoyed miraculous economic growth
provided great business opportunities for companies in electrical engineering. Broadly speaking, Siemens and AEG had similar strategies and structures. Both companies were geared toward growth, and both were eager
to establish themselves in foreign markets. Both companies should have
fared very well in the 1970s, but AEG did not. While it had been able to
catch up to Siemens in the 1950s, profit margins started to fall at the end
of the 1960s, never to recover. What happened?

Considering their similar strategy and structure, the decline of AEG
is certainly puzzling. As is so often the case, the devil lies in the details.
While both companies aspired to grow rapidly in all fields of electricity and electrical engineering, Siemens qualified its hopes in ways that
AEG did not. Growth mattered to Siemens, but so did profits. To ensure continuous profitability, Siemens faced difficult strategic questions.
Would it be possible to continue activity in all major areas of electricity, as founder Werner von Siemens had urged, or should the company
abandon some areas? Should the company reorganize? What should the
new structure look like? Was it even possible to reform such a giant as

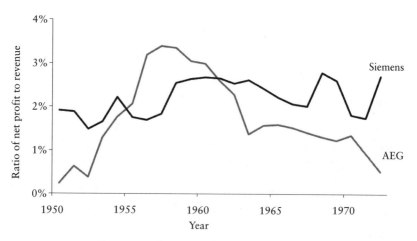

FIGURE 3.19. Siemens and AEG Profit Margin, 1952–1970
SOURCE: Data from annual reports.

Siemens? While the direction of the change initiatives certainly played an important role, the process of how the key choices were made and the subsequent implementation approach were equally important. Siemens took time and care in addressing these issues, and chose a deliberate approach to change. In contrast, AEG struggled on both counts: it shied away from difficult decisions as it failed to set a process in motion that would have enabled it to make them. Then AEG broke down and ultimately collapsed when it undertook too much change too fast.

Change proved unavoidable at Siemens for four reasons, any one of which would on its own have provided ample justification. First, management recognized that the historical separation between its high-current (power generation) and low-current (telecommunications) technologies was no longer appropriate. Indeed, lack of cooperation between its Siemens & Halske (low-current) and Siemens Schuckert (high-current) subsidiaries was resulting in costly duplication of research and other activity. Second, as the group faced pressure to merge these two subsidiaries, management also became aware that the company's long-standing consumer business fit less and less well with the high- and low-current activities that were driving growth. Third, on top of these strategic considerations was the fear of what would happen when the chairman, Ernst von Siemens, retired. In the absence of another member of the founding family to take over, many employees worried that the company's independent subsidiaries would no longer work together effectively. Finally, the German government was preparing legislation that would force the corporation to reveal sensitive business information about its operations unless it consolidated its subsidiaries.

Recognizing these pressures for change, Siemens proved very deliberate in responding. Although it set in motion a process for change in the mid-1960s, the direction of change had been set much earlier. In the 1930s, Siemens had assumed full ownership and control of Siemens & Halske, Siemens Schuckert, and Siemens Reiniger (medical technology). Integration on an operational level was first contemplated then—giving employees an early indication that this might become serious at some point—but was postponed during World War II and its immediate aftermath. In the 1960s, when the topic reappeared on the agenda, top managers knew they had to take the time to engage the units in the process of integration. When decisions were finally made about the future structure, in 1965, Siemens took another four years to implement it. By 1969 the three subsidiaries had disappeared and six new decentralized divisions were in full operation. Aware of the strong cultures of the former subsidiaries, management took a culturally sensitive approach toward change. Not only did the new structure take the old setup into account, but in some cases old practices were left untouched to ensure that the organization would be able to keep moving ahead. As the cultures of the separate units started to converge, additional changes were introduced step by step.

Another decision made around the same time involved businesses that did not fit the core competencies of the firm. In a world progressively influenced by specialists, it was impossible to compete successfully in all areas of electricity and electrical engineering. In particular, the company's top leadership recognized that the consumer business no longer fit with Siemens's core interests. A careful and prudent approach to major change became evident once again: difficult decisions were made, but in a way that did not alienate employees. Siemens began laying the groundwork for the divestiture of its consumer business in 1957, when it brought its radio, TV, and appliances businesses together to create a new subsidiary, Siemens Electrogeräte. Over the following years, it closed or sold off the radio and TV production businesses, leaving it with a rump appliance business. In 1967, a full decade after beginning the change process, it finally spun off the appliance business into a joint venture with Robert Bosch.[118] Initially, BSH Bosch und Siemens Hausgeräte was hardly more than a joint sales force, and only over the years did it start to integrate production.[119]

AEG, meanwhile, failed to act with the same determination and sensitivity for process. In 1962 the authoritarian Hans Heyne became the new CEO, with great plans for AEG. By then, however, the company was already struggling as a consequence of aggressive growth. As a board statement explained: "We have to concentrate all our forces on the reduction of costs. This should be achieved particularly through reorganization."[120] Five new divisions were formed to restructure a company with more than 20 subsidiaries. At about the same time, AEG's large Telefunken subsidiary (telecommunications, radio, and TV) was reorganized as a single group and fully integrated into AEG.

From the outside, the reorganization and integration of a major subsidiary looked similar to what Siemens was doing in the 1960s. The activities that the two companies brought together, however, were quite different. At Siemens, integration made sense, as it united high-current-voltage and low-current-voltage businesses that were no longer logically separate. AEG's integration of Telefunken, on the other hand, brought TV and radio activities into the center, although these were dissimilar to the company's other core activities. In addition, consumer products no longer fit the rest of the corporation, though short-term-growth prospects were encouraging. In 1964, 27 percent of AEG's sales were in consumer products. In the next few years this proportion climbed to 31 percent.[121] Yet this was not entirely good news. Rather, it exposed glaring weaknesses in a company whose various businesses were too diverse to manage and control.

AEG's leaders were either unwilling or unable to focus as Siemens did. Trying to sustain world-class performance in both consumer and industrial markets proved impossible. Limited resources were spread across too many different activities. Heyne, moreover, did not get along with middle management. His distrust of AEG's traditional business practices is evident from a statement in which he refers to advice he received from other managers in the industry: "These men advised me well, but they also told me prior to taking over AEG that I need to secure special mandates from the board to cover my back. Otherwise I would not get anything through in AEG, where things have been on the same track for years."[122]

Although he sought to shake up and modernize the company, Heyne actually created a dysfunctional organization in which managers were unable to take responsibility in a culture based on fear. Many top managers left, and those who remained were often referred to as Heyne's *Würstchen* (Heyne's little sausages). His abrasive style and constant interference also frustrated his successor, who resigned after only a few months on the job since Heyne continued to interfere as chairman of the supervisory board.

The man who followed, Hans Bühler, seemed determined to regain the initiative. The press initially praised him for putting AEG back on track. In hindsight his legacy is less flattering. As an empire builder, he went on a spending spree. While AEG was able to catch up with Siemens in terms of revenue, it lagged significantly behind in profitability. The company took on large debts while searching for a viable strategy. Like his predecessors and his successors, Bühler failed to make the really tough decision to focus. Which business should AEG emphasize, consumer products or industrial products and heavy-current technology? AEG's leaders believed that they could outgrow this decision. Instead, crippling debts caught up with them.

In the late 1970s, the board installed a new leader, Walter Cipa, the former CEO of Gelsenberg AG,[123] a chemical company. Cipa understood AEG's desperate condition and launched an ambitious reorganization, concentrating on a smaller number of businesses, but he went about it in a clumsy, authoritarian manner. As an outsider, he lacked a network of allies and followers in the company. Instead of trying to build coalitions and preparing the organization for change, he simply issued orders and directives. The organization proved unresponsive. Between 1977 and 1979, 36 top managers left the company, and many of those who stayed actively sought to undermine Cipa's initiatives.[124]

By 1980 Cipa was gone, replaced by Heinz Dürr, another outsider. Dürr was determined to avoid Ciba's mistakes, and indeed, his style was inspiring and sensitive to AEG's culture. During his first month in office, he visited all the AEG sites in Germany.[125] Employees trusted him and lines of communication reopened. As he explained in an interview,[126] small and symbolic gestures could make a significant difference. At one plant, he chatted with workers on the shop floor and learned that they could be much more efficient if they had a machine that helped them to lift components. The head of the division explained that they unfortunately did not have the budget to purchase this machine. Dürr came up with an unusual solution when he saw a large Persian carpet in the office of the manager. He asked the secretary of the manager to sell the carpet and use the money to buy the equipment needed on the shop floor. From a financial perspective this made little difference, but the message was clear: management was also prepared to make sacrifices to ensure a successful future for AEG.

At first, results seemed encouraging. Orders began to pour in, but not fast enough to offset the company's financial woes. Several decades of accumulated debt bore down on AEG. An eventual solution was a well-managed settlement with the banks in 1984, which afforded AEG a new start. Unfortunately, the otherwise capable leadership team surrounding

Dürr failed to make the vital strategic decision to concentrate on related businesses. AEG attempted to move ahead as a conglomerate, and it was soon caught again in a familiar trap, struggling to succeed in too many different and diverse businesses. An old problem of inefficient financial planning and control also remained. When in 1985 Daimler-Benz bought a majority stake in AEG, the last chapter of its long history began. In 1993 consumer goods were sold to Electrolux. Two years later, a joint venture was formed with ABB (ASEA Brown Boveri) to unite the trains and transportation business. Before AEG's last annual meeting took place in June 1996, further businesses were either sold off or closed.[127] The final days of a long-established German institution came to an end.

At Siemens the crisis was never so dire. Nonetheless, the company knew that it had to continue to adapt as global competition mounted. By the 1980s, the organization that had been created two decades earlier was under heavy strain. Too many specialists attempted to manage pieces of integrated processes. While a consensus-seeking leadership at the top had the ability to listen, a lack of responsibility and accountability among operational leaders was a serious problem.

Siemens's large central organization in Munich was part of this issue. According to Dr. Hermann Franz, who headed strategy for Siemens, "The company fell into the familiar trap of concentrating too many services at the center. While this made sense considering the competencies [we had in Munich] the head count was simply too high."[128] Once previously protected markets such as telecommunications in Germany were deregulated, Siemens came under attack from competitors focusing on particular segments of the industry. Starting in IT and semiconductors, the threat spread to other core activities, such as electrical power generation. The smaller competitors proved more flexible and target-driven. Siemens, in contrast, operated with huge divisions, which complicated efforts to coordinate plans and actions. Another problem was a centralized sales organization that often found itself at odds with the heads of the operating units.

Siemens's leaders were well aware of these problems. In the 1980s, they had initiated a change program in marketing and sales. While this program had little immediate effect, it did underline the careful, step-by-step approach to change embraced by top management. They were preparing the company for bigger changes to come. In 1987, the decline of the dollar and a weak market for power plants provided the context for the internal merger of all electrical power, energy, and automation-related activities. At the same time, the semiconductor business was moved into a newly created division.

Soon thereafter, it became apparent that more steps would be necessary. According to Franz, who led the effort in the first phase when structural changes were implemented, "The transformation was organized in a snowball-like system"[129] that started from a small beginning and rolled into a bigger activity. At the top level the executive board developed an overall concept and decided on the main framework. Next, the top three people for each division were announced and put in charge of developing concept and structure for their units. Finally, the third level of the organization, the last to have general managerial responsibility, was designed.

Several managers who had led divisions prior to the transformation lost their jobs, and some were asked to retire early. While this represented a radical step for Siemens, the entire process was still characterized by the deep engagement of leaders at all levels. Describing the company's mood at the time, Franz notes:

You always have to ensure that the number of those who benefit from the changes exceeds those who see disadvantages. Once the number of those who see disadvantages is larger, it will not be possible to implement fundamental changes. If the number of those who benefit is larger, you will be able to feel the momentum and motivation.[130]

Siemens took care to ensure that the transformation process was not driven from the center alone. Those who would be in charge of the business had a major stake in the process. In fact, the main goal of the transformation was to create entrepreneurs inside the company. These people, in turn, became responsible for creating concepts and structures to continue the transformation.

Overall, the initiative showed quick returns, partly because of a booming market and new business opportunities in the former East Germany. Nevertheless, the goal of creating entrepreneurs took still more time to accomplish. Old functional thinking died slowly. While the new setup made it possible for general managers to assume larger responsibilities, many of them lacked the necessary training and skills. In 1991 Siemens reported a profit of DM 1.797 million, the equivalent of 2.5 percent of sales. Top management was not satisfied and formed a project team to investigate. This team blamed a lack of process orientation, finding that the old specialist culture was still alive and well in the company. Marketing, R&D, production, sales, and services remained fairly autonomous functions. In response, Siemens commissioned a team of internal consultants to manage ongoing change under the rubric of "the TOP (time-optimized processes) movement."

As we observed in a number of successful transformation efforts—for example, in Shell or Glaxo—effective teams of change agents share common characteristics that were on display in TOP.

Shared Vision: Drive the organization in one direction and speak with one voice. Mixed messages cause confusion.

High-Profile Project: Reporting directly to the CEO increases the chances of being taken seriously outside headquarters.

Considerable Team Size (50 is a magic number): Sufficient size makes a clear statement that the company is serious about change. Moreover, size guarantees a broader impact.

FIGURE 3.20. Characteristics of Successful Change Teams

Achievable Target: Change agents focus on processes and behaviors. If structures are not sorted out beforehand, people are likely to fall back into old behaviors once they leave.

Clear Positioning: Change agents are consultants. They are not sent from central offices to implement change. Operational units are accountable for change.

High-Profile People: The right personnel is another must. Upon leaving the team—usually after about two years—change agents occupy key positions, implementing their ideas.

Strong Marketing: Marketing is not an option, but a must. Successful changes have to be communicated widely, in order to get new customers (operational units) on board.

Previous programs to improve processes at Siemens had concentrated on specific functions. In the new structure, it became possible to look at overall processes for the first time. The TOP movement focused on a new culture of broad involvement in process improvement, innovation, and growth. It became a great success, increasing productivity from 2.7 percent in 1991 to 9.5 percent in 1997 (Siemens estimates that 60 percent of this gain was the result of TOP). To follow up on this success TOP+ was created. The new program concentrated on managerial aspects like benchmarking and asset management and had strong line management involvement and a stronger management attention from the board. Both TOP and TOP+ helped promote entrepreneurs at Siemens. Having the right structures in place beforehand was an essential prerequisite.

The Siemens approach to change was similar to that of the other outstanding companies in our sample. These companies engaged the organization, made sure that those who implemented change were also involved in the design, and adopted a long-term approach. They understood that a large organization will not change the way it behaves overnight. Franz explained that he "initially expected to take five years. Some people at the top were rather perplexed and thought that this should probably be over much faster. Once the transformation started they started to understand that this is a process which cannot be directed. The change of behaviors takes time. In the end it was closer to 10 than five years."[131] The extended period was due in part to the unwillingness or inability of some divisions to change. The older, more traditional parts of the company resisted the program, while newer divisions, such as that responsible for automation, proved much faster at changing their thinking.

While the contrasting stories of Siemens and AEG demonstrate the importance of cultural sensitivity during major organizational transformations, a closer look at mergers and acquisitions shows how cultural sensitivity is also required under these circumstances. Consider the case of HSBC.

CULTURAL SENSITIVITY AND POST-MERGER INTEGRATION—A STORY FROM HSBC

HSBC's acquisition of Midland Bank in 1992 created one of the largest financial institutions in the world. The group headquarters was relocated from Hong Kong to London, and for the first time HSBC had a considerable presence in the UK retail market. A long-term process was set in motion whereby HSBC made itself over from a commercial bank to a retail bank.

HSBC undertook this transformation carefully, beginning with its initial investment in 1987, when it acquired a 14.9 percent stake in Midland Bank. At the time HSBC had not decided whether it would eventually pursue a full merger. Rather, HSBC saw the investment as an opportunity to get to know both Midland and the European market. At the top level, HSBC managers sat on Midland's board, and vice versa. This enabled the two institutions to develop a deeper understanding of how each operated. The two banks also began to coordinate business development across Europe, with one party withdrawing from a particular country while distributing its products through the branches of its partner. Key employees were exchanged to gain an appreciation for each other's cultures and processes. The differences were actually quite pronounced. While Midland Bank was used to relying on management committees and put its emphasis on creativity and innovation, HSBC stressed execution and personal accountability. The long period of engagement prior to the eventual marriage helped Midland get accustomed to the way HSBC went about its business.

When HSBC finally took control of Midland in 1992, many of Midland's top managers left. This was not disruptive, however, as Midland's performance had not been strong and the rank and file was ready for new leadership. HSBC installed some of its own people but also promoted some middle managers from Midland. Decision-making power was moved down to the branch level. Individual accountability replaced the old committee-based style. While this change disturbed a few traditionalists, most employees had gained familiarity with the HSBC way prior to the merger and understood the reasons for the changes. As Stephen Green, HSBC's chairman, explains, "Midland was not a happy ship at the time it was bought. So it was very far from being seen as an aggressive one to take over; on the contrary, for a very large number of Midland people this was seen as the lifeline."[132] Meanwhile, HSBC's policy of promoting from within, which contrasted with Midland's tendency to hire senior people from the outside, boosted the morale of middle management. HSBC also took care to blend Midland managers into the London headquarters organization. Of the top 450 employees, 200 came from Midland.

Overall, HSBC's acquisition of Midland affords a good example of how a company can implement extensive and thoroughgoing changes if top management is prepared to take its time and engage people in the process. HSBC's patience paid dividends, while ongoing communication ensured transparency and established a high level of trust among employees. As Stephen Green puts it: "What had been a very cumbersome bureaucratic and over-politicized culture has become leaner, more efficient, and apolitical!"[133]

CAUTION AND OVER-CAUTION

Another pair of companies in our sample, Munich Re and Cologne Re, illustrate how cautious or bold a firm should be in its change initiatives.

The reinsurance industry is known for its conservatism, as befits an industry that thrives on deep understanding of risk. The story of Munich Re confirms the point. The company has seldom undertaken change, and when it has, it has tended to move deliberately. Between the end of World War II and the 1990s the company operated without any significant reorganization. Even the formation of a primary insurance arm—ERGO—was hardly dramatic. Many of the units that constituted ERGO had been owned by Munich Re since the 1920s. With the establishment of ERGO, what changed was the perception of the outside world, not the internal workings of Munich Re's units.

After World War II, Munich Re had a hierarchical organization with 11 layers of leadership[134] and a divisional structure. Different types of insurance, such as life, fire, transport, and marine, were gathered in separate divisions, more or less reflecting the structure of Munich Re's major customers, the primary insurance companies. To compete abroad, Munich Re needed to find structural solutions to manage its expanding international business. It formed a matrix organization by adding regional units to the established product divisions. This was not a revolutionary change but resulted in slow, incremental adaptation. In the major part of the business, life went on as usual. In Germany and most of Europe, for example, the product divisions were dominant actors. Only in international markets outside of Europe did the regional organizations operate with greater influence. In Japan, for example, it was not feasible to send numerous specialists to deal with the variety of customers and issues there. It made more sense to deploy a generalist, who understood the local marketplace, to handle multiple types of insurance. In a few types of insurance, such as life and transport, the product divisions based in Europe ran their businesses worldwide. Overall, because no clear priorities were assigned in Munich Re's matrix structure, decision rights devolved upon those best positioned to wield them at the time.

In the 1980s, however, the market started to change. New forms of communication prompted primary insurance companies to reorganize their businesses. Power shifted from country units to global product divisions. Reinsurance, however, remained outside the competencies of the primary insurers' powerful global divisions. Intending to reduce complexity and cut costs, most insurers formed new centralized departments to deal with reinsurers. As a result, Munich Re no longer dealt with life, transport, and liability insurers separately. Instead, major customers such as Allianz or AXA wanted a single global account manager who would be able to offer a comprehensive package. Specialists would continue to work out the details, but the final decision would rest with a single individual. Munich Re responded to these demands with the most radical structural reform since World War II. Nonetheless, it proceeded cautiously, taking care to avoid losing existing capabilities.

Reform at Munich Re began in 1993 after Dr. Hans-Jürgen Schinzler became CEO. Instead of hiring external consultants, the leadership team decided to form internal groups to investigate different alternatives. Seven task forces were formed representing different perspectives and interests in the company. This proved a clever approach. Although it might seem risky to expect people invested in a certain way of managing to consider radical change, it worked well at Munich Re for two reasons. First, a company with a strong culture is likely to reject ideas that do not fit. Substantial changes are much more likely to be accepted when powerful constituencies are involved in their design. As Christian Kluge, a member of the board at the time, commented,

People from all hierarchical levels were chosen. Although some had limited knowledge of some of the issues in the beginning, these people had the capabilities required to handle such questions. They were asked to contemplate the end of the matrix structure, although they worked in functional departments for the past 40 years.[135]

Second, Munich Re's top management was sure that people would be prepared to put the good of the company above their own personal interests. The loyalty of Munich Re's employees was legendary. As Kluge observed,

Usually you cannot expect such people to recommend the phaseout of functional departments. But they did it. Considering their authority and the expectation that they would try to boycott any decision that would harm their position, this was very important. It provided us with the opportunity to refer to their reputation.[136]

Kluge tells an old story that emphasizes why top management was so certain that people would act primarily in the interest of the company: in the 1940s times were difficult, as the sizable international business had collapsed entirely during the war. For the first time, the company felt obliged to ask someone to leave. The man who performed a simple manual task refused to accept the decision. The day after he was fired he simply turned up for work again. He was reminded that he was no longer working for the company but responded that he liked his job so much that he would do it for free. After several meetings the directors decided to forbid him to enter the premises. This, too, made little difference! The man knew his way around and always managed to enter the building somehow to show up at work. Eventually the directors gave in to so much loyalty and reinstated the former employee in his old position.[137]

Top management's judgment in the 1990s turned out to be correct. Members of the special task forces effectively talked themselves out of their jobs and positions, trusting that there would be comparable or better opportunities in a newly structured Munich Re. The board reinforced the willingness to take such risks by guaranteeing that the new structure would not result in layoffs. Kluge recalled: "As we restructured ourselves, groups were formed that knew that they [would] talk themselves out of their jobs. Regardless, they tried to develop something which was appropriate for the company at the time."[138]

Munich Re also hired consultants but engaged them only to support the internal task forces, provide them with perspectives from the outside world, and suggest implementation options. The board kept the entire organization up to date and engaged by informing them every week about news and progress.

The first results of the process included the elimination of layers of bureaucracy, from 11 levels to three. Accountability was pushed down to the lowest possible layer. This change took time to take root, as employees were used to looking to their bosses for direction. Now they slowly began to realize that accomplishing the task of management was best achieved through delegation. The adaptation and fine-tuning of this new approach took most of the 1990s. The final stage of the transformation, the structural reform, was no longer controversial or difficult to explain and understand. The company was well prepared for the change. Though it had taken nearly a decade to reach this stage, it took only a little over a year for a new group—under the leadership of one of the company's directors—to formulate and execute plans for the change in structure. Special units were formed to deal with global customers such as Allianz. The other units were organized around markets. The product divisions disappeared.

At Cologne Re, the approach was slightly different. Although it, like Munich Re, was a conservative institution, Cologne Re was even more wedded to tradition. A paternalistic climate presided over by a strong CEO reinforced this attitude. The company also faced little pressure from shareholders, as the small number of institutional investors that held the majority stake did not really require management to improve performance. In fact, it was only after General Re had acquired Cologne Re in 2000 that fundamental structural changes were introduced.

Cologne Re's structure reflected the company's historical development. Traditionally Cologne Re had a structure built around departments responsible for different markets in Germany. Failing to understand the significance of diversifying into international markets after World War II, the company postponed significant change until the late 1970s, when it at last began to expand abroad. Cologne Re lacked the resources to establish foreign subsidiaries with the required expertise and capabilities in all fields, so it set up a divisional structure. The foreign subsidiaries were required to gain approval from the divisions before signing a major contract with a customer.

These arrangements worked well enough for the international business, which was starting from scratch. In Germany, however, the old market-based departments remained in place after the introduction of the divisional structure. Confusion and conflict ensued. The old units retained their expertise and underwriting authority, although as the divisions developed specialist knowledge over the years, they could have benefited from authority to underwrite. This situation proved especially damaging in the reinsurance industry. Employees who dealt directly with customers often developed close relationships with them. This connection was important for bringing in business but frequently carried with it the problem of negotiating contracts at prices that were too low to cover the potential risk. Handing underwriting authority to others would mitigate this problem, and in 2000 Cologne Re finally made the necessary adjustments.

In retrospect, it is difficult to understand why the company took so long to modify its policies, procedures, and structures. In fact, Cologne Re's management was never concerned about organizational issues. Without pressure from competition or shareholders, and without reason to question deeply rooted traditions, the company was reluctant to make controversial decisions. Unlike his counterpart at Munich Re, Cologne Re's chairman and then CEO Peter Lütke-Bornefeld seemed reluctant to talk about managing change when we interviewed him in 2007. The company's aversion to change is deeply rooted. Richard Wiedemann, CEO from 1976 to 1987, for example, was known to meet personally with customers in Monte Carlo. It is hardly surprising, then, that he was reluctant to contemplate a more specialized organization that would relieve the sales force of its underwriting authority. Again, in retrospect, Cologne Re would clearly have benefited if Wiedemann had been willing to focus on organizational matters, to build teams and act more like a coach and less like a player.

SUMMARY

Old, large firms are traditional creatures. Change does not come naturally to them. Given a constantly changing business environment, however, it is clear that companies can thrive over the long run only if they repeatedly make adaptations and adjustments—this is Management 101. But the greatest companies distinguish themselves markedly in the ways they change. Although it seems counterintuitive, they adapt successfully because they are intelligently conservative. They avoid jumping into each management fad. Instead they take considerable time to try and understand broad trends and to distinguish between those that require significant responses and those that do not. When leadership starts to contemplate new organizational solutions, it does so with great cultural sensitivity. Management does not try to implement concepts that seem great on paper but clash in fundamental ways with tradition and culture. When the gold medalist Siemens, for example, began to exit its consumer goods business in the 1960s and to unite its high-current and low-current power businesses, it took its time, engaged employees in the process of change, and allowed them to get accustomed to a new situation. Silver medalist AEG, on the other hand, acted in a much clumsier fashion, with consecutive CEOs attempting to lead the company in different directions. While AEG was not conservative enough, there can also be too much of a good thing. Cologne Re was locked into a paternalistic leadership structure well into the 1980s, when pushing more responsibility farther down the line would have been beneficial. Only after General Re acquired it did more fundamental transformation become possible.

4   WHO — A COMMENTARY ON LEADERSHIP

Fairy tales are exciting and fun. They are told from generation to generation also because they teach important lessons. Children love these stories, but managers may also benefit from reflecting on the wisdom they convey.[1] Take the story "Puss in Boots,"[2] for example:

Once upon a time there was a poor miller whose only inheritance to his three sons was his mill, his donkey, and his cat. The youngest received nothing but the cat. While he was contemplating his fate, the cat approached him: "Do not be so concerned, my good master. If you will but give me a bag, and have a pair of boots made for me, then you shall see that you are not so poorly off with me as you imagine." Although the miller's son was skeptical at first, he did as the cat suggested. The cat went into the woods and laid out the bag, which he had filled with corn. He had scarcely laid it down before some partridge went for the corn. The master cat immediately closed the bag and killed the partridge. Proud of his prey, he went with it to the palace, and straight to the king: "Sir, I have brought you some partridge from my noble lord, the Marquis of Carabas" (for that was the title which the cat was pleased to give his master). "Tell your master," said the king, "that I thank him, and that I am very pleased with his gift." In the following months the cat repeated his visits to the king, bringing back little gifts from the king to his master, the miller's son.

As in most fairy tales, things turn out to be even better for the miller's son. One day, when the king took a drive along the riverside with his daughter, the cat convinced his master to take off his clothes and jump into the water. When the king passed, the cat cried out: "Help! Help! Thieves have stolen the clothes of my Lord Marquis of Carabas." The king immediately commanded the officers of his wardrobe to run and fetch one of his best suits for the Lord Marquis of Carabas. He then invited the marquis to join him for a drive in the carriage. The cat, quite overjoyed to see how his project was succeeding, ran on ahead. Meeting some countrymen who were mowing a meadow, he said to them, "My good fellows, if you do not tell the king that the meadow you are mowing belongs to my Lord Marquis of Carabas, you shall be chopped up like mincemeat." So when the carriage passed the mowers told the king that the meadows belonged to the Marquis of Carabas. The same thing happened in the woods.

But the cat did not stop before arriving at the castle, which belonged to a powerful magician, the actual owner of the land the king was passing at the same time. Standing in front of the vain magician, the cat started to tease him: "I have heard that you are able to change yourself into any kind of creature that you have a mind to. Personally I think it is possible that you transform yourself into an elephant. That is easy. But you will never be able to transform yourself into the smallest of animals, for example, a mouse." "Impossible!" cried the magician. "You shall see!" He immediately changed himself into a mouse. The master cat in turn fell upon the mouse and ate it. When the king and his daughter arrived together with the miller's son—now the Marquis of Carabas—the cat welcomed them: "Your majesty is welcome to this castle of my Lord Marquis of Carabas." Impressed by the castle and estate, the king was sure that there was only one way to proceed: "Dear Marquis of Carabas, would you like to marry my daughter?" The marquis, making several low bows, accepted the honor which his majesty conferred upon him, and forthwith they lived happily ever after.

While the story is certainly amusing, it also has an important message: the miller's son was successful because he had chosen—or in his case inherited—the right employee, made sure that his employee had the right equipment, and was prepared to listen to his sage advice. The situation is not all that different for leaders of large companies. It is an illusion for them to think that they should be able to single-handedly decide the fate of large and complex institutions. Their first and foremost duty is to choose the right people to work with. After taking the time and care to create systems that support the selection of the right people, leaders should then be prepared to let those people get on with their jobs. Leaders need to understand their own limitations. Listening might be more difficult than acting, but it is often more effective.

Our research showed us that the days of the larger-than-life personalities atop corporations are not over. They never existed. In hindsight, we tend to see those leaders who were successful as charismatic superheroes. In reality, only some of them were. What really distinguished the most successful among them was their ability to understand their company and industry, support their staff, and only in very limited cases intervene directly. The most successful leaders in our outstanding companies excelled in four different areas.

Leaders who do not follow these principles can do great damage. This truth is best demonstrated by looking at a company that was not in our sample but should have been, given its generally positive history. Daimler-Benz was set for greatness long before 1987, the year when Edzard Reuter became CEO. In the 15 years before he took over the top position, the

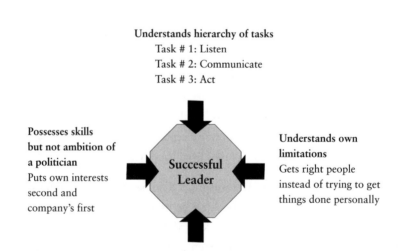

FIGURE 4.1. Characteristics of a Successful Leader

company's share price outperformed the DAX 30 Index by a factor of two. Daimler operated almost at par with Munich Re and Allianz and slightly ahead of Siemens. Once Reuter became CEO, however, the company's performance relative to the market and certain peers fell off dramatically. The year Reuter retired, the company declared the largest loss in German corporate history. In the 15 years following Reuter's rise to the top, other large German companies outperformed Daimler by a factor of 15!

So what happened to Daimler under Reuter? In many ways he symbolizes those characteristics that we admire in a leader. The son of Ernst Reuter, the legendary mayor of Berlin after World War II, he came from a distinguished and talented family and grew up with many advantages. Like his father, he was a well-educated intellectual who knew how to use the media. He could be charming and charismatic, friendly and talkative. He appeared to be a good listener but often voiced strong opinions about business matters. When we met him in a small coffeehouse in Berlin to talk about Daimler under his leadership, he created a relaxed atmosphere in which it was easy to ask questions.[3] His arguments sounded plausible, his vision compelling. Unfortunately they did not work.

In the early 1980s Daimler started to worry about its future as a niche player. Reuter, who had joined the board as an outsider—having previously worked in media, most recently as a top executive in Bertelsmann—saw this as a chance to position himself for the top job. In 1984 he distributed a position paper to fellow board members, stressing the increasing competition in the luxury automobile sector with BMW creating its 7-series,

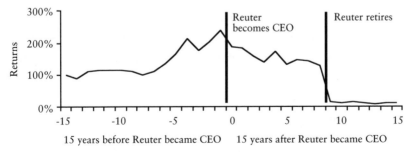

FIGURE 4.2. Daimler's Performance under the Leadership of Edzard Reuter
SOURCE: Data from Thompson Datastream.

Fiat's acquisition of Maserati, Ford's of Jaguar, and Toyota's introduction of Lexus. His proposed solution: diversification, a recipe that was highly popular at the time. Applying his political skill, he was able to convince his colleagues and the supervisory board that the creation of an integrated technology conglomerate would be the best way forward. Promoting the acquisitions of MTU and Dornier (aircraft manufacturers), AEG, MBB (an aerospace company), Cap Gemini (an IT consultant), and Fokker (an aerospace company), Reuter was able to secure the top job.

Once at the top, Reuter started implementing major structural changes. A holding company was created, consisting of five divisions (cars, utility vehicles, aerospace, electricity, and services). Reuter's intention was to ensure integration merely by bringing the CEOs of the divisions onto the board of Daimler-Benz, which according to German law had collective accountability. In reality, the vision turned out to be problematic. Expected synergies between divisions did not materialize. The car division, for example, preferred to buy equipment from Siemens rather than from Daimler's AEG to stay competitive. Meanwhile, rank-and-file employees resisted the new strategy and structure. Employees who had been proud producers of high-quality cars in the past suddenly faced criticism for being associated with a conglomerate that had a considerable interest in the arms industry.

What should have been obvious from the start soon became clear enough: Reuter was a very bright man, but he had a limited understanding of the foundations of Daimler's greatness. He had always been an outsider, and he had no previous experience in the car industry when he joined Daimler's board. As a liberal intellectual and a member of the Social Democratic Party (a party closely wedded to the unions and eyed with great suspicion by conservative managers), he did not fit with the conservative, down-to-earth, engineering-dominated culture of Daimler. In a company in which generations of workers had taken great pride in the Mercedes star, he turned up in a Peugeot on his first day of work! His greatest failure was his bias toward hasty action. Rather than taking the time to understand the organization and then developing plans and policies compatible with its particular context, he started an acquisition spree, assembling a number of companies that did not fit well together. In hindsight, it almost seems as if Daimler fell prey to his ambition to become CEO in a company where most senior managers were against him. He rejected offers for top jobs at Lufthansa, Veba, and Volkswagen and viewed Daimler as an opportunity to make a radical statement by creating an integrated technology conglomerate.

The fact is, many expensive mistakes could have been avoided if he had listened to employees instead of heeding the advice of outsiders. By the time Daimler started to take its problems seriously, it had only limited room to maneuver. Restructuring some of the divisions turned out to be impossible because of uncooperative minority shareholders with opposing interests, although a program to bring the car division back on track worked pretty well. In 1995 Reuter was urged to retire. His successor, Jürgen Schrempp, announced a DM 5.7 billion loss, the largest in German postwar history.

Edzard Reuter failed in all four areas that characterize successful leaders:

(1) He did not understand the hierarchy of tasks. He proved to be a man of action, which is a liability when the actions are the wrong ones. He concentrated his energy on new acquisitions instead of ensuring a flawless integration of earlier purchases and thinking through the entire strategy. Listening more carefully to his people—the first task for a leader—would certainly have urged him to be more cautious. Even his praised communication skills were more for the outside world than for the company itself. His deal making in the early days made him a darling of the media, a celebrated CEO who single-handedly saved struggling icons such as AEG, but it was much less obvious to the core automobile producers how those characteristics could benefit them.

(2) Limitations did not seem to be of any concern to Reuter. For example, after the Daimler fiasco, he tried to position himself as a future mayor of Berlin in an interview with *Der Spiegel*, an influential German magazine in 1994.

(3) As a man who spent his entire career in the media industry, Reuter should have been well aware of his limitations, particularly with regard to Daimler and the automobile industry. He clearly did not understand why his plans were not feasible in a proud automobile business with a tradition of engineering talent.

(4) While he certainly possessed the skills of a politician, he had his ambitions too. Gaining Daimler's top job as an outsider was a strong display of his political savvy. Moving the quest to diversify to the top of the agenda allowed him to outshine the CEO who had little experience in that area. With the help of Alfred Herrhausen, the Deutsche Bank CEO who chaired Daimler's supervisory board, he introduced a task force to review structure and synergy potentials, which reported directly to the supervisory board. Sometimes this task force was seen as the actual decision-making center of the firm,[4] and not surprisingly, the sidelined CEO soon resigned. The plans that helped Reuter to take the top job were less successful for the company, though. Certainly this judgment is easier to make with the benefit of hindsight, but Reuter's love for the media and his failure to listen to the many warning signals over the years should have indicated that he was not the right person to lead Daimler. Leaders in our top companies certainly were of a different kind.

Understand the Hierarchy of Tasks

The leaders of outstanding companies have clear priorities. They recognize that a key challenge is to understand what really is going on in their organizations and where adjustments may be necessary. At Glaxo, for example, top executives displayed a keen interest in learning from their scientists at an early date, when the company started the transition from being a producer of milk powder to being a drug company in the 1920s. This was evident during Harry Jephcott's annual trips to international subsidiaries and also the frequent visits of his successors to the company labs.

At Lafarge, we are able to document the determination of managers to learn from their staff as early as 1833. Léon Pavin de Lafarge, a graduate of the École Polytechnique and the second leader of the young corporation, spent considerable time at the plant, where workers shared their ideas about the production process with him.[5] His successors observe the same principles. Auguste Pavin de Lafarge, who was part of the leadership team in the late 19th century, for example, recommended that leaders spend time at construction sites and make sure that they know all their workers by name—measures that create trust and enable leaders to listen.

Shell is another great company in which leaders are famous for taking the time to listen to employees and other stakeholders. Sir Mark Moody-Stuart, the company's leader from 1998 to 2001, lives in the English countryside. One day a group of about 15 activists came to his home, carrying posters displaying unflattering slogans such as "Murderer." It turned out that the protesters were surprised, both by the modesty of the house and by the friendly greeting they received from Sir Mark and his wife. Over tea served by Mrs. Moody-Stuart, Sir Mark hosted an intensive discussion of the company's policies and actions. The two parties did not reach agreement, but the protesters were disarmed by the willingness of Shell's top boss to listen and communicate.

This ability to listen and communicate has been particularly evident in times of significant change. In the early 1990s, Shell's return on average capital employed (a key performance indicator in the industry) fell below 7 percent, putting the company well behind its major competitors. The country subsidiaries underwent a number of cost-cutting exercises, but the overall results did not improve. The committee of managing directors (Shell's top leadership) became well aware that something more had to be done. A common approach in situations like this is to undertake a structural reorganization. No doubt a more centralized organization could have reduced costs immediately. But the members of the CMD also knew that such an approach would endanger a proven system of strong country organizations. Rather than change the structure, the CMD decided first to listen to the organization. As Cor Herkströter, the leader of Shell at the time, put it,

We did not have a blueprint. We did not say this is what is going to happen. We allowed for input from the organization. The feeling was that we have to arrive at something that is sufficient, that is proactive, that is highly professional. We looked at the environment around us, but it had to be something that is supported by the organization because we realized that many people would be affected by the fundamental changes that did arise out of this process.[6]

A number of themes were compiled by the CMD, and over a period of several months each of the members engaged a wide group of senior managers in conversations about the future of the company. Members of the CMD who themselves were used to finding solutions together with their colleagues had always expected the same from the people who reported to them. Likewise, these people would have expected the same from the people reporting to them. At this crucial time of change, the CMD relied on this proven approach. They engaged, they listened, and they were prepared to make changes. Said Herkströter:

Management became much more visible, management became much more part of the organization, management was prepared to be vulnerable, saying we are not the ones who know everything. Yes, we are indeed in charge of this, but we are prepared to demonstrate our weaknesses and share them with you. At the same time this is not simply to be open and honest without development but to show that together we have to learn a lot. And I think it was also then that we decided that managing is much more coaching rather than directing or saying that is what we want you to do. It is much more coming to the conclusion that this is the right thing for the organization. At the same time—and that is something I expressed very much—at the same time not forgetting that someone has to manage the organization.[7]

The final act in preparing for transformation was a meeting at the end of 1995 in which 50 top executives were asked to write a resignation letter to the "old Shell" before committing themselves to the new one. Afterward, in groups of four, the participants started to map out the company's transformation journey. Following further engagements, a vision, termed the Shell Business Framework, was created.[8]

In sum, it was only after the intensive period of listening, communicating, and engaging that the CMD decided to act. And in fact the early implementation period consisted primarily of communication and efforts to engage other employees in the transformation. A team of change agents was formed to assist with changes in personal behaviors. Only in 1998, after the fall of the oil price below $10 per barrel, was stronger action set and a new structure implemented. The leadership team took four years to reach this point. As they moved ahead, Shell's leaders continued to show patience. Leadership took great care to understand how the organization was responding to the new system. For example, an employee survey (targeting the entire staff of 100,000) was introduced to gain insights into how people were affected. In some cases adjustments followed. Rather than centralizing the entire organization as originally intended, Shell did so only when that was beneficial for the business. Country organizations in Asia, for example, received more competencies at the expense of a regional downstream organization (refining and retail) when staff from this region made it clear that a loose integration made more sense in their fragmented markets.

Understand Your Own Limitations

There is no greater danger to a corporation than a superstar CEO who tries to take all matters into his own hands. Great leaders understand their own limitations. For starters, they know that they will not be around forever. They ensure that the company has a pool of talented top managers who are able to run the firm in case something happens to them. Sir David Prosser from Legal & General, for example, recalls that he regularly talked with his colleagues about promising members of the firm and how they could develop their leadership skills further. This includes training but also, and more importantly, assignments where they can gather experience. To ensure continuity, the board also talks about potential successors for all senior positions every year.[9]

Great leaders also understand that they will not be able to excel in all areas of their business. Some companies develop unorthodox solutions to overcome this limitation. Rather than having a single CEO, they sometimes divide leadership responsibilities among several executives. In the mid-19th century, for example, the two brothers Edouard and Léon de Lafarge formed a talented team at their family cement company. While Edouard was a dynamic and entrepreneurial businessman, his brother was a diligent technician who made sure the company kept up to date with technology developments.[10] Lafarge also resorted to an old Roman concept at various points in its history: the triumvirate. This approach was first taken at the end of the 19th century and once again in the 1970s. In 1971 Marcel Demonque's heir apparent, Jean-Charles Lofficier, left the company. Instead of hiring an outside CEO to replace him, Lafarge decided to divide responsibilities for different core activities (domestic market, foreign market, and diversified products) among Olivier Lecerf, Jean Bailly, and Jean François.[11] While Olivier Lecerf had the title of chief executive, it was clear that he was only first among equals. The different talents of the three leaders allowed Lafarge to survive one of the most challenging times in the French cement industry, when markets collapsed in the wake of the first oil crisis. In fact, the crisis energized the firm's internationalization and diversification process.

The 1970s also proved a crucial period for Lafarge's comparison company, Ciments Français. In 1969 Robert Alexandre, its CEO since 1941, passed away. He had failed to identify and develop a successor, and Ciments Français decided to hire an outsider, Marc Hannotin, who had previously been a member of its supervisory board. This decision turned out to be a fatal mistake. As is often the case with CEOs hired from outside a company, Hannotin's limited knowledge of the company and its business made him inclined to concentrate on expansion through acquisition. In 1971 Ciments Français merged with Poliet et Chausson, resulting in the largest cement producer in France. It was bad timing, however, as the French market was suffering a major recession. The company struggled for many years and was eventually sold to Italcementi in 1992.

Understand the Company and the Industry

In their influential study of long-lived U.S. companies, Collins and Porras pointed out that outstanding corporations did not recruit their CEOs from outside.[12] This was an interesting insight for the United States, but it seemed hardly sensational for Europe, where there is a long tradition of promoting internal candidates. We did not expect any difference between our top and comparison companies in this respect. However, we were surprised to find a significant difference: in 23 cases (23.5 percent of our total sample) comparison companies hired external candidates to become their CEOs, while top companies did so in only five cases (4.2 percent of our total sample).[13]

This finding raises a question about why companies decide to hire outsiders. Conventional wisdom holds that outsiders are not locked into the old ways of a company and thus are particularly well placed to lead change. Our research provides a different answer. Outsiders were not hired to initiate change. They were hired when no suitable internal candidates were available due to the company's failure to nurture its own talent.

Consider the case of Aachener und Münchener between 1914 and 1924. From 1896 to 1914, Fritz Schröder had been in charge of the company and had successfully diversified and modernized the old insurance giant. Like many other powerful leaders, however, he seemed to have forgotten that he would not be around forever. When he died in 1914 there was no successor. The only other person who might have been suitable, his deputy, was ill himself. He took the job for an interim period until an external candidate was finally found. When the new leader fell ill in 1917, the company once again did not have an insider who could move up. Looking outside, the company eventually found an executive from another fire insurance company. Meanwhile, Aachener und Münchener Versicherung also had problems in filling the position of chairman of the supervisory board during this period. One of the people in the position died after just four months in office and another one after 10 months.[14] Not surprisingly, the company was not capable of making important and farsighted decisions during this period.

The gold medalist Allianz, on the other hand, had a strong leadership team and no problems in filling the top job. From 1900 to 1921, Paul von der Nahmer, a close associate of the company's founder, Carl von Thieme, was in charge. With the help of other financial institutions, he built up foreign currency reserves, which came in handy during the war and the subsequent inflation period,[15] a time when he was no longer in charge. This policy is a clear indication that he not merely concentrated on the performance under his leadership but also took care to prepare for the time after his retirement. As a result of this approach, Kurt Schmitt, his successor, was able to excel. While Aachener und Münchener struggled to fill its top position and keep operations running at the same time, Allianz surged ahead by means of timely acquisitions and carefully planned restructuring.[16]

Overall, the development of our gold medalists indicates that large changes are not dependent on the force of an outside CEO. The most dramatic and successful transformations of our outstanding corporations happened under the leadership of executives who had spent their entire career with the company. Alec Nathan, for example, transformed Glaxo's forerunner, a New Zealand wholesaler, into a thriving British milk powder producer. Sir John Bond was at the helm of HSBC when the corporate colonial bank changed into a leading global financial institution. John Loudon, Shell's leader in the 1950s and 1960s, overhauled the entire structure of the oil giant, creating a business model that generated growth for more than 30 years. These leaders succeeded because of—not despite—their long experience in the companies. Large, established corporations with strong cultures are difficult for outsiders to understand. If you want to change them, you need intimate knowledge of how they work, including the unstated and unwritten policies and rules that constitute the company culture. Some outsiders, such as Aachener und Münchener's Fritz Schröder, managed to develop such an understanding. But others failed. AEG's Walter Cipa, for example, wanted to implement radical reforms. From the outside, his ideas looked sensible and necessary. AEG, however, rejected Cipa and his radical ideas. Thirty-six top managers left the company, while others who remained worked to undermine his plans. To no one's surprise, he left after four fruitless years.

The insight from our research is that the apparent advantage of an outside CEO's freedom from existing ways of working is double-edged. Dramatic change works only if it is the right change. Meanwhile, insiders may be just as likely to come up with fresh ideas, while also possessing the intimate contextual understanding and the power base required to make those ideas succeed.

Have the Skills of Politicians, but Not Their Ambition

Leading a large corporation like Legal & General, Nokia, or Lafarge requires high-level political skills. What it does not require is the ambition of leaders to become superstars. It is no coincidence that celebrated superstar CEOs often fail. In a fascinating study of narcissistic CEOs, Arijit Chatterjee and Donald C. Hambrick[17] from Pennsylvania State University measure the prominence of the CEO's photograph in the annual report, the number of times he is mentioned in press releases, the length of his *Who's Who* entry, the use of first-person pronouns in interviews, and his relative pay compared to that of the second-highest-paid executive. Firms with narcissistic CEOs display more extreme and volatile organizational performance. We observed a similar trend in our study and were particularly aware of the downside potential. Superstar CEOs divert too much attention from the actual duty of managing their organization to building their own profiles in the media. Edzard Reuter and Jürgen Schrempp were both celebrated as "manager of the year" by the German *Manager Magazin* before Daimler-Benz tumbled. Even leaders who have clearly done an outstanding job are in danger of falling into this trap. Lord John Browne from BP, for example, became the most celebrated leader in the oil industry, but his high visibility and reputation did not prevent the company from having problems. Following an explosion in a refinery, and an embarrassing report underlining management mistakes, Browne decided to step down earlier than intended. A disruption at the vital Alaska site and a criticism related to an artificial hike in bottled gas prices convinced him that it was best to allow for a new start under a new leader.[18] His retirement was subsequently brought forward by another three months when legal issues erupted concerning a story from his private life that was published by a British tabloid.[19] In contrast to BP's celebrated CEO, Shell's top managers have never been prominent in the public eye. They have preferred a low-key approach, working as a team rather than gathering around a charismatic leader.

The question that a leader has to ask himself is pretty simple: am I focused on the organization or on my own career and reputation? The temptation to promote oneself is always there, especially because the media love to trumpet the titans of industry and sometimes lure them toward public office. Take the German insurance companies that we studied, for example. The founder of Allianz and Munich Re, Carl von Thieme, had one interest only: building a successful organization. He devoted his entire life to this cause. Gustav von Mevissen, founder of Cologne Re, and David Hansemann, founder of Aachener und Münchener, both had ambitions beyond their company. In fact, for them, the company was partly a stepping-stone to gain high public office. Hansemann was a member of the city council, the provincial parliament, and president of the chamber of commerce.[20] In 1848 he became Prussia's finance minister and remained in various advisory positions thereafter. He was aware that his devotion to public office came at the expense of his insurance company but was prepared to sacrifice some of its potential performance to this end.[21] Mevissen, a close acquaintance of Hansemann, was also active in the public arena.

He was a member of the Prussian parliament and president of the chamber of commerce, and he took an important role in the campaign for the administration that Hansemann joined as finance minister. Mevissen also took an active role in the founding of numerous other companies. At one point he asked his cousin to join him to coordinate his multiple offices.[22] From the perspective of Cologne Re, it would have been better for him to devote his considerable talents to that company exclusively.

Summary

Children love the "Puss in Boots" tale, but so should managers. The story about a poor miller's son who inherits a clever cat and "strikes gold" provides an object lesson for corporate leaders: support your troops, but let them do their job. It is unwise as well as unnecessary for top management to take all matters into their own hands. Leaders at our gold medalist companies excelled in four different ways:

> Understand the hierarchy of tasks: The main strength of a successful leader is listening for the best advice. After carefully listening and weighing different options, the leader then communicates to a wider audience and finally initiates action. The temptation to turn this hierarchy upside down is great. Orchestrating a merger is certainly more glamorous than spending months trying to understand the culture and dynamics of a company. Unsolicited action is one of the greatest dangers, though. Edzard Reuter's "destruction" of Daimler, a company once set for greatness, is a perfect example.

> Understand your own limitations: Great leaders understand their own limitations. One of their first and most important tasks is to prepare potential successors. AEG, for example, experienced a frightful shortfall in talented CEOs in the 1970s when one leader suddenly passed away. Without a successor in place, the company compounded its troubles.

> Understand the company and the industry: Reading the names floated by the press when companies look for a new leader seems to sometimes suggest that successful leadership bears no relation to industry experience. The development of our gold medalists certainly points in the opposite direction. In only 3.4 percent of cases did they choose a CEO

from outside the company. The silver medalists, on the other hand, relied on an outsider to take the top job in 23.5 percent of cases. These statistics suggest a link between hiring outsiders and less-compelling performance. And often the outsiders proved unsuccessful. Either their ideas did not fit the problem or they lacked the understanding required to implement new ideas in complex organizations.

Have the skills of politicians but not the ambitions of politicians: Ask the leaders of any large companies whether they feel more like generals or politicians. The answer, most often, is the latter. In fact, many generals would agree that leading an action-oriented institution such as an army requires significant political skills. Great corporate leaders, however, should not confuse skills and ambitions. Leaders of our gold medalists focused their ambitions on the success of their company. In some comparison companies, however, leaders occasionally took themselves too seriously. Cologne Re's and Aachener und Münchener's founders, for example, both ended up in public office. Even great leaders can overstretch themselves.

5   SO WHAT? — A COMPARISON
WITH PRIOR STUDIES

More than 25 years ago, Tom Peters and Robert Waterman published *In Search of Excellence*. Ten years ago, Arie de Geus's *The Living Company* and Jim Collins and Jerry Porras's *Built to Last* started to climb the best-seller lists. Our book provides a fresh perspective on the long-term sources of excellence in great companies in two ways: it is a European study, and it takes into account new insights from management scholars. Some of our findings dovetail with those of earlier authors, but there also are notable differences.

In *Built to Last* Collins and Porras focus on 17 U.S. companies and one Japanese company (plus a matching comparison company for each of them) that had stood the test of time up to the point at which their study was published. These companies were founded between 1812 and 1945, with a median founding date of 1902. Collins and Porras consider whether truly exceptional companies differ from other companies, and if so, how they differ. Their key conclusion is that exceptional companies overturn the conventional wisdom about what it takes. These companies employ leaders who are primarily organization builders, with an ability to balance continuity and change—they distinguish between enduring fundamentals and factors that can and should be changed. The result is an impressive performance. The 1990 return on a 1926 investment of $1 is

15 times higher than that of the general market (NYSE, AMEX) and six times higher than that of the comparison companies.

Built to Last stresses the importance of stimulating progress while preserving the core. Our research, however, suggests that not only great but also good companies preserved their core in Europe. The great companies were adept at handling the constant challenge to adapt. As we've seen, when Siemens changed in the 1960s and in the 1990s, it did so in a culturally sensitive way. AEG, on the other hand, took more dramatic, even radical steps toward change but in so doing created a situation in which employees proved unable or unwilling to implement the solutions sought by top management.

We also take a slightly different view of innovation than Collins and Porras do. While we agree that incremental innovation is important, we are less convinced about breakthrough innovation. Our data indicates that great companies stress exploitation more than exploration. Companies are able to buy exploration capabilities, but it is not possible to outsource efficiency. For example, Glaxo's greatest commercial success, an ulcer medication, resulted from efficient marketing, not breakthrough innovation. Glaxo's comparison company, Wellcome, on the other hand, was known as an innovation machine and was less interested in the commercial end of the business. Glaxo outperformed Wellcome and eventually bought it.

Collins and Porras did not emphasize handling of risk as a theme in their study of U.S. companies. In our sample of European companies, risk management is an important factor. In the course of a long history, companies inevitably and repeatedly confront unexpected events. While it is impossible to predict what will happen, great companies usually have contingency plans in place. For example, when fire destroyed a factory supplying a vital component, Nokia shifted quickly to other suppliers. Its comparison company, Ericsson, had no backup.

The Living Company, by Arie de Geus, pays less attention to year-to-year performance over the long term than Collins and Porras, and it focuses on survival. While there is evidence of corporate longevity, e.g., Japan's Sumitomo originating in 1590 or Sweden's Stora with roots more than 700 years in the past, the average life expectancy of a company is well below 20 years. De Geus's research, based on a study he initiated as the head of

TABLE 5.1. Our Research and the Work of Other Scholars
on Enduring Success

Collins and Porras's main message	Insights from our research
Build an organization rather than relying on a single idea or charismatic leader.	We agree.
Identify vision and mission.	While vision and mission are important, those two characteristics do not distinguish great from good companies.
Embrace paradoxes such as being conservative around the core and bold in your operations.	We agree to a certain extent, but great companies also need to have priorities. For example, they value both exploration and exploitation, but they concentrate on exploitation first.
Stimulate progress with breakthrough new goals, incremental innovation, and avoidance of compliance.	Constant adaptation is needed to keep organization and strategy aligned with changing environment, but unlike Collins and Porras we see incremental innovation and diversification into related products and markets as the most promising approach.
Preserve the core through homegrown management and cult-like cultures.	We agree with observation on homegrown management but take a different view on culture. Culture matters particularly in the sense that it has to be handled in a sensitive way during times of change.
Ensure consistent alignment.	We agree.

De Geus's main message	Insights from our research
Companies need to display sensitivity to the environment to learn and adapt.	We agree.
A company's identity (values, culture) represents its innate ability to build a community and a persona for itself.	We agree, but a strong culture cannot explain the difference between good and great companies.
To survive, companies need to display tolerance and decentralize.	We agree, and we also see a strong role of management by supporting diversification into related activities.
Conservative financing allows companies to govern their own growth effectively.	We agree, but conservatism is important beyond finances. Great companies, for example, do not rely on a single supplier, customer, or market.

TABLE 5.1. (*continued*)

Peters and Waterman's main message	Insights from our research
A bias for action, active decision making—"getting on with it."	A bias for action has its merits on the operational side of a business, but decisions affecting the entire corporation should be made with great care and without rush.
Close to the customer—learning from the people served by the business.	We agree but want to draw attention to the limitation of this concept in some businesses.
Autonomy and entrepreneurship—fostering innovation and nurturing "champions."	While we acknowledge that autonomy and entrepreneurism are important, exploitation is even more important.
Productivity through people—treating rank-and-file employees as a source of quality.	We agree.
Hands-on, value-driven management philosophy that guides everyday practice—management showing its commitment.	We agree.
Stick to the knitting—stay with the business that you know.	We disagree. Companies with a single business structure have no choice other than decline, merger, or sale once their primary offering reaches the end of its life span.
Simple form, lean staff—some of the best companies have minimal headquarters staff.	Headquarters size was not a significant variable in our research.
Simultaneous loose/tight properties—autonomy in shop-floor activities plus centralized values.	We agree but observe that strong values do not distinguish great companies from good ones.

Shell Planning in 1983, collects evidence suggesting that corporations fail because their policies and practices are based too heavily on the thinking and the language of economics. Managers focus on producing goods and services and forget that organizations are communities of human beings and they are in business to stay alive. To explore the personality of companies, which de Geus calls living companies, the Shell team identified 27 companies that were older than 100 years in 1983 and had reasonably well-documented histories. These companies shared four characteristics: (1) conservatism in financing, (2) sensitivity to the world around them, (3) awareness of their identity, and (4) tolerance of new ideas.

We share de Geus's claim that financial conservatism is important, but we see conservatism as the best approach in dealing with other aspects of risk as well. Our research is also in line with de Geus's view that companies need to change their business over time if they want to survive. More precisely, we think the best way to prepare is through constant diversification into related new technologies and markets. Allianz, for example, built new businesses right from the start, taking long periods of minor growth in some areas into account. Its comparison company, Aachener und Münchener, on the other hand, concentrated solely on fire insurance for almost 100 years. As society evolved, markets changed and Aachener und Münchener lost its competitive advantage.

We do not fully agree with de Geus in his view of the importance of culture—which is similar to that of Collins and Porras. Their overlapping views most likely reflect the prominence of interest in corporate culture at the time of their research. As mentioned above, we believe that culture is important but it does not illuminate the difference between good and great companies. AEG, Prudential, and other comparison companies all have or had strong cultures.

We fully agree with de Geus about the role of learning. Our analysis underlines the importance of transferring knowledge across time and distance and explains how this can best be done. More than *The Living Company*, we stress the power of stories to transfer knowledge across time and distance and we provide some tools for achieving this.

In Search of Excellence was the product of a research project conducted at McKinsey & Company. In 1977 the firm launched two projects:

a business strategy project and a project concerned with organization, structure, and people. While the former received more attention in the beginning, it was the latter—managed by Peters and Waterman—that provided the truly interesting results. With no particular theory in mind, Peters traveled the world to interview a wide-ranging group of people. In 1979 Peters presented 700 slides to Siemens in a two-day event. PepsiCo got interested, but wanted a slicker version of the presentation, resulting in the well-known eight themes.

The central message of *In Search of Excellence* is that people, customers, and action matter more than what previously had been considered the hard factors driving success. While this was an important contribution, subsequent research put more emphasis on the organizational aspect—taking people seriously but viewing them primarily as members of groups and networks.

We differ significantly from Peters and Waterman on diversification. They suggest that companies need to stick to their knitting. This view might be the result of the shorter observation period of their research. If companies want to survive and perform successfully over time, they need to diversify into related products and markets. Companies with a single business structure have no choices other than decline, merger, or sale once their primary offering reaches the end of its life span.

In conclusion, we want to pay tribute to the work we discussed above. While *In Search of Excellence* was probably the most influential management book in the 1980s, *Built to Last* and *The Living Company* profoundly shaped the thinking and behavior of managers in the 1990s. We might take a different view on some of the issues discussed above, but we do not intend to challenge the value of these contributions. Our intention is to follow where they led and maybe walk a little farther down the same path.

6   E P I L O G U E

Learning from the History of Outstanding Corporations

Can we really learn from the history of a handful of large corporations? At first, a critic noting the way that circumstances evolve over time would obviously object: "How can the challenges faced by HSBC in 19th-century China, by Siemens in the aftermath of World War II, or by Lafarge during the oil crisis be compared to what corporations have to deal with in the globalized world of the 21st century? And, surely, the current economic crisis challenges the way we have done business, making observations from the past somewhat passé." Well, the 21st century is no doubt different from 19th-century Europe or China, and certainly the current turbulences are dramatic. However, we also have a tendency to view our times as unparalleled and uniquely challenging. In fact, every generation does that. When the Romans learned that Julius Caesar had been assassinated in the Senate in 42 B.C., they surely thought the world would come to an end. When farmers in rural England saw the first steam-powered train passing through their pastures, they no doubt wondered what was going on. When, in 1966, Neil Armstrong raised the American flag on the moon, the exploration of space no longer seemed pure science fiction. And when, in 1989, the Berlin Wall tumbled down, millions of people cheered a new world order. Yes, every generation faces a unique set of challenges. The outstanding companies in our sample survived and prevailed during the Great Depression, two world wars, and two energy crises, not to mention the advent of the telephone, television, and computer technology. Studying their history does not provide the solutions for today's business problems, but it does provide profound insights into how companies can approach the challenges they face and which strategies can help them prevail. As this is an observation of a limited number of companies, the results are essentially propositions. Nonetheless, the consistent differences between gold and silver medalists suggest that the distinction is not purely a coincidence. A trip into history is bound to be exciting and beneficial.

Our trip consisted of a tour through Europe. Europe is the natural place to search for the secret of corporate longevity and business models that endure. Half of the Fortune Global 500 companies older than 100 years are European. Seventy-two of the 100 oldest family businesses in the world are European. International trade in its modern form originated in 16th-century Holland and the modern manufacturing company was born in 18-century Britain. To gain solid and comparable data, we decided to select only publicly quoted companies that were on the 2003 Fortune Global 500 list, that were older than 100 years, and that were outperforming the general market (Dow Jones, DAX, and FTSE) by a factor of at least 15 over a 50-year period starting in 1953. Nine gold medalists made the cut: Allianz, Glaxo, HSBC, Lafarge, Legal & General, Munich Re, Nokia, Shell, and Siemens. They beat the general market by a factor of 115 since 1953. For each of them we found a comparison company, the silver medalists, who beat the market still by a factor of 16. An additional advantage of choosing large multinational corporations is that the threats and opportunities that they deal with are similar to those faced by other international companies, regardless of whether they identify as Chinese, Indian, or American. And so the study of these companies is most useful to readers who have an interest in large enterprises around the globe.

So what did we learn by comparing our nine gold medalists with our nine silver medalists? The fundamental requirement for achieving enduring success is straightforward and not surprising: companies need to align their strategy and organization with the environment in which they operate. HSBC performed considerably better than its main competitor in

Southeast Asia, Chartered Bank (later Standard Chartered), due to an organizational setup that fit perfectly with the immediate business environment. It was the only British overseas bank headquartered in Asia. This provided the bank with a better understanding of the market and a closer connection to customers. For example, in the mid-1860s, London-based banks like Chartered reduced the period allowed for their customers to repay trade bills, but HSBC's management understood that this would not work for China-based trading houses, as they needed a longer time frame to complete the trade between China and the UK. Therefore, HSBC picked up a substantial amount of new business from its competitors! Today the basic requirement for companies with an ambition to be successful in the long run continues to be the same. Companies like Barclays or Goldman Sachs that are able to adjust quickly to new tight credit markets by tapping into reserves as well as picking up new investors and using government money turn out to be the winners. Their strategy and organization are in line with the new environment.

While the framework for enduring success provides you with an explanation of what you need to do, the most exciting insights from our research concern the strategic choices that enable great corporations to achieve strategic and organizational fit. How can an organization ensure that it is in harmony with the environment in which it operates? How can it make the adjustments required to master today's shifting business landscape? We observed five principles or strategies that companies need to follow:

First, companies need to put exploitation first and exploration second. In an ideal world, companies would manage both to explore and to exploit. Unfortunately, innovation and efficiency call for radically different approaches. Outstanding companies know that innovation is important, but their first priority is exploitation, the efficient use of existing assets. Nokia, for example, succeeded by emphasizing logistics and efficiency. Sure, it was also innovative, but so was its comparison company, Ericsson. As a proud leader of technology development for mobile phones, Ericsson employed more than 30,000 people in 100 R&D centers. It pioneered general packet radio system (GPRS) and third-generation mobile technology standards but was hit hard by the telecom recession after 2000. It had put exploration first and exploitation second.

Second, companies need to act conservatively with their finances—and beyond. Most of us do this in our personal lives. In good times we put money aside to save for retirement, the education of our kids, and possible leaner years in the future. Companies that have a natural drive to grow sometimes forget about the risks associated with relying too heavily on outsiders to finance their operations. Some companies also underestimate the risk of relying on a single supplier, market, or outside investor. Throughout history Siemens's approach to finance, for example, was more conservative than AEG's. AEG also lost 74.5 percent of its assets when the Russians occupied East Germany; Siemens, on the other hand, had spread its assets throughout Germany and avoided similar losses. Today the virtue of a conservative financial approach is more evident than ever. In 2008 Lehman Brothers asked Shell why it did not take a more aggressive financial approach. In 2009 the investment bank, with its appetite for risk, was no longer around to ask questions. As the markets start to recover, companies need to remember to grow not only their revenues but also their reserves!

Third, companies need to develop mechanisms that allow them to learn over time and space. Top companies have a culture that facilitates knowledge sharing, their leaders encourage learning, they started systematic training long before others did (for example, Nokia opened a school for employees in 1891), and they use established processes, such as the budgeting process, as a means to spread experience and insights. In addition, they use stories from the past, including bad experiences, as a powerful way to preserve lessons learned. In the 1930s Shell narrowly escaped disaster when the powerful leader Henri Deterding, who was sympathetic to Nazi Germany as a bulwark against the communists, retired without setting up any embarrassing links. The company did not forget its narrow escape. Deterding's successors were never allowed to be so powerful. In 1964 the board rejected advice from McKinsey & Company to install an American-style chief executive officer, whose official powers would have matched those once wielded by Deterding. Naturally, the financial crisis that started in 2008 also provides many valuable lessons. Companies that want to succeed in the future had better think of some stories to remember.

Fourth, companies need to diversify into related businesses. Conglomerates are hard to manage, since top managers often fail to understand some part of their corporation, while narrowly focused companies are left out in the cold if the preference of the market shifts to other businesses. Successful companies like Allianz are ready to branch out into nearby markets, milking their capabilities and extending their reach. Starting in machine insurance, Allianz was able to benefit from the dynamic industrialization of Germany at the end of the 19th century. The cash generated along the way was used to build up first transport insurance, then automobile insurance, and finally life insurance. Allianz's comparison company, the older Aachener und Münchener, was narrowly focused on fire insurance for the first 100 years of its existence. The company lost out when Germany shifted to an industrial economy. When Aachener und Münchener tried to widen its scope in earnest—in the 1970s—it was too late. Its lack of experience with mergers finally led to an ill-advised merger, creating financial constraints that eventually prompted the takeover of the company. Promising companies today act like Allianz. Google, for example, is constantly extending its scope in related areas: Gmail, Google Maps, Chrome, Google News, Google Scholar, Google Books.

Fifth, companies need to manage change in a culturally sensitive way. Although it seems counterintuitive, our gold medalists adapt successfully because they are intelligently conservative. They avoid embracing each management fad. Instead, they invest considerable time in understanding broad trends and distinguishing between those that require significant responses and those that do not. When leadership starts to contemplate new organizational solutions, they do so with great cultural sensitivity. They do not try to implement concepts that seem great on paper but clash in fundamental ways with tradition and culture. When Glaxo's Zantac patent was getting close to expiration in the early 1990s, the firm needed to adapt. Leaders decided to take a culturally sensitive approach, starting with training and workshops. The merger of two separate sales forces and the integration of the acquired Wellcome sales force followed. Meanwhile, key members of the staff were empowered with increased responsibility and budgets. Eventually the different steps added up. The sales force transformed from a product-based hierarchical group into a fast-moving, well-trained force fit to face the new challenges of the 1990s.

Cultural sensitivity and an ability to listen are also core characteristics that we observed in leaders who enabled enduring success. Essentially they reminded us of soccer coaches. Soccer coaches, or leaders, are hardly the ones that score the goals themselves. Their responsibility lies elsewhere: in creating a winning team. They set guidelines for the players, provide them with more training, and perhaps keep in touch with the transfer market to be alert for additional players. They can also change incentives and substitute players who do not perform well. Occasionally a coach may shout from the sidelines or in other ways try to interfere with operations. But this should not happen too often, as it can create chaos. A strong CEO who thinks he should be all over the field will soon notice that his actions result in chaos, not superior performance. Direct action—such as the substitution of a player—is important, but it has to be selective and limited. What coaches have to be strongest at is training their staff and creating learning opportunities.

As I am finishing this book, dramatic events are threatening the well-being of many fine corporations. The storm of the economic crisis might attract less attention than it did during the collapse of Lehman Brothers and Bear Stearns, but we do not know if we have reached the bottom yet. Some commentators already point out that a new bubble is developing. Besides these immediate worries, companies also have to figure out how new technologies, political changes, and globalization can benefit them. The door is wide open for failure or success. My hope in writing this book is that enough people choose to profit from the experience of some of the world's finest corporations to avoid repeating some of their mistakes while adopting some of their successful strategies. We do not know if these corporations themselves will succeed in the future, but we do know that they did something right in the past. In this book I have tried to capture that "something."

Brief Histories of Gold and Silver Medalists

Aachener und Münchener

In the early 19th century the German insurance industry was in its infancy. David Hansemann was an investor and agent of Vaterländische Feuerversicherung. When his request to increase the firm's capital was turned down, he decided to start his own fire insurance business. In an industry dominated by the English and the Dutch in the Rhineland and struggling with a reputation for reluctant payouts, Hansemann decided to build a firm that customers would be able to trust. In 1825 King Wilhelm III approved the enterprise, which wanted to dedicate half its profit to charitable causes. Operations were started with 300 agents in the Rhineland, Hamburg, Königsberg, and Danzig. Agents had more authority than in other firms, keeping central administration slim. Capital grew quickly, which allowed Aachener Feuerversicherungs AG to contribute to charity for the first time in 1934 and to pay dividends to its shareholders for the first time in 1939.

A real boost to its business came after a fire destroyed large parts of Hamburg in 1842. Although it cost the young firm (now called Aachener und Münchener) almost a third of its share capital of one million taler, the willingness to pay without much fuss was quickly acknowledged by potential customers. Premium income doubled between 1841 and 1850, giving Aachener und Münchener a market share of 25 percent in German fire insurance.

In the 1860s premium growth slowed as a result of increasing competition. Shareholders demanded a reduction in charitable contributions at the 1875 annual meeting. Although the management followed this advice, some disgruntled shareholders left nonetheless, founding Aachen-Leipziger Versicherungs AG. Aachener und Münchener also failed to adapt to changing market conditions. When the second industrial revolution provided great opportunities for new insurance products, its agents were unwilling to approach industrial customers, claiming that they lacked relevant experience. The firm concentrated on international expansion instead, setting up offices in 56 countries by 1900. About half of its premiums were collected abroad before World War I. During the war they were forced to take over more industrial risks, expanding the product portfolio.

After the war, the insurer had its headquarters in French-occupied territory and survived a period of hyperinflation thanks to considerable real estate and large foreign reserves. The company was able to expand by taking over struggling competitors such as Thuringia, Aachen-Potsdamer Life Insurance, and Oldenburger, a move that also marked its entry into life insurance.

During the Nazi era, the firm at first expanded as the troops occupied new territories but lost its assets again with the defeat of Germany. Its fire insurance business decreased by 40 percent when Russian-occupied East Germany nationalized its insurance industry. The company was able to compensate for the loss during Germany's postwar economic miracle, however, tripling premium income in the 1950s and doubling it again in the 1960s. Car insurance replaced fire insurance as the most important product.

In the 1970s, losses were reported for the first time since 1906, because of the oil crisis. Aachener und Münchener reorganized its operative business and started to cut costs. Cooperation with financial consulting firms that sold their products on a commission basis provided access to an additional sales force of 20,000, which brought in 25 percent of the new business in the 1980s.

In 1987 Aachener und Münchener bought BfG Bank to create a financial services firm. The plan did not work, and after heavy losses the company sold BfG Bank once again. Another acquisition, that of Volksfürsorge Holding AG, was more successful, making Aachener und Münchener the second-largest life insurance company in Germany.

In 1998 Aachener und Münchener's independence ended when Italy's Generali took over a majority stake in the company. In 2006 the new company, called AMB Generali, had a premium income of almost 2 billion euros, generated from 13.5 million customers. In 2009 Generali's subsidiary had a premium income of $6.4 billion.

AEG

In 1882 Emil Rathenau formed a consortium together with Sulzbach, the Prussian National Bank, and the French Compagnie Continentale to purchase the Edison patent licenses for electric lighting in Germany. Despite initial skepticism from German banks, the new venture had a good start. The first streets were lit in Berlin later the same year. At an industrial fair in Munich, the consortium's display, particularly the lighting provided for a ballet, was well received, attracting new business—from the Munich Hoftheater and the Royal Residence Theater, for example.

Siemens noticed that it had missed a great opportunity and tried to negotiate with Compagnie Continentale. The latter, however, stuck with Rathenau and helped him to form Deutsche Edison-Gesellschaft (DEG) with a capital base of 5 million marks in 1883. A major problem at the time was access to electricity. The new firm therefore decided to concentrate on the construction of small generators, forming a separate company to build the first central generating station in Berlin in 1884. Although DEG built a lightbulb factory and started to produce an arc lamp invented in Belgium, continuous disagreements about Edison patent holders around the world and brawls with powerful Siemens threatened DEG. In 1883 a contract was signed with Siemens, allowing both firms to build power stations and severing ties with Compagnie Continentale. DEG's name was changed to Allgemeine Elektricitäts Gesellschaft (AEG).

AEG expanded rapidly during the following years, opening factories in Russia, Finland, Sweden, and Norway and sales offices in Paris and Belgium. The company also became interested in electric trains. Growth continued throughout the first third of the 20th century, with AEG temporarily even overtaking Siemens. World War II, however, was disastrous for the firm. AEG had most of its production in what became East Germany, Poland, and the Soviet Union. After the war it lost 90 percent of its production facilities.

In the era of postwar growth in West Germany, AEG tried to catch up with Siemens once again. Particularly in the 1960s, under the leadership of Hans Bühler, the company threw caution to the winds and financed growth through massive debt. In a period of just four years, 50 firms, almost all of them in household goods, were acquired. Once consumer demand slowed with the recession of the 1970s, AEG's fortunes declined rapidly. Investing in the wrong technology in nuclear power stations added to the company's problems. A long struggle for revival began. In 1979 a group of German banks put a rescue package together. In the 1980s the search for partners began, with partial success in some areas such as a video deal signed with JVC, Thomson-Brandt, and Thorn-EMI. New hope emerged in 1982 when Heinz Dürr managed to reach a settlement with AEG's creditors, resulting in the sale of its television production to France's Thomson S.A. and a reduction in staff from 120,000 to 75,000. In 1985 Dürr convinced Daimler-Benz to buy a majority stake of AEG. New cash allowed it to expand once again, but it did not return to sustained profitability. Eventually, in 1996, Daimler-Benz decided to break up AEG, selling off and closing down the various businesses. Household goods and the famous brand were purchased by Electrolux.

Allianz

Munich Re's Carl Thieme and the private banker Wilhelm Finck founded Allianz Versicherungs AG (Allianz) in 1890. Anticipating the advent of rapid mechanization, they began to offer accident and liability insurance, though most of the company's income before World War I was in freight insurance. Almost 45 percent of its premium income came from this division in 1913. Allianz used its income to diversify into new products such as fire insurance.

In the 1920s Allianz achieved a dominant position in the German market. The firm's leader at the time, Paul von der Nahmer, had accurately predicted the importance of building foreign currency reserves. These reserves enabled him to establish Allianz in all classes of insurance. Acquisitions of struggling competitors during the 1922–1923 hyperinflation played an important role. The acquisitions were particularly successful because of Allianz's rationalization capabilities, an implementation of Frederick Winslow Taylor's scientific management principles. The most significant move during these times was the foundation of Allianz Life in 1922 together with Munich Re. By 1927 it was the largest life insurer in Europe. In the same year Germany's largest accident and liability insurance company, Stuttgarter Verein Versicherungs AG, was taken over. In 1929 Allianz took over Frankfurter Allgemeine Versicherungs AG, Germany's second-largest insurance company, after its collapse.

During World War II, Allianz was able to grow considerably, but at the same time the Berlin headquarters was destroyed. After the war, successful branch offices were lost in the East, and specialized sections were scattered all over Germany. Management decided to move to Munich.

In the 1950s and 1960s Allianz concentrated on the home market, growing in the postwar boom and rationalizing its own operations. When the economy slowed in the 1970s and motor insurance for the first time moved into the red, Allianz had to change. A cost reduction program was introduced, and large-risk industrial and commercial business received more attention. In a final move, the company began to take international markets more seriously. At first this was accomplished by offering industrial clients insurance for their foreign investments. Allianz set up new subsidiaries abroad.

In the 1980s Allianz also began to be more aggressive in its acquisition policy. In 1981 it bought a 30 percent stake in Britain's Eagle Star Insurance Company, which it sold in 1981 for a considerable profit after losing a takeover battle against BAT Industries. In 1984 the company acquired a majority stake in Italy's RAS, and in 1986 it finally established itself in the UK when it took over the Cornhill Insurance Company. Further international mergers followed, the most notable being the acquisition of the Firemen's Fund Insurance Company of Novato, California, making Allianz the 14th-largest insurer in the United States.

In the late 1990s Allianz began to pay more attention to Asia. The firm also started to take a broader approach, expanding into financial services. The well-publicized takeover of Dresdner Bank, Germany's third-largest bank, was the most visible sign of this strategy. Today Allianz is one of the world's largest financial services companies, with 2009 sales of almost $120 billion generated by 153,000 employees in more than 70 countries.

BP

In 1901 the Grand Vizier of Persia granted William Knox D'Arcy a concession to explore for oil. The adventurer who had made a fortune in Australian mining was soon forced to look for partners to finance expensive exploration in a politically unstable country without proper infrastructure. The Burmah Oil Company joined the syndicate in 1905 in return for operational control. Eventually oil was struck in 1908 in Masjid-i-Sulaiman, and Anglo-Persian (which later became BP) was formed the following year. The new company hired Charles Greenway, who had been a partner in a managing agent handling the marketing of Burmah Oil products in India. It was to a certain extent his ability that helped the young venture to survive the difficult first few years. Although the company had substantial oil reserves, it had problems in refining its crude oil and lacked both a tanker fleet and a distribution network for its products. Greenway was able to fend off potential predators such as Shell through an agreement with the British government. Under the leadership of the First Lord of the Admiralty Winston Churchill and Admiral Fisher, the Royal Navy had decided to switch from coal to fuel oil. In more general terms, this event prepared the way for oil to become the world's most important energy resource. For Anglo-Persian the signing of a long-term contract with the navy guaranteed independence. At the same time additional funds were provided to build an integrated oil company as the British government invested £2 million to take a majority share. The government held its share until the 1980s but did not interfere with the company's practice.

World War I provided Anglo-Persian with a great opportunity as demand soared. Production increased tenfold in Iran despite pipeline destruction by local tribesmen and the Germans. Greenway also used the opportunity to build a fleet of 30 tankers. The most important move during the war was the acquisition of the British Petroleum Company—the British marketing subsidiary of a continental alliance with significant Deutsche Bank participation—in 1917.

By the end of the war Anglo-Persian was one of the world's largest oil companies, ready for further expansion. It built new refineries and established marketing subsidiaries in many European countries. Meanwhile the firm came under considerable pressure in Persia in the 1930s when its concession was canceled. Negotiations at the League of Nations resulted in a new agreement in 1933. Although the concession area was reduced to one-quarter of its original size and new royalty payments were fixed, the negative effects for the firm were limited.

Following World War II, an era of decolonization began. Anglo-Iranian—as the firm was called after 1935—was formally nationalized in 1951. When the Iranian government under Mossadegh was overthrown in 1953, the company, now named BP, was allowed to return, but under new, less favorable terms. BP now held a 40 percent share in a consortium of Western oil companies exploring for and producing oil in Iran.

In the following decades BP diversified into new regions, trying to reduce its dependence on Iran. The eventual breakthrough was the discovery of oil in the North Sea, first in 1965 and then, most importantly, in the Fortis Field in 1970. In 1969 BP also discovered oil in Alaska, which opened the U.S. market. In the same year it acquired ARCO's downstream activities on the East Coast and then signed an agreement with SOHIO that gave SOHIO control over the Alaska lease and BP's U.S. downstream activities in return for a 25 percent holding, which became a majority stake in 1978 before BP acquired the rest of SOHIO in 1987.

In the 1970s BP diversified into other industries, with limited success, and the acquired holdings were later sold off or shut down. In the 1990s the company decided to concentrate on its core competencies in the upstream and downstream oil and gas industry. At the same time fundamental changes in the organizational makeup were initiated; under Robert Horton, a reduction of bureaucracy resulted in major job cuts, and between 1990 and 1992 almost 20,000 people were asked to resign. The dwindling of morale, combined with major losses, forced Horton to resign. Nonetheless, his reforms continued under his successors. BP's strong revival finally became evident under John Browne, who had led the U.S. business with a strong hand. He acquired Amoco and ARCO, establishing BP once again as one of the most celebrated oil companies. In 2009 BP had revenues of $246 billion generated by 80,000 employees.

Ciments Français

The origins of Ciments Français can be traced back to the industrialist Emile Dupont, who started the production of Portland cement together with Charles Demarle in 1846. By 1855 the volume had increased from the original 50 tons to 580 tons per year.[1]

In 1881 the Société des Ciments Français et des Portland was registered in Boulogne-sur-Mer. With 250 employees the company produced 10,000 tons of cement per year. Large construction projects initiated by Baron Haussmann in Paris at the turn of the century created increasing demand for cement and provided a great opportunity. Ciments Français used the boom to open subsidiaries throughout France. The positive development was interrupted by World War I, but after the war ended, the firm continued to expand, acquiring five other French cement producers between 1925 and 1939. In addition to integrating these firms, Ciments Français concentrated on extending its product portfolio.

World War II once again reduced production. The headquarters was moved to Guerville after the complete destruction of the center in Boulogne. The postwar reconstruction boom after the defeat of Nazi Germany allowed for an extended period of economic growth, which peaked in the 1960s. Ciments Français opened its first foreign plant in Morocco in 1951 but continued to be primarily a French player. In 1971 the company took over Poliet et Chausson, making Ciments Français the largest cement producer in the domestic market. As a result of the merger, the French bank Paribas held 30 percent of Ciments Français. Unfortunately the expansion in France was ill timed, as the first oil crisis caused a major recession. A number of plants were closed down and international expansion was finally started in earnest, with most attention being paid to North America, Spain, and Belgium.

In the 1990s Paribas was in financial difficulties and decided to sell its Ciments Français holdings. Italcementi acquired the 30 percent stake and took a more active role than Paribas had. A new strategy was implemented: concentrating on core competencies, geographic expansion, cost reduction, and reduction of liabilities. While Ciments Français originally enjoyed substantial independence, allowing the company to expand in the Mediterranean region, the United States, India, Gambia, Mauritius, and Sri Lanka, Italcementi continued to increase its stake, which stands at 76 percent today. In 2009 Ciments Français was the second-largest cement company in France, with sales of $5.1 billion and almost 18,000 employees.

Cologne Re

In 1843 a number of important inhabitants of Cologne met to establish the world's first independent reinsurance company.[2] Independence from a primary insurer should avoid potential conflicts of interest, as there is no danger that the reinsurance company would favor its own parent company over other firms it insures. Due to an economic recession, the initial capital of three million taler was not sufficient. In 1952 a contract was signed with Rothschild in Paris and Oppenheim in Cologne to sell shares for an additional 2 million taler.

In the following years the company was able to pick up new business from fire, transportation, life, and hail insurance firms. Nonetheless, an increase of fire-related incidents and losses in transport and hail, as well as bad investments, resulted in a difficult start for the young venture.[3] By the end of the 1860s, increasing losses forced Cologne Re to renegotiate premiums. The hail and transport parts of the company were also closed down, reducing the firm primarily to fire reinsurance.

In the 1880s Cologne Re started to intensify its international business. In the United States the company initially did this primarily by selling its products through the German American Insurance Company in New York,[4] before opening its own agency in Hartford, Connecticut.[5] The U.S. business grew more after the San Francisco earthquake in 1906; the natural disaster resulted in losses of DM 88,000, and the company's willingness to pay was well received by potential customers.

In World War I, Cologne Re lost its international business. Rebuilding it in the 1920s, it had to retreat from the United States after the crash of the stock exchange. To create a stronger capital base in Germany, the two independent subsidiary companies were integrated and new capital was signed by existing shareholders and Colonia Versicherungs AG and National Allgemeine Versicherungs AG.

The positive development was halted by World War II and the company lost all international business for the second time in less than 30 years. Nonetheless, the business was quickly rebuilt after the war, and by 1970 Cologne Re had 30 offices in 26 countries. During this time losses in the transport reinsurance business were offset by well-performing capital investments.

In the 1970s Cologne Re introduced a matrix organization and started to use computer systems to evaluate risk. While its product mix was more or less similar to that of other reinsurance firms, life reinsurance played a more important role then.

In 1994 General Re acquired a majority in Cologne Re by purchasing the shares that were previously held by Colonia and the French Union des Assurances de Paris. General Re itself was bought by Berkshire Hathaway in 1998, making Cologne Re part of the U.S. investment firm.

Ericsson

In 1876 Lars Magnus Ericsson founded a workshop to repair telegraph machines in Stockholm. Within a couple of years he also began selling telephones—unfortunately with little success, as AT&T had a virtual monopoly on phone services and used its own equipment. This changed with the arrival of Stockholms Allmänna Telefonaktiebolag (SAT) in 1883. Although the firm soon set up its own production, Ericsson eventually bought SAT's manufacturing operations, in 1901. Ericsson also started to export its phones and telephone exchanges in the late 19th century. By 1900 exports accounted for 90 percent of total sales. The establishment of foreign production sites began in St. Petersburg in 1899, followed by Great Britain, the United States, France, and Austria-Hungary.

The 1930s proved a particularly troublesome period for the company when Ivar Kreuger, a Swedish investor, managed to acquire a majority stake of Ericsson. When his empire crumbled, he sold his stake to ITT, one of

Ericsson's main competitors. Swedish law prohibited a takeover, but the situation was nonetheless unsatisfactory. It was finally resolved in 1960 when the Wallenbergs, a Swedish industrial family, bought ITT's share.

Ericsson fell behind its competitors in the 1960s in terms of technology development but made a great comeback in 1976 when it introduced its computer-controlled exchange system AXE. Inspired by this success, the firm diversified into computers and office furniture in the early 1980s, introducing the "office of the future." Profits never materialized, however, and Electrolux chairman Hans Werthen was called in to split his time between his old firm and Ericsson to save the latter. He sold the firm's data business to Nokia in 1988 and refocused on telecom equipment, thus luring customers back. Ericsson also became the world leader in mobile phones, capturing a 40 percent market share. In 1989 it beat AT&T and Motorola to become the standard in the United States, solidifying its position.

By the end of the 1990s Ericsson's position in mobile phones had dwindled, though the company remained strong in the mobile infrastructure market. Infrastructure accounted for 70 percent of its revenue and handsets for only 21 percent. Heavy losses in the latter in 2000 resulted first in the outsourcing of production to Flextronics International and finally the formation of a joint venture with Sony.

Glaxo

In 1861 founder Joseph Edward Nathan created the company as a general merchant in New Zealand. In 1905 a subsidiary was started to commercialize a patent that the firm had purchased for manufacturing dried milk. Thanks to a well-organized marketing campaign waged by his son Alec, the company quickly became Britain's leading supplier of dried infant milk. After World War I distribution was expanded to India and South Africa.

When Harry Jephcott, a chemist who later became chairman, visited the International Dairy Congress in Washington in 1923, the company's history took a decisive turn. He observed the potential of vitamin D–fortified products, resulting in Ostelin Liquid, Britain's first commercial vitamin concentrate, and therefore opening the path for pharmaceutical products.

During World War II Glaxo produced anesthetics, penicillin, and a variety of vitamin supplements. After the war pharmaceutical activities were enhanced through both acquisition and consolidation. A chemical firm and a medical supply business were acquired and an independent veterinary department established. The most important takeover was Allen & Hanburys in 1958. Glaxo's laboratories also proved successful, when, for example, Britain's first commercial cortisone was produced.

The next dramatic event in Glaxo's history was Beecham's takeover attempt in 1972. Fighting back, Glaxo sought a merger of its own, courting Boots. The Monopolies Commission ruled against both bids, arguing that innovation declines in larger firms. In the same decade Glaxo also established its first U.S. subsidiary through the purchase of Meyer Laboratories. Overall, most of its business remained in the Commonwealth, though, and Glaxo remained a medium-sized pharmaceutical firm. All this changed with Zantac, an ulcer medication. Zantac was less a triumph of research—as SmithKline had a similar product on the market before—than a success in marketing. Under the leadership of Paul Girolami, the product was first introduced in Europe and then, through a joint venture with Hoffmann–La Roche, in the United States. By 1984 Zantac had captured 25 percent of the new prescription market, making it the best-selling drug ever.

In 1995, as the Zantac patent neared expiration and Glaxo had no replacement in its pipeline, the firm decided to acquire Wellcome for $14.9 billion. Leveraging existing products brought the firm back on track. Eventually, in 2000, another huge merger, this time with SmithKline, followed to keep up in a consolidating industry. The world's largest drug company with sales of $22.5 billion was formed.

In recent years takeovers and joint ventures with smaller companies, particularly in the biotech sector, followed to ensure the future development of drugs. In 2009 Glaxo's 99,000 employees generated revenues of $42 billion.

HSBC

In the 1860s trade in the Far East was financed by London- or India-based banks. When a group of Bombay-based financiers intended to start a "Bank of China," Hong Kong's European trading houses, called "hongs," decided to take matters into their own hands. Led by Thomas Sutherland, the local superintendent of the Peninsular and Oriental Steam Navigation Company, they set up the Hongkong and Shanghai Banking Corporation (later HSBC) in 1865. The first branch in Hong Kong was soon followed by a second one in Shanghai. An office in London was also opened in 1865. The close link to the merchant community ensured a constant flow of business, which was particularly helpful during the international financial crisis in 1865–1866. Instead of dying, the young institution thrived, picking up new business and experienced staff from failing competitors. By 1900 the bank had branches in Japan, Thailand, the Philippines, Singapore, Malaysia, Myanmar, Sri Lanka, and Vietnam. The bank acted as the government's banker in Hong Kong, built up impressive reserves, and became an active investor in local businesses.

To strengthen its link with London, the world's main financial center at the time, the bank set up a Consultative Committee, which the City often viewed as a second board. This organizational structure was particularly helpful during the two world wars, when managers in London were able to take over the leadership of the firm once Japan had occupied Hong Kong.

After World War II the bank played a major role in the rebuilding of the East. Its entrepreneurial spirit, expressed by the keen investment in new start-ups such as Cathay Pacific Airways, turned out to be highly profitable in the next few decades. At the same time, the bank lost one of its main territories when the communists took over in China in 1949 and all offices except the one in Shanghai were closed.

From the early 1950s to the 1970s, the bank adopted a new expansion strategy under Michael Turner. Subsidiaries were formed to create local banks, which enjoyed great independence. The first one was established in California in 1955. Others followed in the Middle and Far East when HSBC acquired the Mercantile Bank and the British Bank of the Middle East in 1959, Wayfoong (a consumer financing group) in 1960, and Hang Seng Bank in 1965.

The 1980s saw a standoff between HSBC and Standard Chartered when both wanted to take over the Royal Bank of Scotland, a venture that was stopped by the British Monopolies and Mergers Commission.

After the 1990s HSBC sped up its international expansion once again. First, a long-anticipated friendly takeover of Midland was completed in 1992. As a consequence, the headquarters was moved from Hong Kong to London. Second, acquisitions in both the United States (e.g., Household Finance in 2003) and Europe (e.g., Crédit Commercial de France [CCF] in France in 2005) followed. Today HSBC is the world's second-largest bank in terms of assets. With 10,000 offices in 80 countries, it provides consumer and commercial banking services, credit cards, asset management, private banking, securities underwriting and trading, insurance, and leasing. Its 302,000 employees generated revenues of $104 billion in 2009.

Lafarge

In 1831 Auguste Pavin de Lafarge, a French aristocrat, built a small lime kiln in the south of France. In 1833 he handed it over to his oldest son, Léon, who was later joined by his brother Edouard. Lime had been used in the region for centuries, but the newly founded company succeeded in expanding into new markets. As a result of the geographic expansion on the Mediterranean coast, the Marseilles-based firm of Gueyraud et Fils Cadet was invited to manage the business. The engagement brought much-needed engineering talent to the firm, as Felix Gueyraud was a graduate of the École Centrale des Arts et Manufactures at Paris.

A landmark event for Lafarge was the 1864 contract to supply 110,000 tons of hydraulic lime for the construction of the Suez Canal. The medium-sized French company became an international player. This improved position was further enhanced throughout the 19th century, partly through acquisitions. By the turn of the century Lafarge supplied such markets as New York, Rio de Janeiro, and Saigon. The annual production of cement products reached 800,000 tons before World War I. During the war, business slowed, as French industry turned its attention to arms production.

In 1928 Jean de Waubert became the first non-family director of Lafarge. He moved the headquarters to Paris and introduced a new four-level management structure: general management, technical operations, sales, and finance. The transformation of a family business into a modern cement producer prepared the firm for further growth. The cement producer diversified into new products such as Portland cement and expanded through acquisitions. During the Great Depression, for example, struggling competitors were bought despite Lafarge's own difficulties.

Following the difficulties of World War II, Lafarge concentrated on organic growth and modernization of its production system. By the end of the 1950s it had regained the lead position in France, producing 3.2 million tons of cement annually. Operations started in Canada, soon enhanced by the acquisition of two ready-mix cement companies. In 1969 a merger with Canada Cement, its main competitor in the country, and a series of acquisitions in the United States finally established Lafarge as a major player in North America. In 1980 Canada Cement Lafarge merged with General Portland to create a new holding company in North America, resulting in headquarters in both Paris and Dallas.

In Europe a merger with Evence Coppée in 1981 fueled Lafarge's growth and allowed diversification into biochemical, specifically amino acids. At the same time, the integration of General Portland and Evence Coppée presented a challenging task. In France the workforce was reduced from 30,000 to 25,500 in two years.

Through a number of acquisitions, particularly in Europe (such as Redland in 1997 and Blue Circle in 2001), Lafarge became the world leader in building materials. In 2009 Lafarge had sales of US19 billion and a workforce of 78,000 people in 70 countries. More recently the focus has turned to the fast-growing economies of Asia.

Legal & General

A growing population and increasing personal incomes started a boom in the British life insurance business in the early 1830s. Founded by six lawyers in 1936, Legal & General proved the most durable firm of the 310 joint-stock life insurers that came into being between 1934 and 1936. The first policy was sold to a man called Smith, who died after four years, obliging the young company to pay a policy of £1,000 after receiving £177 in premiums.

Selling 100 policies in its first year and opening six provincial agents, Legal & General soon started to offer loans to corporate and individual customers—for example, to finance the construction of railway infrastructure. In the 1850s the firm also diversified into real estate, investing heavily in the development of Birkenhead, near London, and other projects. By the turn of the century, Legal & General was Britain's second-largest life insurer in terms of capitalization, with total assets exceeding £2 million.

In 1920 the company listed at the stock exchange and diversified into fire and accident insurance. The 1920s and 1930s brought further change, as membership was opened also to those who had been in professions other than the law and the first overseas office was opened in Johannesburg. Continuing growth was not affected by the Great Depression. In 1933 Legal & General acquired the London office of New York's Metropolitan Life Insurance. The acquisition of Gresham Life and Gresham Fire and Accident followed a year later, strengthening the overseas business considerably.

During World War II Legal & General had to relocate its offices to escape German bombs. The war efforts were supported through the purchase of low-interest government bonds and the release of personnel. After the war the company increased its efforts to expand both its product portfolio and its international business. Fire and accident policies were signed in South Africa, and life insurance was added to non-life in Australia. Throughout this period Legal & General remained Great Britain's second-largest life insurance company, ranking behind Prudential. Nonetheless, by the late 1960s shareholders were dissatisfied about the low dividends. The rumor that the shareholders would sell out to policyholders, however, did not materialize.

The 1970s started off with a reorganization of the executive office, opening the way for further international expansion. A number of alliances and mergers took place, which made further structural reform necessary by the end of the decade. The partner company Legal & General Group became a non-insurance company consisting of British insurance operations, international operations, and investment-management activities. This provided a clear operational focus and greater financial flexibility. The new organization prepared the ground for entering the U.S. market through the acquisition of Government Employees Life Insurance Company. In the 1980s Legal & General also struggled with a poorly performing pension fund—which was resurrected when David Prosser was hired from the Coal Board's pension fund—and sold off operations in France, Australia, and South Africa.

In 1997 the company started to offer instant access deposit account services in the UK after securing a banking license. Around the same time, the firm also became entangled in a pension scandal, with agents having lured customers away from lucrative occupational retirement plans into personal pensions from Legal & General. After a fine from the organization that self-regulated the UK life insurance industry and much negative publicity, Legal & General compensated its customers. Although rumors of a takeover spread, the firm was able to stay independent, with new business growing by 40 percent the following year. Today Legal & General is a strong insurance firm that is primarily concentrated on the UK. It generated $7.8 billion and had close to 10,000 employees in 2009.

Munich Re

In 1880 Munich Re was incorporated as the world's first independent reinsurance company. Carl von Thieme, an experienced insurance agent, convinced a group of investors—among them the widely regarded founder of Merck, Finck & Company, Theodor Cramer-Klett—of the potential of such a venture. He argued that dependence on a primary insurer was harmful in the sense that often poor-quality risks had to be insured. In the firm Thieme promoted mutually binding treaties between insurer and reinsurer instead of the traditional individual placement of risks.

Thieme signed his first contract with his former employer, Thuringia Insurance Company. Within one year premium income passed 1 million marks. In the following years the firm continued to grow. Listed in 1888, the firm's capital base stood at some 20 million marks by 1914 already. By then 450 people worked for the firm, up from its initial five. Munich Re also embarked on foreign markets right from the start, establishing offices in Vienna and Hamburg in 1880, signing a contract with a Danish insurance firm, setting up another office in the 1880s in St. Petersburg, and starting operations in London and the United States before the turn of the century. It was particularly the prompt payment after huge disasters, like the 1906 San Francisco earthquake, that facilitated Munich Re's subsequent growth.

Munich Re understood that the company could best benefit from a growing primary insurance market if it supported its clients rather than directly competing with them. This interpretation was slightly stretched when Thieme founded Allianz—a primary insurer—in 1890. While keeping their independence, the two firms always enjoyed a unique relationship: first through Thieme's leadership in both firms and then through a special treaty formalizing their cooperation, such as when new subsidiaries were formed.

The period between 1914 and 1945 was marked by great difficulties. Munich Re lost its foreign business twice. During the Great Depression the firm was hit hard. At the same time its decision to support a number of ailing primary insurance companies proved to be farsighted, creating loyal customers for the future.

During the postwar years Munich Re's fortunes quickly improved. By the mid-1950s turnover surpassed all previous levels. It was particularly Munich Re's investments that grew in importance. By the mid-1970s its reinsurance business experienced a loss, but it was easily offset by investment income. The difficulty in the reinsurance business resulted from overcapacity and rate competition, as well as from primary insurers' organizing their own reinsurance cover.

In the 1990s this trend continued. In addition, the decade began with a number of expensive natural catastrophes. Munich Re reacted by strengthening its core business through several acquisitions such as American Re in 1996, establishing a new asset management subsidiary, and reorganizing its shareholdings in primary insurers to form ERGO, Germany's second-largest insurer.

In 2001 Munich Re had to cope with the largest man-made disaster in its history, the terrorist attacks on September 11. Even worse was the subsequent crash of the stock exchange. Due to its conservative approach toward finances, however, the firm could cover the losses. It was also able to weather the financial crisis well and reported revenues of $50 billion (up from $46.6 billion the previous year) generated by 47,000 employees in 2009.

Nokia

The origins of the world's largest mobile phone producer go back to 1865, when Fredrik Idestam established a paper and pulp mill in a small town named Nokia in central Finland.[6] A pioneer in this industry, the company even started its own power plant to meet its large energy demand. As the energy production increased, Finnish Rubber Works became one of Nokia's major customers. Founded by Eduard Polón and a group of investors in 1898, this firm produced shoes, boots, overshoes, and belts for industrial use. After the initial struggle, Russia's withdrawal from the world market on the eve of World War I became a turning point, providing Polón with sufficient financial resources to purchase a controlling stake in Nokia Ab in 1918. In 1922 he also gained control of Finnish Cable Works, founded by Arvid Wikström in 1912 to supply electrical wires and cables for industrial customers. Over the next four decades the three companies continued to operate independently and more or less unnoticed by anyone outside Finland. This changed in the 1960s when Nokia wanted to expand beyond its borders to become a regionally recognized conglomerate. Encouraged by the government, the three separate companies merged in 1967. The most important division was the cable business, which generated roughly the same revenue as the remaining businesses together.

In 1973 Nokia had to rethink its business model, which relied heavily on trade with the Soviet Union. Finland and the Soviets had an arrangement to keep trade—mainly Finnish lumber products and machinery in exchange for Soviet oil—strictly in balance. When oil prices rose as a result of the oil crisis, the value of Nokia's goods was greatly reduced. Although the firm was never in real danger, a reorientation toward the West nonetheless followed. The greatest changes came after Kari Kairamo was appointed as the new CEO in 1975. He understood that Finland was too small a market. Though he viewed electronics as one of the most promising divisions, he was not willing to shed traditional heavy industries such as paper, chemicals, machinery, and electricity generation. To ensure flexibility as far as a later sale was concerned, each division had to finance its own modernization and growth.

In 1992 Jorma Ollila became president and CEO of Nokia.[7] Following the collapse of the Soviet Union, Finland was hit by a serious recession, which was also painful for Nokia. Ollila was given 18 months to bring the company back on track. Uniting the corporation behind the bold vision of becoming a telecom company, he was able to achieve just that. In the same year Nokia broke even, generating 73 percent growth in telecommunications, particularly mobile phones.[8] Nokia had in fact been a pioneer in mobile phones in the 1980s when it developed Europe's first operational mobile phone network. Under the leadership of Ollila the firm decided to concentrate on mobile phones and networks. Non-core businesses such as cable (a profitable business) were sold off. Nokia's success in mobile phones is attributed to both its efficiency and its consistent ability to come up with high-margin products that are superior to those offered by its competitors. In 2009, 125,000 employees generated revenues of $50 billion.

Prudential

The Prudential Assurance Company Limited, originally registered as Prudential Mutual Assurance, Investment, and Loan Association, was founded by George Harrison and a diverse group of people that included both a doctor of divinity and an auctioneer. Seeing the revolutions that shocked Europe in 1848 as an opportunity to offer people much-desired security, the company targeted an established middle-class clientele. This strategy brought it, like many of its competitors, to the brink of bankruptcy. By 1851 the company's premium income was still under £2,000 per year.

In 1852 Prudential decided to change course and target working-class people, a potentially huge market only recently served by some "friendly societies," associations that provided benefits for members. Cautious expansion into this market with so-called industrial policies provided the Prudential with a rising premium income. In the 1860s the insurer acquired six firms, and by 1880 it was the leading provider of industrial policies. By 1905 it had issued 25 million policies to 43 million people. Prudential's strength was its good customer relations through its "man of the Pru," agents who had a specific territory assigned in which they called on a set number of homes every week. Prudential's customer focus was particularly evident during the two world wars when it chose to honor also those policies it would not have been obliged to and provided the government with dollar securities.

Until the 1970s the firm made few changes. In 1978 a holding was established to gain a more decentralized structure. Through a more thorough reorganization in 1984, seven operating divisions were created: UK individual, UK group pensions, international, Mercantile and General Reinsurance, Prudential Portfolio Managers, Prudential Property Services, and Prudential Holborn (a unit trust investment branch). Foreign expansion and acquisitions received increasing attention. Although there was already a limited presence in Europe, South Africa, and the Commonwealth, that did not alter the British character of Prudential. The most important acquisition was Jackson National Life Insurance Company in 1986, one of the fastest-growing insurers in the United States. A more efficient and computerized firm, it helped Prudential to modernize its operations.

With increasing diversification Prudential was for the first time confronted with limited customer recognition. For example, in a 1986 survey only 20 percent of those who knew Prudential also knew about its mortgage business. The Pru reacted with more advertising—for example, in the wake of a new State Earnings-Related Pension Scheme after deregulation in 1988.

In 1994 Prudential Corporation Asia was created. In 1997 Egg Banking plc was started as a branchless bank originally operating through telephone and mail but then going online in 1998. In 1999 M&G Group plc was acquired to strengthen the mutual fund business. The same year another restructuring and a 20 percent reduction in the domestic workforce marked a shift from the traditional "man of the Pru" to more online and phone-based customer services. Efforts to expand into new markets continue. The long-term goal to build a global retail financial services business guides the organization. In 2009, 25,000 employees generated revenues of $30 billion.

Shell

In 1907 the Royal Dutch/Shell Group of Companies was formed through a merger of the Royal Dutch Petroleum Company and the Shell Transport and Trading Company. The latter was founded by an East London merchant in 1830. In 1870 Marcus Samuel and Samuel Samuel took over the business and soon began to transport oil from Russia to Japan. Breaking the monopoly of Standard Oil in the Far East, they gained permission to transport oil in bulk through the Suez Canal in 1892. Toward the end of the century Shell discovered oil in Borneo and started to produce closer to its main market.

The Royal Dutch Petroleum Company received a concession to explore for oil in Sumatra in 1890. Founded by Aeilko Zijlker, the young venture exported its first oil in 1892. The firm experienced rapid growth under the leadership of Henri Deterding, who took over in 1901.

The two companies formed a marketing alliance in Asia together with the Rothschild family in 1903. When Shell Transport and Trading made a series of costly mistakes, its financial position deteriorated and Deterding was able to dictate his own terms for a merger, leaving the Dutch with 60 percent ownership of the new group.

The period until the end of World War II brought mixed fortunes. While the British Navy's switch from coal to oil marked the rise of oil as the world's foremost energy resource, the firm lost access to its oil fields in Russia in 1917 and Mexico in 1938 when the oil industry was nationalized there. And in 1936, when Henri Deterding retired, a committee-based top management started to emerge. This rather unusual organizational approach was formalized in the 1960s.

During a period of growth after the war, Shell diversified into natural gas, started to operate offshore, and expanded its chemical business. Shell and the other major oil companies continued to dominate the international oil business at the time. It was in 1973, when OPEC introduced production caps and thereby triggered the first oil crisis, that the balance of power began to shift toward the oil-producing countries. Shell had come to resist the pressure from the UK government to reserve a greater portion of its production for Britain. The company also began to produce in more technically challenging but politically stable territories, such as the North Sea, and also to diversify into other businesses like coal production and mining, such as through the acquisition of Billiton. These activities did not prove to be particularly profitable, and Shell sold Billiton again in 1994 and 1995.

In the mid-1990s Shell came under major criticism by environmental groups for its involvement in Nigeria and the proposed decommissioning of Brent Spar, an oil storage facility in the North Sea. Changing some of its policies, the company became a vocal supporter of sustainable development.

In 2004 it became apparent that Shell had overstated its proven reserves. The chairman, Phil Watts, was asked to resign, and the old committee-based structure was transformed, leaving Jeroen van der Veer as the first "classic" CEO in the firm's history. His successor, Peter Voser, reported revenues of $278 billion in 2009. The company has 102,000 employees in more than 90 countries.

Siemens

In 1847 Werner Siemens and Johann Georg Halske started to manufacture and install telegraphic systems. Their first major contract was a line between Frankfurt and Berlin that reported the traditional election of the emperor in Frankfurt. In 1853 the young firm established a presence in Russia—which came in handy when contracts dried up at home. One of Werner's brothers opened an office in London, which became particularly well known for deep-sea telegraphic cables, receiving a contract to build a line between London and Calcutta or Ireland and the United States.

When Alexander Graham Bell's telephones reached Berlin for the first time in 1877, Siemens[9] was quick to patent an improved version and begin production. The company was equally fast to patent a X-ray tube one year after Wilhelm Conrad Roentgen's discovery of the X-ray in 1895, proving its ability to exploit successful trends and products.

In 1897 Siemens went public to generate capital in the new power business (high-current business), but the family remained in control of the firm. The increasing importance of electricity generation and transition motivated Siemens to take over Schuckert and establish Siemens Schuckert.[10]

During World War I all assets in Russia and the UK were seized. While international business was rebuilt in the 1920s and 1930s, all assets were lost again during World War II. Before the end of that war the firm learned about Allied plans to divide Germany into zones, and it moved both assets and headquarters into the Western zones. The new headquarters was in Munich. By the end of the 1950s, Siemens was once again involved in a wide range of products such as railroads, telephones, and power-generating equipment.

The 1960s and 1970s saw major international expansion, and between 1966 and 1969 a transformation that brought the different subsidiaries, which has been linked only at the very top, under a single roof to form Siemens AG.

The 1970s also saw Siemens enter the high-tech arena. The first mainframe computers were sold and the company invested heavily in an effort to catch up with Silicon Valley in microcircuit technology, which was not successful. Despite a joint venture with Philips, the company lost money until 1988 and had to buy components from Toshiba.

In the 1980s the company continued to invest heavily in R&D and acquisitions to build up its high-tech business, with limited success.

In the 1990s the firm transformed its organization once again and started to act more global. The first non-engineer in the top position led the company to a more commercial approach. Eventually, in the 2000s, a sale of mobile phones and a joint venture in phone networks followed, putting a clear focus on energy and infrastructure. In 2006 the eruption of a bribery scandal shook the firm. Despite heavy fines in the United States and Germany, Siemens continued to generate solid profits throughout this period as well as during the financial crisis. In 2009 revenues of $93.7 billion were reported. Siemens operates in more than 190 countries and has 420,000 employees.

Standard Chartered

Standard Chartered was formed in 1969 through a merger of the Standard Bank, operating primarily in Africa, and the Chartered Bank, concentrated in India, China, and Southeast Asia. The latter was originally incorporated as the Chartered Bank of India, Australia, and China in 1853 in London. James Wilson, a politician, editor, and businessman, who also started the *Economist*, was the driving force behind the new venture. Due to difficulties in coming up with the capital required for a Royal Charter, it was not until 1858 that the first branch opened, in Bombay. Others followed in the same year in Calcutta, Shanghai, Hong Kong, and Singapore.

The Standard Bank was started only a few years later, in 1862, by the schoolmaster John Paterson in South Africa. He had a wide range of interests, including mining, railroad promotion, and real estate development. Through a number of acquisitions of smaller banks, he was soon able to establish the bank as one of the primary financial firms in the region.

In fact, both companies were able to grow quickly, as trade in their respective regions flourished. At the beginning of the 20th century, they opened offices in the United States. Like other banks, they suffered during the two world wars, drastically reducing the branch network, particularly in Asia. After the wars a period of expansion followed. Like HSBC, the Chartered Bank tried to diversify into new regions through acquisitions, most significantly that of the Eastern Bank. While this was an important move, Chartered did not operate on the same scale as its main competitor—HSBC did more and better deals. By the mid-1960s both firms had become potential takeover targets. To fend off a bid from Barclays, Chartered proposed the merger with Standard. Following the integration of the two institutions, the bank decided to continue its strategy of focusing on overseas commercial banking. To offset some of the fluctuations, it also tried to strengthen its European position and in 1979 acquired Union Bancorp of California. During this time, no domestic retail base was established, though other overseas banks managed to do that. A bid for Royal Bank of Scotland in 1981 failed when HSBC made a counterbid and the British Monopolies Commission ruled against both banks. As important countries such as Malaysia and Singapore entered recession in the mid-1980s, the company's overexposure to the developing world hurt profits considerably. Union Bancorp of California and the United Bank of Arizona had to be sold to raise capital. Nonetheless, a takeover attempt by Lloyds Bank was warded off with the help of three businessmen who purchased 35 percent of Standard Chartered shares.

In the 1990s Standard Chartered consolidated divesting holdings in Europe, the United States, and Africa, as well as shedding jobs. Management decided to concentrate on consumer, corporate, and institutional banking in Asia, Africa, and the Middle East. In 2000 ANZ Grindlays Bank's South Asian and Middle Eastern banking operations and Chase Manhattan Corp.'s Hong Kong consumer banking and credit card operations were bought. The Asian crisis was also used to expand cheaply.

In 2001 the bank once again experienced some turbulence when its CEO, Rana Talwar, agreed to consider takeover bids when the price was right. Sir Patrick Gillam, the chairman, replaced him with Mervyn Davies, and the bank kept its independence. In recent years the bank has performed well as emerging markets are experiencing a period of growth. In 2009, 74,000 employees generated revenues of $19 billion.

Wellcome

In 1880 two Americans named Silas M. Burroughs and Henry S. Wellcome started to distribute pharmaceutical products from a shop in London. While Wellcome concentrated on the UK market, Burroughs took care of business in continental Europe, Australia, and the United States. Only two years after the establishment of Burroughs Wellcome,[11] the new firm produced its first medication, then soon started to also register patents. High quality and innovative marketing fueled remarkable growth in this early phase. New production sites and warehouses had to be built.

Despite the commercial success, the two founders had a difficult relationship. After Burroughs was ill for an entire year, Wellcome asked him to leave. When the partnership was about to be dissolved in 1895, Burroughs unexpectedly passed away. Over the next decades Wellcome presided over international expansion in Africa, Canada, the United States, China, Argentina, and India. He also established a strong research orientation, best shown by the widely regarded research labs of Wellcome and the founding of Britain's first tropical institute, the Wellcome Bureau of Scientific Research.

During World War I the firm was part of the Allied supply chain, concentrating on the production of vaccines and pain relievers. In 1924 Wellcome consolidated its various activities and the founder handed over operational control to George E. Pearson. While the firm's scientific capabilities remained undiminished, its commercial success began to fade. Substantial funds were used to build a medical museum, and in 1936 the whole ownership passed to the Wellcome Trust after the founder's death. The trust was set up to advance basic research and philanthrophic projects.

In the 1950s a new marketing concept and Wellcome's role in the development of new treatments such chemotherapy revived some of the firm's fortunes. Subsidiaries were opened in New Zealand, Brazil, Kenya, and Pakistan. The firm also entered niche markets such as veterinary medication through acquisitions in the 1960s and 1970s.

In 1986, 20 percent of the firm was listed on the London stock exchange to fund the transformation into a modern pharmaceutical company. Wellcome developed one of the most promising drug pipelines in the industry with successes, for example, in fighting AIDS. Commercially, though, the development was less convincing. In 1995 the Wellcome Trust decided to sell its shares to Glaxo and invest its proceeds otherwise.

Methodology and Selection
of Comparison Companies

Methodology

In management studies longitudinal research is rare. There are some notable exceptions, such as the classic work of Alfred Chandler,[1] tracking
the development of the modern firm, but most empirical studies have an
observation period of five to a maximum of 15 years.[2] Such an approach
implicitly carries a bias toward short-term development and is particularly odd, considering the age of many firms. As Connie Helfat, a widely
recognized strategist from the Tuck School of Business, suggests, "Those
who ignore history are doomed to repeat it. Thus, if we look only at a
cross-section of resources and capabilities, we may draw incorrect infer-
ences about why some firms have better resources than other firms. We also
may draw the wrong lessons for the future. Retrospective understanding
of competitive success and failures therefore can help to provide a firmer
foundation for prospective advice."[3]

Exploring the past to learn for the future is exactly the goal of our
study. In order to achieve this outcome, we first selected a group of 18
long-living corporations and then went on to study them in great detail.
It is important to note that we do not claim that the companies we study
will be successful in the future. They have done a great job in the past,
and we are trying to find out how they did that. There is no guarantee

that they will continue down the same track. Likewise, we want to stress the explorative nature of our approach. Case study research provides a good understanding of how things were done, but larger samples would be required to conduct statistical tests of our findings. Consequently, we would like to encourage some caution as far as the applicability of our work is concerned. We provide ideas and insights, but we do not provide a recipe that you can simply follow in order to be successful.

SAMPLE SELECTION

To avoid what Wittgenstein calls "a one-sided diet"[4] of similar examples (i.e., all strong performers), we selected pairs of cases to untangle the similarities and differences between them.[5] We started by identifying a number of outstanding firms and then selected a comparison company for each of them. The following criteria were used:

Size: The project targeted major corporations for two reasons. First, this increased the chances of finding relevant data for our study. Second, it would not make sense to have both small and large companies in our sample, as they face different issues. We would be trying to compare apples and oranges.

Age: Each of the selected companies had to have been a major stand-alone company for at least 100 years.

Performance: Following Jim Collins and Jerry Porras[6] (who conducted a study of long-lived American companies), total shareholder return (TSR) was used as the performance criterion in order to avoid distortions based on industry or market characteristics. Firms had to perform 15 times better than the major markets (Dow Jones, DAX, FTSE) over a period of 50 years (this translates into an annual performance advantage of 5.57 percent, slightly more stringent than the 4.6 percent that Collins and Porras calculated in their study).

Industry and country: We wanted to compile a sample that included companies from different countries and industries so that we could observe how companies in general were able to achieve outstanding performance rather than ending up with results based purely on the effects of industry or country.

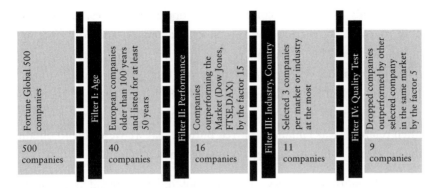

FIGURE B.I. Selection of Top Companies

In order to compile a sample of companies that meet these criteria, we applied a filter process, starting with the world's largest companies in 2003.

Filter I: Age   The first filter ensured that all companies selected met the age criteria. To collect the data necessary to trace a company back to its origins, we relied on a number of different sources: company Web sites, annual reports, company archives (i.e., Historical Institute Deutsche Bank), and corporate histories. All companies that were founded before 1904 and remained independent passed this filter. Since some firms re-register, or change their name in the course of a merger, we did not focus on strict legal criteria but tried to determine the origin of a corporation. State-owned companies (e.g., most postal service and telecommunication companies) were not included unless they had become independent before 1903. In the case of a merger, the acquirer was considered to be the survivor. Besides the requirement of having origins dating back before 1903, this filter required companies to be listed on a stock exchange since 1953, to make a performance calculation possible. Forty European companies passed the first filter.

Filter II: Performance   The 40 companies that passed the age filter were then subjected to our performance criteria. For any firm to pass this filter, the total shareholder return[7] had to be at least 15 times above the performance of the major European markets (Dow Jones, DAX, FTSE) over a period of 50 years.

Collecting the data we needed to make this estimation was trickier than we expected. Centralized financial databases[8] for British companies go back only to 1964; for continental European companies, they extend only to 1972. By visiting libraries, stock exchanges, and corporate archives, we were able to find old reports and newspapers containing most of the information we sought. Finland turned out to be particularly tough. It was only when Seppo Ikäheimo from the Helsinki School of Economics kindly pointed us toward Kim Lindström, an elderly investor who is often referred to as Finland's Warren Buffett, that we were able to obtain the necessary numbers. Sixteen companies passed Filter II.

Filter III: Industry, Country   Filter III took industry spread and country distribution into account. It ensured that the results of the research on the selected companies did not merely reflect industry- or country-related aspects but more universal success factors. To ensure this spread, no more than three companies from the same country or industry were taken into the last step of the selection process. Four companies from Great Britain dropped off the list, leaving the sample at 11 companies.

Filter IV: Quality Test   We installed one additional filter to test the relative performance of companies against potential comparison companies. Two companies were deselected. Ericsson's performance was substantially lower than Nokia's, and Ahold, a Dutch grocery chain, scored below most potential comparison companies. This left nine companies in the final set.

These companies—which we call the gold medalists—outperformed the market by a factor of 62. We then looked for a set of comparison companies, ideally a match in terms of country, industry, and age. As their longevity implies, these silver medalists also turned in solid performances (outstripping the market by a factor of eight in 2003—when we made the selection) and even beating out the gold medalists at times and for relatively short periods (six years in one exceptional case, but usually for only a year or two).

SELECTION OF COMPARISON COMPANIES

We used three criteria to find an ideal comparison company:

Country fit: The comparison company had its origins in the same country or had its main business interest in the same country as the outstanding company.

TABLE B.1. Selection of Comparison Companies (1 = perfect fit, 5 = no fit)*

Allianz	Country Fit	Business Fit	Age Fit	Overall Fit
Aachener und Münchener	1	1	2	1.3
Nürnberger Lebensversicherungen AG	1	2	1	1.3
Württembergische Versicherungs AG	1	1	2	1.3
Zurich Financial Services	2	1	1	1.3
Gerling	1	3	1	1.7
Gothaer	1	2	2	1.7
AXA	3	1	2	2.0
ING Group	3	1	2	2.0
Munich Re	1	4	1	2.0
Swiss Life Insurance & Pension	2	2	2	2.0
Generali	3	1	3	2.3
Swiss Re	2	4	1	2.3
Aviva	5	2	1	2.7
Prudential	5	1	2	2.7
CNP Assurances	5	2	2	3.0
Legal & General	5	1	3	3.0
Royal & Sun Alliance	5	1	4	3.3
HBOS	5	3	4	4.0

Glaxo[1]	Country Fit	Business Fit	Age Fit	Overall Fit
Wellcome	1	2	1	1.3
Novartis	4	1	1	2.0
Roche	4	1	2	2.3
AstraZeneca	2	2	4	2.7
Aventis	4	2	2	2.7

HSBC	Country Fit	Business Fit	Age Fit	Overall Fit
Standard Chartered	1	2	1	1.3
Barclays	3	1	1	1.7
Lloyds TSB	2	1	2	1.7
Royal Bank of Scotland	2	1	2	1.7
Deutsche Bank	4	1	1	2.0
HBOS	2	2	2	2.0
ABN AMRO	5	1	1	2.3
Banca Intesa	5	1	1	2.3
BBVA	5	1	1	2.3
BNP Paribas	5	1	1	2.3
Credit Suisse	5	1	1	2.3
Dexia Group	5	1	1	2.3

*Primary and secondary material as well as interviews with industry experts were used to determine how similar firms were to the gold medalists in terms of geographical location, product offering, and age. An almost perfect similarity would result in a score of 1 while very different companies would yield a score of 5 on a specific criterion.

[1] Today GlaxoSmithKline

(continued)

HSBC	Country Fit	Business Fit	Age Fit	Overall Fit
Nordea	5	1	1	2.3
Banco Santander	5	1	1	2.3
Société Générale	5	1	1	2.3
UBS	5	1	1	2.3
UniCredito Italiano	5	1	1	2.3
Bayerische Landesbank	5	2	1	2.7
Crédit Agricole	5	2	1	2.7
Europhypo	5	2	1	2.7
Groupe Caisse d'Épargne	5	1	2	2.7
Almanij	5	1	3	3.0
Landesbank Baden-Württemberg	5	1	3	3.0
HypoVereinsbank	5	2	3	3.3
Rabobank	5	2	3	3.3
WestLB	5	1	4	3.3
DZ Bank	5	2	5	4.0
Fortis	5	3	5	4.3

Lafarge	Country Fit	Business Fit	Age Fit	Overall Fit
Ciments Français	1	1	1	1.0
Heidelberg Cement	2	1	1	1.3
Holcim	2	1	2	1.7

Legal & General	Country Fit	Business Fit	Age Fit	Overall Fit
Prudential	1	1	1	1.0
Aviva	1	2	1	1.3
HBOS	1	2	2	1.7
Royal & Sun Alliance	1	2	2	1.7
AXA	5	1	1	2.3
CNP Assurances	5	1	1	2.3
Generali	5	1	1	2.3
Swiss Life Insurance & Pension	5	1	2	2.7
Zurich Financial Services	5	1	2	2.7
Allianz	5	1	3	3.0
ING Group	5	1	3	3.0
Swiss Re	5	4	2	3.7
Munich Re	5	4	3	4.0

Munich RE	Country Fit	Business Fit	Age Fit	Overall Fit
Cologne Re	1	1	1	1.0
Swiss Re	2	1	1	1.3
Allianz	1	4	1	2.0
Gerling	1	3	2	2.0
Hannover Re	1	1	5	2.3
Zurich Financial Services	2	4	1	2.3
Credit Suisse	2	5	1	2.7
Generali	3	4	2	3.0
Legal & General	3	4	2	3.0
Prudential	3	4	2	3.0
HBOS	3	4	3	3.3
Royal & Sun Alliance	3	4	3	3.3

Nokia	Country Fit	Business Fit	Age Fit	Overall Fit
Ericsson	2	2	1	1.7
Metsä Tissue (Serlachius Oy)	1	4	1	2.0
Stora Enso	1	4	1	2.0
UPM Kymene	1	4	1	2.0
Alcatel	4	4	1	3.0
Siemens	4	3	2	3.0

Shell	Country Fit	Business Fit	Age Fit	Overall Fit
BP	1	1	1	1.0
Moeara Enim Petroleum	1	2	1	1.3
Fina	3	1	3	2.3
ENI	3	1	5	3.0
Fortum	5	2	3	3.3
Repsol YPF	5	2	3	3.3
Statoil	4	2	5	3.7

Siemens	Country Fit	Business Fit	Age Fit	Overall Fit
AEG	1	1	1	1.0
ABB	2	1	2	1.7
Philips	3	3	2	2.7
Alcatel	4	3	2	3.0
Ericsson	4	3	2	3.0
Nokia	4	3	2	3.0
Electrolux	4	4	3	3.7
Alstom	4	4	4	4.0

TABLE B.2. Key Performance Indicators for Top and Comparison Companies

	Siemens–AEG	Nokia–Ericsson	Allianz–Aachener und Münchener	Legal & General–Prudential	Munich Re–Cologne Re	Shell–BP	Glaxo	HSBC–Standard Chartered	Lafarge–Ciments Français
Return on equity (ROE)	■	■	▨	■	■	■	■	■	■
Operating margin	□	□	■	■	■	□	■	□	□
Profit margin	■	■	■	■	■	■	■	□	■
Equity ratio	■	□	▨	■	■	■	■	□	■
Return on investment (ROI)	■	■	▨	■	■	■	■	■	■
Liquidity ratio	■	■	■	■	■	■	■	■	■
Growth in sales (premiums)	□	□	■	▨	■	▨	□	■	■
Personnel costs as % of sales	■	■	□	□	□	□	□	■	■
Capital expenditure (CAPEX) as % of sales	■	■	□	□	□	■	■	■	■
Return on capital employed (ROCE)	■	■	□	□	□	■	■	■	■
Debt-to-equity ratio	■	■	□	□	□	□	■	■	□

Growth in total assets

Return on invested assets

Cost-to-income ratio

Payout ratio

Earning per share (EPS)

Dividends per share (DPS)

Earnings before interest and taxes
(EBIT) margin

Earnings before taxes (EBT)
margin

gold medalist beats silver medalist

silver medalist beats gold medalist

SOURCE: Data from annual reports.

Business fit: The comparison company offered similar products and services as the outstanding company.

Age fit: The comparison company was founded in the same era as the outstanding company.

In our search for these companies, we studied the corporate histories of our gold medalists and industry lists to compose a list of potential comparison companies from the same industry. Then we used a Likert scale in interviews with industry experts and historians to determine how close a match the potential comparison companies were in terms of age, industry, market, and size. Next we consulted secondary material to challenge the scores. In cases where interviews and secondary data did not correspond, additional interviews were conducted before a final decision was made as to which firm fit best. Not all of the comparison companies are independent companies today. Over a period of 55 years our comparison companies—which we called silver medalists—outperformed the market by a factor of 16.

To test the robustness of our company pairs, we identified additional key performance indicators.[9] On the basis of secondary literature and five interviews with financial analysts, we compiled a list of 21 key performance indicators. The list was then sent to 893 equity researchers from investment institutes in 11 European countries.[10] They were asked to name the 10 most important performance indicators for each relevant industry (ranking them from 1 to 10). The return rate was 14 percent (125 questionnaires). Data to calculate the key performance indicators was collected from annual reports. The results of a Mann-Whitney U-test[11] showed that the top companies in 83 percent of all cases also significantly outperformed the comparison companies in terms of the 10 key performance indicators. Thus the goal of pairing a very strong performer with a significantly weaker secondary firm was realized.

Once we had compiled our sample of gold and silver medalists, we started our analysis. Before we explain the research approach, we will briefly explain the data we used.

DATA

It was crucial to use the appropriate data for our analysis if we were to obtain meaningful results. In his recent book *The Halo Effect*, Philip Rosenzweig[12] points out that a major issue facing a number of prominent management books is the correlation between dependent and independent variables. In our case the dependent variable is the performance measured as TSR. This means any data that was derived retrospectively with this outstanding performance in mind has a bias. If we had relied solely on interviews with top managers who explained why the firm has been successful we would have been faced with problematic data. To avoid such a bias, we needed to collect truly independent data. Sources for such data include annual reports (which have to adhere to specific standards) but also descriptive, fact-based accounts of a company's history. Such corporate histories, written by respected historians, exist for almost all of the companies in our sample. To increase the robustness of our study, we combined different sources of data. Comparing the conclusions we reached on the basis of annual reports and corporate histories, for example, provides not only a richer but also a more solid picture. In this light interview data is also useful, providing information about a firm's view of certain events. Keeping these considerations in mind, we used three different types of data:

Publicly available data: All firms were publicly traded and therefore released financial statements, management discussions, stock market data, and press materials. Most importantly, extensive histories were published on most companies. These presented the most significant data source in our study (in the case of HSBC, for example, the corporate history comprised four volumes totaling 3,114 pages).

Archival material: We conducted intensive research in corporate archives and collected materials such as change plans, organization charts, internal memos, and material for training exercises.

Interviews: While secondary items and archival material were the most important sources (considering the historic nature of the analysis), we also conducted 46 interviews with 42 individuals, most of whom were either active or retired executives.

TABLE B.3.   Interviews

	First Interview	Repeat Interview
Active and retired chairmen and/or CEOs	17	4
Board members	8	
Senior executives	7	
Experts	5	
Company historians	5	

In order to keep some order in the thousands of pages of material, we initially sorted the data in nine categories (adapted from *Good to Great*[13]):

Category I: Market, competitors, business environment. How did the relevant markets develop and affect the companies? What did their competitors do? How did the companies react? What impact did the business environment have on the companies?

Category II: General development of the companies. How did the companies develop over time? What were the main events that shaped the companies?

Category III: Technology and products. What role did technology play in the companies? What types of products did the companies produce? Did the companies change their product range substantially? Did technology have considerable influence on products?

Category IV: Value statements, visions. Did the companies define value statements and visions? At what point in their history did they do so? Are the values stated reflected in the companies' behaviors? Can the values be traced back to the origins of the companies?

Category V: Business strategy, strategic process. What are the primary elements of the companies' strategy? What was the process that assisted them in setting this strategy?

Category VI: Change management. When did the companies engage in major change exercises? Why did they do so? How did they manage change? Who played a vital role in these processes?

Category VII: Leadership. What role did leadership play in the companies? Which leadership style works well in which environment? Is there a different approach at different levels in the companies?

Category VIII: Financial data. How did the companies perform? How did profits, earnings, sales, etc., develop?

Category IX: Rest category. All aspects that did not fit into the more conventional categories.

DATA ANALYSIS

We chose a qualitative research approach. Since capabilities are processes embedded in firms, organizational and empirical lenses are more suitable than economic and formal modeling.[14] To untangle the roots of competitive advantage, we followed the tradition of in-depth historic case studies. Prominent examples using such an approach include Danneels's studies of U.S. high-tech firms and Belgian apparel retailing firms, Burgelman's studies of Intel, Rosenbloom's study of NCR, Sull's study of Firestone, and Tripsas and Gavetti's study of Polaroid.[15]

Other than the grounded theory approach,[16] the extended case study method[17] does not try to build new theory; rather it extends existing theory. Empirical case study data is used to reconceptualize and extend existing theory. The researcher confronts data and theory in many cycles. In each cycle new data and additional concepts and theories are identified to be explored further. Burawoy[18] identifies two "running exchanges" between literature and data analysis, and between data analysis and data collection, represented as: literature review _ data analysis _ data collection. In the first, intensive data analysis and exploration of the scholarly literature occur simultaneously. While the data analysis points to relevant concepts and theories in the literature, at the same time the literature provides conceptual frameworks to support the data interpretation. The second running exchange calls for continuously moving back and forth between data collection and analysis. The analysis of initial data identifies additional information to be collected.[19]

Using a historical case study approach, we were able to develop a new understanding of how companies achieve outstanding success without reinventing the wheel, but by relying on more than 100 years of management sciences.

NOTES

PREFACE

1. From 1915 to 1946 Glaxo was part of Joseph Nathan & Co. The company was then rebranded as Glaxo Laboratories in 1947. From 1962 to 1972 the company was called Glaxo Group and from 1972 to 1995 Glaxo Holdings. After the merger with Wellcome, it was renamed Glaxo Wellcome. The merger with SmithKline Beecham resulted in the last name change. Today the company is called GlaxoSmithKline.

2. Allgemeine Electricitäts-Gesellschaft, but commonly referred to as AEG.

3. In 2005 the Royal Dutch/Shell Group of Companies changed its name to Royal Dutch Shell plc, following an integration of its London-based Shell Transport and Trading Company with its Royal Dutch Petroleum Company, based in The Hague. Subsequently the company will be referred to as Shell.

4. The original name was Allianz Versicherungs-Aktiengesellschaft. Subsequently it will be referred to as Allianz.

CHAPTER I

1. Christian Stadler, *Unternehmenskultur bei Royal Dutch/Shell, Siemens, und DaimlerChrysler*, ed. Hans Pohl, vol. 18, *Beiträge zur Unternehmensgeschichte* (Stuttgart: Franz Steiner Verlag, 2004).

2. Arie de Geus, *The Living Company* (Boston: Harvard Business School Press, 1997); Arie de Geus, "The Living Company," *Harvard Business Review* (1997).

3. James Collins and Jerry I. Porras, *Built to Last: Successful Habits of Visionary Companies*, 1st paperback ed. (New York: HarperBusiness, 1997); James C. Collins and Jerry I. Porras, "Building Your Company's Vision," *Harvard Business Review* (September–October 1996).

4. Data used for this study is from Bureau van Dijk (Amadeus database) and Eurostat, the statistical office of the European Communities.

5. List of local data providers: Coface Mope (Portugal), Coface SCRL (France/Monaco), CreditInfo Group (Iceland/Malta/Cyprus), CreditInform AS (Norway), Creditreform Austria (Austria), Honyvem (Italy), ICAP (Greece), Informa (Spain), Jordans (United Kingdom/Ireland), Københmandstandens OplysningsBureau (Denmark), LexisNexis (The Netherlands), Suomen Asiakastieto Oy (Finland), UC (Sweden), Verband der Vereine Creditreform (Germany), World'Vest Base Inc. (Worldwide—listed non-U.S. companies), Fitch Ratings (Worldwide—banks/insurance)

6. Austria, Belgium, Cyprus, Denmark, Finland, France, Germany, Gibraltar, Greece, Iceland, Ireland, Italy, Liechtenstein, Luxembourg, Malta, Monaco, Netherlands, Norway, Portugal, San Marino, Spain, Sweden, Switzerland, Turkey, United Kingdom.

7. In the qualification process, Amadeus disregarded the following types of shareholders, collectively labeled, because it is considered that they cannot, as such, exert a voting power: "public" (for publicly traded companies); "unnamed private shareholders, aggregated"; "other unnamed shareholders, aggregated."

8. Jane Banaszak-Holl, "Incorporating Organizational Growth into Models of Organizational Dynamics: Manhattan Banks, 1791–1980" (Cornell University, 1991); William P. Barnett, "The Organizational Ecology of a Technological System," *Administrative Science Quarterly* 35 (1990); Joel A. C. Baum and Stephen J. Mezias, "Localized Competition and Organizational Failure in the Manhattan Hotel Industry, 1898–1990," *Administrative Science Quarterly* 37 (1992); Jacques Delacroix and Anand Swaminathan, "Cosmetic, Speculative, and Adaptive Organizational Change in the Wine Industry: A Longitudinal Study," *Administrative Science Quarterly* 36 (1991); Michael Hannan and John Freeman, "The Population Ecology of Organizations," *American Journal of Sociology* 82 (1977); Daniel A. Levinthal, "Random Walks and Organizational Mortality," *Administrative Science Quarterly* 36 (1991); James Ranger-Moore, "Ecological Dynamics and Size Distributions in the Life Insurance Industry" (Cornell University, 1990).

9. This was calculated based on 2005 data. De Geus and his team calculated an average life expectancy of 12.5 years for European and Japanese firms. Other than this, we are not aware of any studies on the subject.

10. David N. Barron, Elizabeth West, and Michael T. Hannan, "A Time to Grow and a Time to Die: Growth and Mortality of Credit Unions in New York City, 1914–1990," *American Journal of Sociology* 100, no. 2 (1994); C. Wright Mills, *The Power Elite* (New York: Oxford University Press, 1956); Michael Useem, *The Inner Circle* (New York: Oxford University Press, 1984); Beth Mintz and Michael Schwartz, *The Power Structure of American Business* (Chicago: University of Chicago Press, 1985).

11. Banaszak-Holl, "Incorporating Organizational Growth into Models of Organizational Dynamics"; Barnett, "The Organizational Ecology of a Technological

System"; Baum and Mezias, "Localized Competition and Organizational Failure in the Manhattan Hotel Industry, 1898–1990"; Delacroix and Swaminathan, "Cosmetic, Speculative, and Adaptive Organizational Change in the Wine Industry"; Hannan and Freeman, "The Population Ecology of Organizations"; Levinthal, "Random Walks and Organizational Mortality"; Ranger-Moore, "Ecological Dynamics and Size Distributions in the Life Insurance Industry."

12. *Encyclopedia Britannica*, http://www.britannica.com/eb/article-63867.

13. Guinness World Records, ed., *Guinness World Records 2006* (Guinness, 2006).

14. The average life span of humans in Neanderthal was 20 years, in Upper Paleolithic 33 years, and in Neolithic 20 years. Compare *Encyclopedia Britannica*, (http://www.britannica.com/eb/article-63867). Rachel Caspari and Sang-Hee Lee, "Older Age Becomes Common Late in Human Evolution," *Proceedings of the National Academy of Sciences* (2004).

15. William T. O'Harra, *Centuries of Success: Lessons from the World's Most Enduring Family Businesses* (Avon, MA: Adams Media Corporation, 2004).

16. Ibid.

17. de Geus, *The Living Company*.

18. Ibid.

19. Data is from EIM Business & Policy Research (EIM BV), an independent research and consultancy organization based in the Netherlands.

20. The Austrian economist Joseph Schumpeter used the term "creative destruction" to describe a transformation process of the economy during which innovative entrepreneurs push established companies out. Despite the disruptions caused to the economy, this is necessary, in Schumpeter's view, to ensure growth in the long run. For more details on "creative destruction," see William J. Abernathy and Kim B. Clark, "Innovation: Mapping the Winds of Creative Destruction," *Research Policy* 14, no. 1 (1985); William J. Abernathy and James M. Utterback, "Patterns of Industrial Innovation," *Technology Review* 80, no. 7 (1978); Clayton M. Christensen and Joseph L. Bower, "Customer Power, Strategic Investment, and the Failure of Leading Firms," *Strategic Management Journal* 17, no. 3 (1996); Arnold C. Cooper and Dan Schendel, "Strategic Responses to Technological Threats," *Business Horizons* 19 (February 1976); Arnold C. Cooper and Clayton G. Smith, "How Established Firms Respond to Threatening Technologies," *Academy of Management Executive* 6, no. 2 (1992); Richard N. Foster, *Innovation: The Attacker's Advantage* (New York: Summit Books, 1986); Rebecca M. Henderson and Kim B. Clark, "Architectural Innovation: The Reconfiguration of Existing Product Technologies and the Failure of Established Firms," *Administrative Science Quarterly* 35, no. 1 (1990); Joseph Schumpeter, *The Theory of Economic Development* (Cambridge: Harvard University Press, 1934); Joseph Schumpeter, *Capitalism, Socialism, and Democracy* (New York: Harper Torchbooks, 1942); Mary Tripsas, "Unraveling the Process of Creative Destruction: Complementary Assets and Incumbent Survival in the Typesetter Industry," *Strategic Management*

Journal 18 (Special Summer Issue 1997); Michael L. Tushman and Philip Anderson, "Technological Discontinuities and Organizational Environments," *Administrative Science Quarterly* 31, no. 3 (1986); Sidney G. Winter, "Schumpeterian Competition in Alternative Technological Regimes," *Journal of Economic Behavior and Organization* 5, no. 3–4 (1984).

21. Compare Raghavendra R. Rau and Theo Vermaelen, "Glamour, Value, and the Post-Acquisition Performance of Acquiring Firms," *Journal of Financial Economics* 49, no. 2 (1998).

22. Data was retrieved from Compustat database.

23. *Fortune* created a list of 351 companies in 30 industries with revenues greater than $8 billion. The Hay Group sent surveys to 8,645 executives and directors at those companies, as well as to analysts. Respondents were asked to rate companies in their industry on nine attributes, on a scale of 0 (poor) to 10 (excellent); the average of those scores was used for country and industry rankings. Respondents were also asked to rank their top 10 companies across all industries. *Fortune*'s Global Most Admired Companies list is based on that result. A total of 611 companies in 70 industries were surveyed. Due to an insufficient response rate, the results for 29 companies in five industries are not reported: advertising; consumer credit; health care, pharmacy and other services; precision equipment; and printing. Thus American Express (no. 17) and 3M (no. 20) are on the overall list even though their industries—consumer credit and precision equipment—did not have enough responses to merit a category. http://money.cnn.com/magazines/fortune/globalmostadmired/full_list/.

24. In *Good to Great*, Collins selects companies that perform at least three times better than the market over a period of 15 years. This translates into 7.75 percent above annual market performance. We chose a slightly lower factor, as an observation period of 50 years increases the difficulty to consistently perform above market over time. On average, the companies we selected would also meet Collins's criteria, which would be 38 times better than the market over a period of 50 years. Compare Jim Collins, *Good to Great: Why Some Companies Make the Leap . . . and Others Don't* (New York: HarperCollins, 2001). Compared to Collins and Porras's performance criteria in *Built to Last*, our method is slightly more rigorous, as we apply the same factor over a 50-year observation period, while they chose an observation period of 60 years. This translates into 4.6 percent above-annual-market performance.

CHAPTER 2

1. Read a more detailed account on the collapse of the Viking society in Greenland and the survival of the Inuit in Jared Diamond, *Collapse: How Societies Choose to Fail or Succeed* (New York: Penguin, 2005).

Further material on the subject: Tom Amorosi et al., "They Did Not Live by Grass Alone: The Politics and Paleoecology of Animal Fodder in the North Atlantic Region," *Environmental Archaeology* 1 (1998); Martin Appelt, Joel

Berglund, and Hans Christian Gulløv, eds., *Identities and Cultural Contact in the Arctic* (Copenhagen: Danish Polar Center, 2000); Martin Appelt and Hans Christian Gulløv, eds., *Late Dorset in High Arctic Greenland* (Copenhagen: Danish Polar Center, 1999); Jette Arneborg, "Contact between Eskimos and Norsemen in Greenland: A Review of the Evidence," in *Tvaerfaglige Vikingesymposium* (Aarhus, Denmark, Aarhus University, 1993); Jette Arneborg et al., "Change of Diet of the Greenland Vikings Determined from Stable Carbon Isotope Analysis and 14c Dating of Their Bones," *Radiocarbon* 41 (1999); Joel Berglund, "The Decline of the Norse Settlements in Greenland," *Arctic Anthropology* 23 (1986); Eric Christiansen, *The Norsemen in the Viking Age* (Oxford: Blackwell, 2002); William Fitzhugh and Elisabeth Ward, eds., *Vikings: The North Atlantic Saga* (Washington, DC: Smithsonian Institution Press, 2000); Finn Gad, *The History of Greenland*, vol. 1, *Earliest Times to 1700* (Montreal: McGill-Queen's University Press, 1971); Bjarne Jakobsen, "Soil Resources and Soil Erosion in the Norse Settlement Area of Østerbygden in Southern Greenland," *Acta Borealia* 1 (1991); Gwyn Jones, *Vikings: The North Atlantic Saga* (Oxford: Oxford University Press, 1986); Christian Keller, "Vikings in the West Atlantic: A Model of Norse Greenlandic Medieval Society," *Acta Archaeologica* 61 (1990); Donald F. Logan, *The Vikings in History* (New York: Routledge, 1991); G. J. Marcus, *The Conquest of the North Atlantic* (New York: Oxford University Press, 1981); Thomas McGovern, "Contributions to the Paleoeconomy of Norse Greenland," *Acta Archaeologica* 54 (1985); Thomas McGovern, "Climate, Correlation, and Causation in Norse Greenland," *Arctic Anthropology* 28 (1991); Else Roestahl, *The Vikings* (New York: Penguin, 1987); Kirsten Seaver, *The Frozen Echo: Greenland and Exploration of North America ca. A.D. 1000–1500* (Stanford, CA: Stanford University Press, 1996).

2. Alfred D. Chandler, *Strategy and Structure* (Cambridge, MA: MIT Press, 1962); Alfred D. Chandler, *Scale and Scope: Dynamics of Industrial Capitalism* (Cambridge, MA: Harvard University Press, 1990).

3. Katherine Doornik and John Roberts, "Nokia Corporation: Innovation and Efficiency in a High-Growth Global Firm," in *Case S-IB-23* (Stanford, CA: Stanford University Graduate School of Business, 2001).

4. Ibid.

5. Interview with Christian Kluge, December 12, 2006.

6. Read more on this period and banks like the Oriental Bank Corporation, Agra Bank, and the Chartered Mercantile Bank in Albert S. J. Baster, *The Imperial Banks* (London: King, 1929); Geoffrey Jones, *British Multinational Banking, 1830–1990* (Oxford: Oxford University Press, 1993); Stuart Muirhead, *Crisis Banking in the East: The History of the Chartered Mercantile Bank of India, London, and China, 1853–93* (Aldershot: Scolar Press, 1996).

7. Read more in Baster, *The Imperial Banks*, and Jones, *British Multinational Banking*.

8. Read more in Frank H. H. King, *The Hongkong Bank in the Period of*

Development and Nationalism, 1941–1984: From Regional Bank to Multinational Group (New York: Cambridge University Press, 1991); Frank H. H. King, Catherine E. King, and David J. S. King, *The Hongkong Bank in Late Imperial China, 1864–1902: On an Even Keel* (New York: Cambridge University Press, 1987); Frank H. H. King, Catherine E. King, and David J. S. King, *The Hongkong Bank between the Wars and the Bank Interned, 1919–1945: Return from Grandeur*, 705 vols. (New York: Cambridge University Press, 1988); Frank H. H. King, David J. S. King, and Catherine E. King, *The Hongkong Bank in the Period of Imperialism and War, 1895–1918: Wayfoong, the Focus of Wealth* (New York: Cambridge University Press, 1988).

9. For convenience, we will refer to the bank as HSBC.

10. Read more in Compton Mackenzie, *Realms of Silver: One Hundred Years of Banking in the East* (London: Routledge & Kegan Paul, 1954).

11. Read more in George T. Amphlett, *History of the Standard Bank of South Africa Ltd., 1862–1913* (Glasgow: Maclehose, 1914); J. A. Henry, *The First Hundred Years of the Standard Bank* (London: Oxford University Press, 1963).

12. For convenience, we will refer to the bank as Chartered Bank.

13. See W. T. C. King, *A History of the London Discount Market* (London: Routledge, 1936); King, King, and King, *The Hongkong Bank in Late Imperial China*. King also refers to a discussion between Woldemar Nissen and Georg T. Siemssen, August 26, 1866, Archives of Siemssen and Co., Hamburg, the Hongkong Bank semiannual report issued in August 1867, and *London and China Express*, June 26 and July 10, 1866.

14. J. W. Maclellan, "Banking in India and China," *Bankers' Magazine* 55, no. 735 (1891).

15. D. McLean to James Greig, July 16, 1875, in McLean Private Letters (London), I, 3, McLean Papers, MS 380401, SOAS. King, King, and King, *The Hongkong Bank in the Period of Imperialism and War*.

16. King, King, and King, *The Hongkong Bank in the Period of Imperialism and War*.

17. Standard Chartered, ed., *Strength in Depth across the World* (1986).

18. Court Minute, December 28, 1899. Similar decisions were in Court Minute, May 15, 1901, and Court Minute, January 15, 1902, in File 3 (II), Box 3, Chartered History Files, SC. Compare Jones, *British Multinational Banking*.

19. Jones, *British Multinational Banking*.

20. Ronald W. Ferrier, *The History of the British Petroleum Company*, vol. 1, *The Developing Years, 1901–1932* (London: Cambridge University Press, 2000).

21. Ibid.

22. Ibid.

23. Ibid.

24. Frederick C. Gerretson, *History of the Royal Dutch* (Leiden: E. J. Brill, 1958).

25. Lafarge, ed., *Pavin de Lafarge, 1833–1933* (Paris, 1933); P. D'Ambly, *Naissance d'une Entreprise: Les Pavin de Lafarge de l'armée du roi à l'industrie de la republique* (Paris, 2000).

26. Société des Ciments Français, ed., *Centenaire de la Société des Ciments Français, 1881–1981* (Paris, 1981).

27. Ciments Français. Annual Report 1979.

CHAPTER 3

1. Peter Feist, *Die Berliner Mauer* (Berlin: Kai Homilius Verlag, 2004), Hans-Hermann Hertle and Katrin Elsner, *Mein 9. November* (Berlin: Verlag Nicolai, 1999).

2. http://www.bbc.co.uk/radio4/history/inourtime/greatest_philosopher_vote_result.shtml.

3. "When Lightning Strikes: How to Maintain Business as Usual in Unusual Times," *Economist*, October 27, 2005; Andreas Norrman and Ulf Jansson, "Ericsson's Proactive Supply Chain Risk Management Approach after a Serious Sub-Supplier Accident," *International Journal of Physical Distribution and Logistics Management* 34, no. 5 (2004); John H. Holland, *Adaptation in Natural and Artificial Systems* (Ann Arbor: University of Michigan Press, 1975); Timur Kuran, "The Tenacious Past: Theories of Personal and Collective Conservatism," *Journal of Economic Behavior and Organization*, no. 10 (1988); James G. March, "Exploration and Exploitation in Organizational Learning," *Organization Science* 2, no. 1 (1991); Joseph Schumpeter, *The Theory of Economic Development* (Cambridge: Harvard University Press, 1934).

4. March, "Exploration and Exploitation in Organizational Learning."

5. Daniel A. Levinthal and James G. March, "A Model of Adaptive Organizational Search," *Journal of Economic Behavior and Organization* 2 (1981); Sidney G. Winter, "Satisficing, Selection, and the Innovating Remnant," *Quarterly Journal of Economics* 85 (1971).

6. Barbara Levitt and James G. March, "Organizational Learning," *Annual Review of Sociology*, no. 14 (1988).

7. Interview with David Prosser, October 20, 2006.

8. For a more detailed account, see Edgar Jones, *The Business of Medicine: A History of Glaxo, a Baby Food Producer, Which Became One of the World's Most Successful Pharmaceutical Companies* (London: Profile Books, Ltd., 2001).

9. Fred A. Coe, Jr., *Burroughs Wellcome Co., 1880–1980*, ed. The Newcomen Society in North America (New York: 1980).

10. Ibid.

11. Charles M. Wenyon, *Protozoology: A Manual for Medical Men, Veterinarians, and Zoologists* (London: Baillière, Tindall, and Cox, 1926).

12. Compare Chris Argyris and Donald A. Schön, *Organizational Learning* (Reading, MA: Addison-Wesley, 1978); Paul A. David, "Clio and the Economics of Qwerty," *American Economic Review* 75 (1985).

13. An exception was vitamin B12.

14. Jones, *The Business of Medicine*; Richard Wright, "How Zantac Became the Best-Selling Drug in History," *Journal of Health Care Marketing* (Winter 1996).

15. "Glaxo Coping with Unwellcome News," *Economist*, April 26, 1997, 59.

16. Jones's interview of Joe Ruvane, CEO of Glaxo, Inc., June 8, 1994, in Jones, *The Business of Medicine*.

17. Ibid.

18. Ibid.

19. Glaxo Holdings, "Annual Report" (London, 1995).

20. Interview with Sir Richard Sykes, April 25, 2003.

21. "Glaxo's Expanding Galaxy," *Economist,* November 23, 2000.

22. Veronica Hope Hailey and Julia Balogun, "Devising Context Sensitive Approaches to Change: The Example of Glaxo Wellcome," *Long Range Planning* 35, no. 2 (2002).

23. F. J. Flynn and B. M. Staw, "Lend Me Your Wallets: The Effect of Charismatic Leadership on External Support for an Organization," *Strategic Management Journal* 25, no. 4 (2004).

24. Interview with Jean-Pierre Garnier, July 9, 2008.

25. Julian Birkinshaw and Cristina Gibson, "Building Ambidexterity into an Organization," *MIT Sloan Management Review* (Summer 2004).

26. Read further on Nokia's mobile story in John Roberts, *The Modern Firm: Organizational Design for Performance and Growth* (Oxford: Oxford University Press, 2004); Katherine Doornik and John Roberts, "Nokia Corporation: Innovation and Efficiency in a High-Growth Global Firm," in *Case S-IB-23* (Stanford, CA: Stanford University Graduate School of Business, 2001); Martti Häikiö, *Nokia: The Inside Story* (Helsinki: Edita, 2001); Martti Häikiö, *Nokia Oyj:N Historia 3: Globalisaatio* (Helsinki: Edita, 2001); Dan Steinbock, *The Nokia Revolution: The Story of an Extraordinary Company That Transformed an Industry* (New York: Amacom, 2001).

27. Nokia Annual Report 1995 and 1996.

28. Interview with Jorma Ollila, June 14, 2007.

29. Häikiö, *Nokia: The Inside Story*.

30. The seven electors were the archbishops of Mainz, Cologne, and Trier, the count on the Rhine, the duke of Saxony, the margrave of Brandenburg, and the king of Bohemia.

31. Richard Ehrenberg, *Das Zeitalter der Fugger: Geldkapital und Kreditverkehr im 16. Jahrhundert*, 2 vols. (Jena: Verlag von Gustav Fischer, 1922); Franz Herre, *Die Fugger in ihrer Zeit*, 12th ed. (Augsburg: Wißner-Verlag, 2005); Hans Herzfeld, ed., *Geschichte in Gestalten* (Frankfurt a. M.: Fischer Taschenbuch, 1980).

32. Ehrenberg, *Das Zeitalter der Fugger*.

33. Herzfeld, ed., *Geschichte in Gestalten*.

34. Ehrenberg, *Das Zeitalter der Fugger*.

35. Interview with Christian Kluge, December 12, 2006, and Dr. Schinzler, October 25, 2006.

36. For more detailed information on Standard & Poor's credit rating methodology and definition, see Standard & Poor's, ed., Corporate Ratings Criteria 2006, obtained at http://www 2.standardandpoors.com.

ISSUER CREDIT-RATING DEFINITIONS

A Standard & Poor's issuer credit rating is a current opinion of an obligor's overall financial capacity (its creditworthiness) to pay its financial obligations. This opinion focuses on the obligor's capacity and willingness to meet its financial commitments as they come due. It does not apply to any specific financial obligation, as it does not take into account the nature of and provisions of the obligation, its standing in bankruptcy or liquidation, statutory preferences, or the legality and enforceability of the obligation. In addition, it does not take into account the creditworthiness of the guarantors, insurers, or other forms of credit enhancement on the obligation. Foreign credit ratings are all forms of issuer credit ratings.

Issuer credit ratings are based on current information furnished by obligors or obtained by Standard & Poor's from other sources it considers reliable. Standard & Poor's does not perform an audit in connection with any issuer credit rating. Issuer credit ratings can be either long term or short term. Short-term issuer credit ratings reflect the obligor's creditworthiness over a short-term time horizon.

Long-Term Issuer Credit Ratings

AAA: An obligor rated "AAA" has extremely strong capacity to meet its financial commitments. "AAA" is the highest issuer credit rating assigned by Standard & Poor's.

AA: An obligor rated "AA" has very strong capacity to meet its financial commitments. It differs from the highest-rated obligors only to a small degree.

A: An obligor rated "A" has strong capacity to meet its financial commitments but is somewhat more susceptible to the adverse effects of changes in circumstances and economic conditions than obligors in higher-rated categories.

BBB: An obligor rated "BBB" has adequate capacity to meet its financial commitments. However, adverse economic conditions or changing circumstances are more likely to lead to a weakened capacity of the obligor to meet its financial commitments.

BB, B, CCC, and CC: Obligors rated "BB," "B," "CCC," and "CC" are regarded as having significant speculative characteristics. "BB" indicates the lowest degree of speculation and "CC" the highest. While such obligors will likely have some quality and protective characteristics, these may be outweighed by large uncertainties or major exposures to adverse conditions.

BB: An obligor rated "BB" is less vulnerable in the near term than other lower-rated obligors. However, it faces major ongoing uncertainties and exposure to adverse business, financial, or economic conditions that could lead to the obligor's inadequate capacity to meet its financial commitments.

B: An obligor rated "B" is more vulnerable than the obligors rated "BB," but the obligor currently has the capacity to meet its financial commitments. Adverse business, financial, or economic conditions will likely impair the obligor's capacity or willingness to meet its financial commitments.

CCC: An obligor rated "CCC" is currently vulnerable, and is dependent upon favorable business, financial, and economic conditions to meet its financial commitments.

CC: An obligor rated "CC" is currently highly vulnerable.

Plus (+) or minus (−): The ratings from "AA" to "CCC" may be modified by the addition of a plus (+) or minus (−) sign to show relative standing within the major rating categories.

R: An obligor rated "R" is under regulatory supervision owing to its financial condition. During the pendency of the regulatory supervision the regulators may have the power to favor one class of obligations over others or pay some obligations and not others. Please see Standard & Poor's issue credit ratings for a more detailed description of the effects of regulatory supervision on specific issues or classes of obligations.

SD and D: An obligor rated "SD" (selective default) or "D" has failed to pay one or more of its financial obligations (rated or unrated) when it came due. A "D" rating is assigned when Standard & Poor's believes that the default will be a general default and that the obligor will fail to pay all or substantially all of its obligations as they come due. An "SD" rating is assigned when Standard & Poor's believes that the obligor has selectively defaulted on a specific issue or class of obligations but will continue to meet its payment obligations on other issues or classes of obligations in a timely manner. Please see Standard & Poor's issue credit ratings for a more detailed description of the effects of a default on specific issues or classes of obligations.

37. Read further on Siemens after World War II in Wilfried Feldenkirchen: *Siemens 1918–1945* (München: Piper, 1995); and *Siemens: Von der Werkstatt zum Weltunternehmen* (München: Piper, 1997).

38. Read further on AEG after World War II in Allgemeine Elektricitäts-Gesellschaft, ed.: *50 Jahre AEG* (Berlin-Grunewald, 1956); *Unsere AEG* (Berlin, Frankfurt, 1957); and *75 Years AEG* (Frankfort am Main, 1959); Peter Strunk, *Die AEG: Aufstieg und Niedergang einer Industrielegende* (Berlin: Nicolai, 1999).

39. Feldenkirchen, *Siemens 1918–1945*.

40. Strunk, *Die AEG*.

41. Ibid.

42. To read more on Ericsson and Ivar Kreuger, see John Meurling and Richard Jeans, *The Ericsson Chronicle: 125 Years in Telecommunications* (Stockholm: Informationsförlaget, 2000); and George Soloveylchic, *Invar Kreuger* (London, 1932).

43. Ronald C. Anderson and David M. Reeb, "Founding-Family Ownership and Firm Performance: Evidence from the S&P 500," *Journal of Finance* 58, no. 3 (2003); Jim Lee, "Family Firm Performance: Further Evidence," *Family Business Review* 19, no. 2 (2006). Danny Miller and Isabelle Le Breton-Miller, "Family Governance and Firm Performance: Agency, Stewardship, and Capabilities," *Family Business Review* 19, no. 1 (2006).

44. See quote in Meurling and Jeans, *The Ericsson Chronicle*.

45. Read more on the fire in Albuquerque in "When Lightning Strikes"; Norrman and Jansson, "Ericsson's Proactive Supply Chain Risk Management Approach after a Serious Sub-Supplier Accident"; Almar Latour, "Trial by Fire: A Blaze in Albuquerque Sets Off Major Crisis for Cell-Phone Giants—Nokia Handles Supply

Shock with Aplomb as Ericsson of Sweden Gets Burned—Was SISU the Difference?" *Wall Street Journal*, January 29, 2001; Yossi Sheffi, *The Resilient Enterprise: Overcoming Vulnerability for Competitive Advantage* (Boston: MIT Press, 2005).

46. Latour, "Trial by Fire."

47. Douglas Adams, *The Hitchhiker's Guide to the Galaxy* (London: Picador, 1979).

48. Kurt Matzler et al., "Methods and Concepts in Management: Significance, Satisfaction, and Suggestions for Further Research: Perspectives from Germany, Austria, and Switzerland," *Strategic Change* 14, no. 1 (2005).

49. Keetie Sluyterman, *A History of Royal Dutch Shell: Keeping Competitive in Turbulent Markets, 1973–2007*, vol. 3 (Oxford: Oxford University Press, 2007).

50. Interview with Gerrit Wagner, June 6, 2001.

51. Interview with Cor Herkströter, June 5, 2001.

52. Peter Nulty and Jessica Skelly von Brachel, "Batman Shakes BP to the Bedrock," *Fortune*, November 19, 1990.

53. Ibid.

54. Roberts, *The Modern Firm*.

55. Daniel Yergin, *The Prize: The Epic Quest for Oil, Money, and Power* (New York: Pocket Books, 1993).

56. In the upstream business, for example, peer groups were formed on the basis of the issues facing teams in specific fields. Engineers and geologists at newly discovered fields were dealing with different issues than those who were working at old and depleting fields.

57. Interview with Jorma Ollila, June 14, 2007.

58. According to Joost Jonker and Jan Luiten van Zanden, it is not possible to determine whether he was forced to retire or retired on his own account. In any case, he was 70 at the time and had recently fallen in love with a young German woman. Joost Jonker and Jan Luiten van Zanden, *A History of Royal Dutch Shell: From Challenger to Joint Industry Leader, 1890–1939*, vol. 1 (Oxford: Oxford University Press, 2007).

59. As Gerrit Wagner, chairman from 1972 to 1977, put it in an interview with us: "There is no chief executive, but there is no doubt that the chairman somehow was more equal than others. I know because I have done it myself."

60. Interview with Jeroen van der Veer, March 21, 2007.

61. Terry Macalister, "BP Goliath Plays David," *Guardian*, November 28, 2005.

62. Christian Stadler and Hans H. Hinterhuber, "Changing Companies with Strong Values: Shell, Siemens, and Daimler Chrysler," *Long Range Planning* 38, no. 5 (2005).

63. Sluyterman, *A History of Royal Dutch Shell*.

64. Royal Dutch/Shell Group of Companies, "What We Look For" (2006).

65. Compare Michael Goold and Andrew Campbell, "Structured Networks: Towards the Well Designed Matrix," *Long Range Planning* 36, no. 5 (2003); Stadler and Hinterhuber, "Changing Companies with Strong Values."

66. Interview with Cor Herkströter, June 5, 2001.

67. Lafarge Coppée, "L'identité d'un groupe: Lafarge Coppée, 1947–1989, an-Goulême" (Paris, 1991).

68. James H. Bamberg, *The History of the British Petroleum Company*, vol. 2, *The Anglo-Iranian Years, 1928–1954* (Cambridge: Cambridge University Press, 2000).

69. Heinrich v. Pierer and Michael Mirow, "Strategie im Praxistest. Unternehmen: Welche strategische. Planungskonzepte haben sich bei Siemens in den vergangenen Jahrzehnten bewährt," *Harvard Business Manager* (October 2004).

70. Arie de Geus, "Planning as Learning," *Harvard Business Review* (March–April 1988).

71. Compare Robert Bood and Theo Postman, "Strategic Learning with Scenarios," *European Management Journal* 15, no. 6 (1997); Paul J. H. Schoemaker, "Multiple Scenario Development: Its Conceptual and Behavioral Foundation," *Strategic Management Journal* 14 (1993).

72. For more about scenario planning in Shell, see Peter Cornelius, Alexander Van de Putte, and Mattia Romani, "Three Decades of Scenario Planning in Shell," *California Management Review* 48, no. 1 (2005); Geus, "Planning as Learning"; Arie de Geus, *The Living Company* (Boston: Harvard Business School Press, 1997); Kees van der Heijden, *Scenarios: The Art of Strategic Conversation* (New York, 1996); Kees van der Heijden et al., *The Sixth Sense: Accelerating Organizational Learning with Scenarios* (New York: John Wiley, 2002); Peter Schwartz, *The Art of the Long View: Planning for the Future in an Uncertain World* (New York: Doubleday Currency, 1991); Pierre Wack, "Scenarios: Shooting the Rapids," *Harvard Business Review* 63, no. 3 (1985).

73. Herman Kahn and Anthony J. Wiener, *The Year 2000* (New York: Macmillan, 1967).

74. Wack, "Scenarios."

75. David Ingvar, "Memory of the Future: An Essay on the Temporal Organization of Conscious Awareness," *Human Neurobiology* (1985).

76. Geus, *The Living Company*.

77. Cornelius, Putte, and Romani, "Three Decades of Scenario Planning in Shell."

78. Interview with Cor Herkströter, November 16, 2006.

79. Martti Häikiö, *Nokia Oyj:N Historia 1: Fuusio* (Helsinki: Edita, 2001).

80. Stephen Howarth and Joost Jonker, *A History of Royal Dutch Shell: Powering the Hydrocarbon Revolution, 1939–1973*, vol. 2 (Oxford: Oxford University Press, 2007).

81. Adolph Berle and Gardiner Means, *The Modern Corporation and Private Property* (New York: Macmillan, 1932).

82. Michael C. Jensen, "The Eclipse of the Public Corporation," *Harvard Business Review* (September–October 1989).

83. Diversification is often associated with mergers. Avery, Chevalier, and

Schaefer found that CEOs are more likely to be appointed to other firms' boards of directors if they undertake acquisitions. Christopher Avery, Judith A. Chevalier, and Scott Schaefer, "Why Do Managers Undertake Acquisitions? An Analysis of Internal and External Rewards for Acquisitiveness," *Journal of Law, Economics, and Organization* 14 (1998).

84. David Besanko et al., *Economics of Strategy* (Hoboken, NJ: John Wiley, 2002).

85. Richard P. Rumelt, "Strategy, Structure, and Economic Performance" (Ph.D. diss., Harvard Business School, 1972). For further research building on Rumelt, see Jay R. Galbraith and Robert K. Kazanjian, *Strategy Implemention*, 2nd ed. (St. Paul, MN: West Publishing, 1986).

86. Gareth P. Dyas, "The Strategy and Structure of French Industrial Enterprise (Ph.D. diss., Harvard Business School, 1972); Gareth P. Dyas and Heinz T. Thanheiser, *The Emerging European Enterprise* (Boulder, CO: Westview, 1976).

87. Derek F. Channon, "The Strategy and Structure of British Enterprise" (Ph.D. diss., Harvard Business School, 1971).

88. Alfred D. Chandler, *Strategy and Structure* (Cambridge, MA: MIT Press, 1962); Leonard Wrigley, "Divisional Autonomy and Diversification" (Ph.D. diss., Harvard Business School, 1970); Channon, "The Strategy and Structure of British Enterprise"; Dyas, "The Strategy and Structure of French Industrial Enterprise"; Dyas and Thanheiser, *The Emerging European Enterprise*.

89. Michael Mayer and Richard Whittington, "Diversification in Context: A Cross-National and Cross-Temporal Extension," *Strategic Management Journal* 24 (2003); Richard Whittington and Michael Mayer, *The European Corporation: Strategy, Structure, and Social Science* (New York: Oxford University Press, 2000).

90. Gary Hamel and C. K. Prahalad, *Competing for the Future* (Boston: Harvard Business School Press, 1994).

91. Robert M. Grant, *Contemporary Strategy Analysis: Concepts, Techniques, Applications*, 4th ed. (Oxford: Blackwell Business, 2002); Gregg A. Jarrell, James A. Brickly, and Jeffry M. Netter, "The Market for Corporate Control: Empirical Evidence since 1980," *Journal of Economic Perspectives* 2, no. 1 (1988).

92. Noel Capon et al., "Corporate Diversity and Economic Performance: The Impact of Market Specialisation," *Strategic Management Journal* 9 (1988); Cynthia A. Montgomery, "The Measurement of Firm Diversification: Some New Empirical Evidence," *Academy of Management Journal* 25 (1982).

93. Leslie E. Palich, Laura B. Cardinal, and Chet C. Miller, "Curvilinearity in the Diversification-Performance Linkage: An Examination of over Three Decades of Research," *Strategic Management Journal* 21 (2000).

94. Sayan Chatterjee and Birger Wernerfeld, "The Link between Resources and Type of Diversification," *Strategic Management Journal* 12 (1991).

95. Peter Borscheid, *100 Jahre Allianz: Menschen machen Geschichte: Der Weg des Unternehmens von seiner Gründung bis Heute vor dem Hintergrund des zeitgeschichtlichen Umfelds* (München, 1990).

96. Wilhelm Kisch, *Fünfzig Jahre Allianz: Ein Beitrag zur Geschichte der Deutschen Privatversicherung* (München: Münchener Rückversicherungs-Gesellschaft, 1940).

97. Ludwig Arps, *Wechselvolle Zeiten: 75 Jahre Allianz Versicherung, 1890–1965* (München: Allianz Versicherungs-AG, 1965); Ludwig Arps, *Auf Sicheren Pfeilern: Deutsche Versicherungswirtschaft vor 1914* (Göttingen: Vandenhoeck & Ruprecht, 1965); Peter Borscheid, *100 Jahre Allianz* (München: Allianz Aktiengesellschaft Holding, 1990); Peter Borscheid, "Allianz Ag," in *International Directory of Company Histories,* ed. Jay P. Peterson (Detroit: St. James Press, 2004).

98. E. Hauser, "Amb Generali Holding Ag," in *International Directory of Company Histories,* ed. T. Grant (Detroit: St. James Press, 2003).

99. Lothar Brückner, "David Hansemann als Versicherungsunternehmer," in *David Hansemann, 1790, 1864, 1964,* ed. Bernhard Poll (Aaachen: Industrie und Handelskammer Aachen, 1964).

100. Aachener und Münchener Feuer-Versicherungs-Gesellschaft, ed., *Aachener und Münchener Feuer-Versicherungs-Gesellschaft: Denkschrift zur Hundertjahr-Feier, 1825–1925* (Aachen: Aachener Verlags- u. Druckerei-Gesellschaft, 1925); Aachener und Münchener Feuer-Versicherungs-Gesellschaft, ed., *110 Jahre Aachener und Münchener Feuer-Versicherungs-Gesellschaft, Aachen: 1825–1935* (1935).

101. Aachener und Münchener Feuer-Versicherungs-Gesellschaft, ed., *Aachener und Münchener Feuer-Versicherungs-Gesellschaft.*

102. Aachener-und-Münchener-Versicherung-AG, ed., *Perspektiven: 175 Jahre Aachener und Münchener Versicherung Aktiengesellschaft: Leistungsstark und Erfolgsorientiert in die Zukunft* (Aachen: Aachener und Münchener Versicherung AG, 2000).

103. Münchener und Aachener Mobiliar-Feuer-Versicherungs-Gesellschaft, ed., *Hundert Jahre Münchener und Aachener Mobiliar-Feuer-Versicherungs-Gesellschaft, 1834–1934: Denkschrift der im Jahre 1825 Gegründeten Aachener und Münchener Feuer-Versicherungs-Gesellschaft Anläßlich ihrer Hundertjahrfeier in Bayern* (München: Bruckmann, 1934).

104. Hoppenstedt, ed., *Versicherungsjahrbuch 1997* (Darmstadt: Hoppenstedt, 1997).

105. Philip Wältermann, *Unternehmenserfolg in der Versicherungswirtschaft: Langfristige Erfolgsfaktoren in der Assekuranz* (Berlin: Erich Schmidt, 2007).

106. William Pitt, "Rude Awakening," *Reactions,* 05/92 (1992).

107. Aachener-und-Münchener-Versicherung-AG, ed., *Perspektiven.*

108. Häikiö, *Nokia: The Inside Story.*

109. Read further on Nokia's mobile story in Roberts, *The Modern Firm;* Doornik and Roberts, "Nokia Corporation"; Häikiö, *Nokia: The Inside Story;* Häikiö, *Nokia Oyj:N Historia 3: Globalisaatio;* Steinbock, *The Nokia Revolution.*

110. Nokia. Annual Report 1992.

111. Doornik and Roberts, "Nokia Corporation."

112. Ibid.

113. Feldenkirchen, *Siemens: Von der Werkstatt zum Weltunternehmen.*

114. Dorothy Leonard-Barton, *Wellsprings of Knowledge: Building and Sustaining the Sources of Innovation* (Boston: Harvard Business School Press, 1995).

115. Interview with Lodewijk van Wachem, June 14, 2001.

116. Paul Bate, Raza Khan, and Annie Pye, "Towards a Culturally Sensitive Approach to Organization Structuring: Where Organization Design Meets Organization Development," *Organization Science* 11, no. 2 (2000); Hope Hailey and Balogun, "Devising Context Sensitive Approaches to Change."

117. Hope Hailey and Balogun, "Devising Context Sensitive Approaches to Change."

118. Feldenkirchen, *Siemens: Von der Werkstatt zum Weltunternehmen.*

119. Interview with Hermann Franz, April 16, 2007.

120. Minutes, AEG Supervisory Board, September 28, 1962, p. 2, FA: "Es muss daher mit allen Kräften versucht werden, die Kosten zu senken. Dies soll insbesondere auch durch eine Umorganisation erreicht werden" (Strunk, *Die AEG: Aufstieg und Niedergang einer Industrielegende*).

121. Annual Reports 1964–1970.

122. Strunk (1999) recalls the following quote: "Die Herren haben mich gut beraten, mir aber bei Übernahme der AEG auch gesagt, dass ich mir auf alle Fälle durch Sonderbefugnisse vom Aufsichtsrat Rückendeckung holen müsse. Sonst würde ich bei der AEG, die sich seit vielen Jahren zu sehr in ausgefahrenen Gleisen bewege, nicht durchkommen."

123. Strunk, *Die AEG.*

124. Ibid.

125. Ibid.

126. Interview with Heinz Dürr, March 20, 2007.

127. Strunk, *Die AEG.*

128. Interview with Dr. Hermann Franz, January 25, 2001.

129. Ibid.

130. Ibid.

131. Ibid.

132. Interview with Stephen Green, January 11, 2007.

133. Ibid.

134. Interview with Christian Kluge, December 12, 2006.

135. Ibid. "Man hat Leute aus den unterschiedlichsten Ebenen ausgesucht. Das waren Leute die Kompetenz hatten so etwas zu durchdenken. Obwohl sie die Materie zum Teil kaum kannten. Somit mussten jemand über die Abschaffung der Matrix nachdenken, obwohl er selbst 40 Jahre in einer der Fachabteilungen gearbeitet hatte."

136. Ibid. "Von so jemanden können sie normalerweise nicht erwarten, dass er die Abschaffung der Fachabteilung empfiehlt. Haben sie aber gemacht. Sie haben die Kompetenzen rein bekommen und die Autorität im Unternehmen zu sagen, wir sind zu dem Entschluss gekommen, wir müssen uns so uns so aufstellen und dann

erklärt warum und das ist gerade dann, weil jeder wusste, das waren eigentlich Fachleute und hatte erwartet, dass sie eigentlich alles torpedieren würden. Haben sie nicht gemacht im Gegenteil."

137. Ibid.

138. Ibid.

CHAPTER 4

1. Cary J. Broussard and Anita Bell, *From Cinderella to CEO: How to Master the 10 Lessons of Fairy Tales to Transform Your Work Life* (New York: Wiley, 2005); Jürgen Fuchs, *Das Märchenbuch für Manager: "Gute Nacht-Geschichten" für Leitende und Leidende*, 2nd ed. (Frankfurt: Frankfurter Allgemeine Buch, 2007); Franz S. Berger, *"Sieben auf einen Streich": Grimms Märchen für Manager* (München: Wirtschaftsverlag Langen Müller/Herbig, 2001); Rolf Wunderer, "Vom Selbst- zum Fremdvertrauen: Konzepte, Wirkungen, Märcheninterpretationen," *Zeitschrift für Personalforschung* 18, no. 4 (2004).

2. Fuchs, *Das Märchenbuch für Manager*; Charles Perrault, "The Master Cat," in *The Blue Fairy Book*, ed. Andrew Lang (London: Longmans, Green, 1889).

3. Interview with Edzard Reuter, December 12, 2001.

4. Hans Otto Eglau, *Edzard Reuter* (Düsseldorf: Econ, 1991).

5. Léon Dubois, *Foundation for the Future: The Lafarge Story* (Paris: Editions Belfond, 1988).

6. Interview with Cor Herkströter, June 5, 2001.

7. Ibid.

8. Compare Noel Tichy and Eli Cohen, *The Leadership Engine: How Winning Companies Build Leaders at All Levels* (New York: HarperCollins, 1997).

9. Interview with David Prosser, October 20, 2006.

10. P. D'Ambly, *Naissance d'une Entreprise: Les Pavin de Lafarge de l'armée du roi à l'industrie de la republique* (Paris: François-Xavier de Guibert, 2000).

11. Dubois, *Foundation for the Future*.

12. James Collins and Jerry I. Porras, *Built to Last: Successful Habits of Visionary Companies*, 1st paperback ed. (New York: HarperBusiness, 1997).

13. The difference might be even more pronounced; we were not able to discover complete records for all comparison companies.

14. Aachener und Münchener Feuer-Versicherungs-Gesellschaft, ed., *Aachener und Münchener Feuer-Versicherungs-Gesellschaft: Denkschrift zur Hundertjahr-Feier, 1825–1925* (Aachen: Aachener Verlags- u. Druckerei-Gesellschaft, 1925).

15. Peter Borscheid, *100 Jahre Allianz: Menschen machen Geschichte: Der Weg des Unternehmens von seiner Gründung bis Heute vor dem Hintergrund des zeitgeschichtlichen Umfelds* (München: Allianz AG, 1990).

16. Ibid.

17. Arijit Chatterjee and Donald C. Hambrick, "It's All about Me: Narcissistic CEOs and Their Effects on Company Strategy and Performance," *Administrative Science Quarterly* 52 (2007).

18. "Browne Out," *Economist*, January 18, 2007; "BP Chief Executive to Retire at the End of July, Earlier Than Expected," *USA Today*, December 1, 2007.

19. "Secrets and Lies," *Economist*, May 3, 2007.

20. Aachener und Münchener Feuer-Versicherungs-Gesellschaft, ed., *Aachener und Münchener Feuer-Versicherungs-Gesellschaft*.

21. Ludwig Arps, *Deutsche Versicherungsunternehmer* (Karlsruhe: Verlag Versicherungswirtschaft, 1968).

22. Josef Hansen, *Gustav von Mevissen: Ein Rheinisches Lebensbild, 1815–1899*, vol. 1 (Berlin, 1906); Kölnische Rückversicherungs-Gesellschaft, *100 Jahre Kölnische Rückversicherungs-Gesellschaft* (Köln, 1953); Gunter Quarg and Klara von Eyll, *Gustav von Mevissen und Seine Bibliothek*, Schriften der Universitäts- und Stadtbibliothek Köln 9 (Köln: Universitäts- und Stadtbibliothek Köln, 1999).

APPENDIX A

1. Pierre Campagne, *La Cimeterie de Gargenville 1916 à 2002* (Paris, 2004).

2. Burkhard Beer, "Ein Blick in die Geschichte der Kölnischen Rück," in *Themen Nr. 5*, ed. General Re/Kölnische Rückversicherungsgesellschaft (Köln, 1996).

3. Kölnische Rückversicherungs-Gesellschaft, *100 Jahre Kölnische Rückversicherungs-Gesellschaft* (Köln, 1953).

4. Ibid.

5. Beer, "Ein Blick in die Geschichte der Kölnischen Rück."

6. Read more about Nokia's history in Katherine Doornik and John Roberts, "Nokia Corporation: Innovation and Efficiency in a High-Growth Global Firm," in *Case S-IB-23* (Stanford, CA: Stanford University Graduate School of Business, 2001); Martti Häikiö, *Nokia: The Inside Story* (Helsinki: Edita, 2001); Elaine Williams, "100-Year-Old Nokia Experiences Fast-Growth Pains," *Electronic Business* (1989).

7. Read further on Nokia's mobile story in John Roberts, *The Modern Firm: Organizational Design for Performance and Growth* (Oxford: Oxford University Press, 2004); Doornik and Roberts, "Nokia Corporation"; Häikiö, *Nokia: The Inside Story*; Martti Häikiö, *Nokia Oyj:N Historia 3: Globalisaatio* (Helsinki: Edita, 2001); Dan Steinbock, *The Nokia Revolution: The Story of an Extraordinary Company That Transformed an Industry* (New York: Amacom, 2001).

8. Nokia. Annual Report 1992.

9. The company's original name was Telegraphen-Bauanstalt von Siemens & Halske.

10 The company's full name is Siemens-Schuckertwerke GmbH.

11. At the time, the company was called Burroughs Wellcome.

APPENDIX B

1. Alfred D. Chandler, *Strategy and Structure* (Cambridge, MA: MIT Press, 1962); Alfred D. Chandler, *The Visible Hand: The Managerial Revolution in American Business* (Cambridge, MA: Belknap Press, 1977); Alfred D. Chandler,

Scale and Scope: Dynamics of Industrial Capitalism (Cambridge, MA: Harvard University Press, 1990).

2. Joseph L. Bower, *Managing the Resource Allocation Process: A Study of Corporate Planning and Investment* (Boston: Harvard University Press, 1970); Shona L. Brown and Kathleen M. Eisenhardt, "The Art of Continuous Change: Linking Complexity Theory and Time-Paced Evolution in Relentlessly Shifting Organizations," *Administrative Science Quarterly* 42 (1997); Robert A. Burgelman, "A Process Model of Internal Corporate Venturing: Strategic Decision Making," *Strategic Management Journal* 13 (1983).

3. Constance E. Helfat, "Guest Editor's Introduction to the Special Issue: The Evolution of Firm Capabilities," *Strategic Management Journal* 21, no. 10–11 (2000).

4. Ludwig Wittgenstein, *Philosophical Investigations* (Oxford: Blackwell, 1989), §593.

5. Kathleen M. Eisenhardt, "Building Theories from Case Study Research," *Academy of Management Review* 14, no. 4 (1989).

6. James Collins and Jerry I. Porras, *Built to Last: Successful Habits of Visionary Companies*, 1st paperback ed. (New York: HarperBusiness, 1997).

7. Dividends, rights issues, gratitude shares, stock splits, and other benefits for the shareholder were taken into consideration when we made our calculations.

8. Thomson Financials DataStream database.

9. For a more detailed description of these tests, see Daniel Blum, *Langfristiger Unternehmenserfolg: Ermittlung Mittels Börsen- und Bilanzkennzahlen* (Berlin: Erich Schmidt, 2007).

10. The Society of Chartered Financial Analysts (CFA) provided the address of equity researchers who were members of the different national industry bodies in Austria, Belgium, Germany, Great Britain, Finland, France, Ireland, the Netherlands, Sweden, Switzerland, and Spain.

11. H. B. Mann and D. R. Whitney, "On a Test of Whether One of Two Random Variables Is Stochastically Larger Than the Other," *Annals of Mathematical Statistics* 18 (1947).

12. Phil Rosenzweig, *The Halo Effect . . . and the Eight Other Business Delusions That Deceive Managers* (New York: Free Press, 2007).

13. Jim Collins, *Good to Great: Why Some Companies Make the Leap . . . and Others Don't* (New York: HarperCollins, 2001).

14. Kathleen M. Eisenhardt and Jeffrey A. Martin, "Dynamic Capabilities: What Are They?" *Strategic Management Journal* 21 (2000).

15. Robert A. Burgelman, "Intraorganizational Ecology of Strategy Making and Organizational Adaptation: Theory and Field Research," *Organization Science* 3, no. 2 (1991); Robert A. Burgelman, "Fading Memories: A Process Theory of Strategic Business Exit in Dynamic Environments," *Administrative Science Quarterly* 39, no. 1 (1994); Burgelman, "Strategy as Vector and the Inertia of Coevolutionary Lock-in," *Administrative Science Quarterly* 47, no. 2 (2002); E. Danneels, "The Dynamics of Product Innovation and Firm Competences," *Strategic Management*

Journal 23, no. 12 (2002); E. Danneels, "Tight-Loose Coupling with Customers: The Enactment of Customer Orientation," *Strategic Management Journal* 24, no. 6 (2003); Richard S. Rosenbloom, "Leadership, Capabilities, and Technological Change: The Transformation of NCR in the Electronic Era," *Strategic Management Journal* 21, no. 10 (2000); Donald N. Sull, "The Dynamics of Standing Still: Firestone Tire & Rubber and the Radial Revolution," *Business History Review* 73, no. 3 (1999); Mary Tripsas and Giovanni Gavetti, "Capabilities, Cognition, and Inertia: Evidence from Digital Imaging," *Strategic Management Journal* 21 (2000).

16. B. G. Glaser and A. L. Strauss, *The Discovery of Grounded Theory* (Chicago: Aldine, 1967).

17. Michael Burawoy, *Ethnography Unbound* (Berkeley, CA: University of California Press, 1991).

18. Ibid.

19. Danneels, "The Dynamics of Product Innovation and Firm Competences"; Danneels, "Tight-Loose Coupling with Customers"; E. Danneels, "The Process of Technological Competence Leveraging," *Strategic Management Journal* 28, no. 5 (2007).

REFERENCES

INTERVIEWS

Régina Boullié-Gugliemi, Ciments Français (Director of Finance)

Keith Daton, Lafarge (Senior Vice President, HR)

Marc Desgranges, Ciments Français (Director of Strategy and Development)

Heinz Dürr, AEG (CEO 1980–1990)

Hermann Franz, Siemens (Chairman 1993–1999)

Jean-Pierre Garnier, Glaxo (CEO 2000–2008)

Stephen Green, HSBC (Chairman since 2006, CEO 2003–2006)

Jean-Pierre Herbinier, Ciments Français (Director of Formation and Development)

Cor Herkströter, Shell (CEO 1993–1998)

Christian Herrault, Lafarge (Board Member since 1998)

Arno Junke, Cologne Re (Board Member 2003–2007)

Klaus Kleinfeld, Siemens (CEO 2005–2007)

Christian Kluge, Munich Re (Board Member 1998–2006)

Martin Lord, HSBC (Head of Government and Community Relations)

Peter Lütke-Bornefeld, Cologne Re (CEO 1993–2009)

Mark Moody-Stuart, Shell (CEO 1998–2001)

Alexander Nieuwenhuizen, Lafarge (Senior Vice President, HR)

Jorma Ollila, Nokia (Chairman since 1992, CEO 1992–2006)

Heinrich von Pierer, Siemens (Chairman 2005–2007, CEO 1992–2005)

David Prosser, Legal & General (CEO 1991–2005)

Hans-Jürgen Schinzler, Munich Re (Chairman since 2004, CEO 1993–2004)

Henning Schulte-Noelle, Allianz (Chairman since 2003, CEO 1991–2003)

Sara Ravella, Lafarge (Board Member since 2008)
Edzard Reuter, Daimler-Benz (CEO 1987–1995)
Peter von Siemens, Siemens (Member of family who founded company)
Reinhard Siepenkort, AEG (Former Company Secretary)
Peter Stileman, Standard Chartered (Head of Corporate Development)
Richard Sykes, Glaxo (Chairman 1997–2002, CEO 1993–2000)
Jeroen van der Veer, Shell (CEO since 2004)
Lodewijk van Wachem, Shell (Chairman 1992–2002, CEO 1985–1992
Gerrit Wagner, Shell (CEO 1972–1977)
Phil Watts, Shell (CEO 2001–2004)
Claus Weyrich, Siemens (Board Member 1996–2006)
Günter Wilhelm, Siemens (Board Member 1992–2000)

LIBRARIES AND ARCHIVES
Allianz Historical Archives, Munich
Annual Report Archives at Cologne University
Annual Report Archives at Saarland University
Archive of Stock Exchange Market (Bolsa Madrid), Madrid
Baker Library, Historical Collection, Boston
Bayerische Staatsbibliothek
Ciments Français Archives, Paris
Cologne Re Archive, Cologne
Deutsche Nationalbibliothek, Frankfurt
Deutsches Technikmuseum Berlin
Euronext Archive, Paris
Guildhall Library, London
Historical Archive of Banco de España, Madrid
Historical Archive BBVA, Bilbao
HSBC Group Archives, London
HWWA, Hamburg
Lafarge, Historical Archives, Paris
London Business School Library, London
Mercedes-Benz Museum und Historisches Archiv, Untertürkheim
National Library of France, Paris
OMX Archives, Stockholm and Helsinki
Royal Dutch Archives, The Hague
Siemens Corporate Archives, Munich
Universidad de Cantabria, Santander
University Library Mannheim
University Library Munich
Wellcome Library, London

BOOKS AND ARTICLES

Aachener-und-Münchener-Versicherung-AG, ed. *Perspektiven: 175 Jahre Aachener und Münchener Versicherung Aktiengesellschaft: Leistungsstark und Erfolgsorientiert in die Zukunft*. Aachen: Aachener und Münchener Versicherung AG, 2000.

Aachener und Münchener Feuer-Versicherungs-Gesellschaft, ed. *110 Jahre Aachener und Münchener Feuer-Versicherungs-Gesellschaft, Aachen: 1825–1935*. Aachen: Aachener und Münchener Feuer-Versicherungs-Gesellschaft, 1935.

————, ed. *Aachener und Münchener Feuer-Versicherungs-Gesellschaft: Denkschrift zur Hundertjahr-Feier, 1825–1925*. Aachen: Aachener Verlags- u. Druckerei-Gesellschaft, 1925.

Abernathy, William J., and Kim B. Clark. "Innovation: Mapping the Winds of Creative Destruction." *Research Policy* 14, no. 1 (1985): 3–22.

Abernathy, William J., and James M. Utterback. "Patterns of Industrial Innovation." *Technology Review* 80, no. 7 (1978): 40–47.

Adams, Douglas. *The Hitchhiker's Guide to the Galaxy*. London: Picador, 1979.

Allgemeine Elektricitäts-Gesellschaft, ed. *50 Jahre AEG*. Berlin-Grunewald, 1956.

————, ed. *75 Years AEG*. Frankfort-am-Main, 1959.

————, ed. *Unsere AEG*. Berlin, Frankfurt, 1957.

Amorosi, Tom, Paul C. Buckland, Kevin J. Edwards, Ingrid Mainland, Tom H. McGovern, Jon P. Sadler, and Peter Skidmore. "They Did Not Live by Grass Alone: The Politics and Paleoecology of Animal Fodder in the North Atlantic Region." *Environmental Archaeology* 1 (1998): 41–54.

Amphlett, George T. *History of the Standard Bank of South Africa Ltd., 1862–1913*. Glasgow: MacLehose, 1914.

Anderson, Ronald C., and David M. Reeb. "Founding-Family Ownership and Firm Performance: Evidence from the S&P 500." *Journal of Finance* 58, no. 3 (2003): 1301–27.

Appelt, Martin, Joel Berglund, and Hans Christian Gulløv, eds. *Identities and Cultural Contact in the Arctic*. Copenhagen: Danish Polar Center, 2000.

Appelt, Martin, and Hans Christian Gulløv, eds. *Late Dorset in High Arctic Greenland*. Copenhagen: Danish Polar Center, 1999.

Argyris, Chris, and Donald A. Schön. *Organizational Learning*. Reading, MA: Addison-Wesley, 1978.

Arneborg, Jette. "Contact between Eskimos and Norsemen in Greenland: A Review of the Evidence." In *Tvaerfaglige Vikingesymposium*, 23–35. Aarhus, Denmark: Aarhus University, 1993.

Arneborg, Jette, Jan Heinemeier, Nils Lynnerup, Henrik L. Nielsen, Nils Rud, and Árný E Sveinbjörnsdóttir. "Change of Diet of the Greenland Vikings Determined from Stable Carbon Isotope Analysis and 14c Dating of Their Bones." *Radiocarbon* 41 (1999): 157–68.

Arps, Ludwig. *Auf Sicheren Pfeilern: Deutsche Versicherungswirtschaft vor 1914*. Göttingen: Vandenhoeck & Ruprecht, 1965.

————. *Deutsche Versicherungsunternehmer*. Karlsruhe: Verlag Versicherungswirtschaft, 1968.

———. *Wechselvolle Zeiten: 75 Jahre Allianz Versicherung 1890–1965.* München: Allianz Versicherungs-AG, 1965.

Avery, Christopher, Judith A. Chevalier, and Scott Schaefer. "Why Do Managers Undertake Acquisitions? An Analysis of Internal and External Rewards for Acquisitiveness." *Journal of Law, Economics, and Organization* 14 (1998): 24–43.

Bamberg, James H. *The History of the British Petroleum Company.* Vol. 2, *The Anglo-Iranian Years, 1928–1954.* Cambridge: Cambridge University Press, 2000.

Banaszak-Holl, Jane. "Incorporating Organizational Growth into Models of Organizational Dynamics: Manhattan Banks, 1791–1980." Cornell University, 1991.

Barnett, William P. "The Organizational Ecology of a Technological System." *Administrative Science Quarterly* 35 (1990): 31–60.

Barron, David N., Elizabeth West, and Michael T. Hannan. "A Time to Grow and a Time to Die: Growth and Mortality of Credit Unions in New York City, 1914–1990." *American Journal of Sociology* 100, no. 2 (1994): 381–421.

Baster, Albert S. J. *The Imperial Banks.* London: King, 1929.

Bate, Paul, Raza Khan, and Annie Pye. "Towards a Culturally Sensitive Approach to Organization Structuring: Where Organization Design Meets Organization Development." *Organization Science* 11, no. 2 (2000): 197–211.

Baum, Joel A. C., and Stephen J. Mezias. "Localized Competition and Organizational Failure in the Manhattan Hotel Industry, 1898–1990." *Administrative Science Quarterly* 37 (1992): 580–604.

Beer, Burkhard. "Ein Blick in die Geschichte der Kölnischen Rück." In *Themen Nr. 5,* edited by General Re/Kölnische Rückversicherungsgesellschaft, 16–17. Köln, 1996.

Berger, Franz S. *"Sieben auf Einen Streich." Grimms Märchen für Manager.* München: Wirtschaftsverlag Langen Müller/Herbig, 2001.

Berglund, Joel. "The Decline of the Norse Settlements in Greenland." *Arctic Anthropology* 23 (1986): 109–35.

Berle, Adolph, and Gardiner Means. *The Modern Corporation and Private Property.* New York: Macmillan, 1932.

Besanko, David, David Dranove, Mark Shanley, and Scott Schaefer. *Economics of Strategy.* Hoboken, NJ: John Wiley, 2002.

Birkinshaw, Julian, and Cristina Gibson. "Building Ambidexterity into an Organization." *MIT Sloan Management Review* Summer (2004): 47–55.

Blum, Daniel. *Langfristiger Unternehmenserfolg: Ermittlung Mittels Börsen- und Bilanzkennzahlen.* Berlin: Erich Schmidt, 2007.

Bood, Robert, and Theo Postman. "Strategic Learning with Scenarios." *European Management Journal* 15, no. 6 (1997): 633–46.

Borscheid, Peter. *100 Jahre Allianz.* München: Allianz Aktiengesellschaft Holding, 1990.

———. *100 Jahre Allianz: Menschen machen Geschichte: Der Weg des Unternehmens von seiner Gründung bis Heute vor dem Hintergrund des zeitgeschichtlichen Umfelds.* München: Allianz AG, 1990.

——. "Allianz Ag." In *International Directory of Company Histories,* edited by Jay P. Peterson, 18–24. Detroit: St. James Press, 2004.

Bower, Joseph L. *Managing the Resource Allocation Process: A Study of Corporate Planning and Investment.* Boston: Harvard University Press, 1970.

Broussard, Cary J., and Anita Bell. *From Cinderella to CEO: How to Master the 10 Lessons of Fairy Tales to Transform Your Work Life.* New York: Wiley, 2005.

Brown, Shona L., and Kathleen M. Eisenhardt. "The Art of Continuous Change: Linking Complexity Theory and Time-Paced Evolution in Relentlessly Shifting Organizations." *Administrative Science Quarterly* 42 (1997): 1–34.

Brückner, Lothar. "David Hansemann als Versicherungsunternehmer." In *David Hansemann, 1790, 1864, 1964,* edited by Bernhard Poll. Aaachen: Industrie und Handelskammer Aachen, 1964.

Burawoy, Michael. *Ethnography Unbound.* Berkeley: University of California Press, 1991.

Burgelman, Robert A. "Fading Memories: A Process Theory of Strategic Business Exit in Dynamic Environments." *Administrative Science Quarterly* 39, no. 1 (1994): 24–56.

——. "Intraorganizational Ecology of Strategy Making and Organizational Adaptation: Theory and Field Research." *Organization Science* 3, no. 2 (1991): 239–62.

——. "A Process Model of Internal Corporate Venturing: Strategic Decision Making." *Strategic Management Journal* 13 (1983): 13–37.

——. "Strategy as Vector and the Inertia of Coevolutionary Lock-in." *Administrative Science Quarterly* 47, no. 2 (2002): 325–57.

Campagne, Pierre. *La Cimeterie de Gargenville 1916 à 2002.* Paris, 2004.

Capon, Noel, James M. Hulbert, John U. Farley, and Elizabeth L. Martin. "Corporate Diversity and Economic Performance: The Impact of Market Specialization." *Strategic Management Journal* 9 (1988): 61–74.

Caspari, Rachel, and Sang-Hee Lee. "Older Age Becomes Common Late in Human Evolution." *Proceedings of the National Academy of Sciences* (2004): 10895–900.

Chandler, Alfred D. *Scale and Scope: Dynamics of Industrial Capitalism.* Cambridge, MA: Harvard University Press, 1990.

——. *Strategy and Structure.* Cambridge, MA: MIT Press, 1962.

——. *The Visible Hand: The Managerial Revolution in American Business.* Cambridge, MA: Belknap Press, 1977.

Channon, Derek F. "The Strategy and Structure of British Enterprise." Ph.D. diss., Harvard Business School, 1971.

Chatterjee, Arjit, and Donald C. Hambrick. "It's All about Me: Narcissistic CEOs and Their Effects on Company Strategy and Performance." *Administrative Science Quarterly* 52 (2007): 351–86.

Chatterjee, Sayan, and Birger Wernerfeld. "The Link between Resources and Type of Diversification." *Strategic Management Journal* 12 (1991): 33–48.

Christensen, Clayton M., and Joseph L. Bower. "Customer Power, Strategic Investment, and the Failure of Leading Firms." *Strategic Management Journal* 17, no. 3 (1996): 197–218.

Christiansen, Eric. *The Norsemen in the Viking Age*. Oxford: Blackwell, 2002.

Coe, Fred A., Jr. *Burroughs Wellcome Co., 1880–1980*. Edited by the Newcomen Society in North America. New York, 1980.

Collins, James, and Jerry I. Porras. "Building Your Company's Vision." *Harvard Business Review* (September–October 1996): 65–77.

———. *Built to Last: Successful Habits of Visionary Companies*. 1st paperback ed. New York: HarperBusiness, 1997.

Collins, Jim. *Good to Great: Why Some Companies Make the Leap . . . and Others Don't*. New York: HarperCollins, 2001.

Cooper, Arnold C., and Dan Schendel. "Strategic Responses to Technological Threats." *Business Horizons* 19 (February 1976): 61–69.

Cooper, Arnold C., and Clayton G. Smith. "How Established Firms Respond to Threatening Technologies." *Academy of Management Executive* 6, no. 2 (1992): 55–70.

Cornelius, Peter, Alexander Van de Putte, and Mattia Romani. "Three Decades of Scenario Planning in Shell." *California Management Review* 48, no. 1 (2005): 92–109.

D'Ambly, P. *Naissance d'une entreprise: Les Pavin de Lafarge de l'armée du roi à l'industrie de la republique*. Paris, 2000.

Danneels, E. "The Dynamics of Product Innovation and Firm Competences." *Strategic Management Journal* 23, no. 12 (2002): 1095–122.

———. "The Process of Technological Competence Leveraging." *Strategic Management Journal* 28, no. 5 (2007): 511–33.

———. "Tight-Loose Coupling with Customers: The Enactment of Customer Orientation." *Strategic Management Journal* 24, no. 6 (2003): 559–76.

David, Paul A. "Clio and the Economics of Qwerty." *American Economic Review* 75 (1985): 332–37.

Delacroix, Jacques, and Anand Swaminathan. "Cosmetic, Speculative, and Adaptive Organizational Change in the Wine Industry: A Longitudinal Study." *Administrative Science Quarterly* 36 (1991): 631–61.

Diamond, Jared. *Collapse: How Societies Choose to Fail or Succeed*. New York: Penguin, 2005.

Doornik, Katherine, and John Roberts. "Nokia Corporation: Innovation and Efficiency in a High-Growth Global Firm." In *Case S-IB-23*. Stanford, CA: Stanford University Graduate School of Business, 2001.

Dubois, Léon. *Foundation for the Future: The Lafarge Story*. Paris: Editions Belfond, 1988.

Dyas, Gareth P. "The Strategy and Structure of French Industrial Enterprise." Ph.D. diss., Harvard Business School, 1972.

Dyas, Gareth P., and Heinz T. Thanheiser. *The Emerging European Enterprise.* Boulder, CO: Westview, 1976.

Eglau, Hans Otto. *Edzard Reuter.* Düsseldorf: Econ, 1991.

Ehrenberg, Richard. *Das Zeitalter der Fugger: Geldkapital und Kreditverkehr im 16. Jahrhundert.* 2 vols. Jena: Verlag von Gustav Fischer, 1922.

Eisenhardt, Kathleen M. "Building Theories from Case Study Research." *Academy of Management Review* 14, no. 4 (1989): 532–51.

Eisenhardt, Kathleen M., and Jeffrey A. Martin. "Dynamic Capabilities: What Are They?" *Strategic Management Journal* 21 (2000): 1105–21.

Feist, Peter. *Die Berliner Mauer.* Berlin: Kai Homilius Verlag, 2004.

Feldenkirchen, Wilfried. *Siemens: Von der Werkstatt zum Weltunternehmen.* München: Piper, 1997.

———. *Siemens 1918–1945.* München: Piper, 1995.

Ferrier, Ronald W. *The History of the British Petroleum Company.* Vol. 1, *The Developing Years, 1901–1932.* London: Cambridge University Press, 2000.

Fitzhugh, William, and Elisabeth Ward, eds. *Vikings: The North Atlantic Saga.* Washington, DC: Smithsonian Institution Press, 2000.

Flynn, F. J., and B. M. Staw. "Lend Me Your Wallets: The Effect of Charismatic Leadership on External Support for an Organization." *Strategic Management Journal* 25, no. 4 (2004): 309–30.

Foster, Richard N. *Innovation: The Attacker's Advantage.* New York: Summit Books, 1986.

Fuchs, Jürgen. *Das Märchenbuch für Manager: "Gute Nacht-Geschichten" für Leitende und Leidende.* 2nd ed. Frankfurt: Frankfurter Allgemeine Buch, 2007.

Gad, Finn. *The History of Greenland.* Vol. 1, *Earliest Times to 1700.* Montreal: McGill-Queen's University Press, 1971.

Galbraith, Jay R., and Robert K. Kazanjian. *Strategy Implementation.* 2nd ed. St. Paul, MN: West Publishing, 1986.

Gerretson, Frederick C. *History of the Royal Dutch.* 4 vols. Leiden: E. J. Brill, 1958.

Geus, Arie de. *The Living Company.* Boston: Harvard Business School Press, 1997.

———. "The Living Company." *Harvard Business Review* (1997): 51–59.

———. "Planning as Learning." *Harvard Business Review* (March–April 1988): 70–74.

Glaser, B. G., and A. L. Strauss. *The Discovery of Grounded Theory.* Chicago: Aldine, 1967.

"Glaxo Coping with Unwellcome News." *Economist,* April 26, 1997, 59.

Glaxo Holdings. "Annual Report." London, 1995.

"Glaxo's Expanding Galaxy." *Economist,* November 23, 2000.

Goold, Michael, and Andrew Campbell. "Structured Networks: Towards the Well-Designed Matrix." *Long Range Planning* 36, no. 5 (2003): 427–41.

Grant, Robert M. *Contemporary Strategy Analysis: Concepts, Techniques, Applications*. 4th ed. Oxford: Blackwell Business, 2002.

Guinness World Records, ed. *Guinness World Records 2006*. New York: Guinness, 2006.

Häikiö, Martti. *Nokia: The Inside Story*. Helsinki: Edita, 2001.

———. *Nokia Oyj:N Historia 1: Fuusio*. Helsinki: Edita, 2001.

———. *Nokia Oyj:N Historia 3: Globalisaatio*. Helsinki: Edita, 2001.

Hamel, Gary, and C. K. Prahalad. *Competing for the Future*. Boston: Harvard Business School Press, 1994.

Hannan, Michael, and John Freeman. "The Population Ecology of Organizations." *American Journal of Sociology* 82 (1977): 929–64.

Hansen, Josef. *Gustav von Mevissen: Ein Rheinisches Lebensbild, 1815–1899*. Vol. 1. Berlin, 1906.

Hauser, E. "Amb Generali Holding Ag." In *International Directory of Company Histories*, edited by T. Grant, 48–75. Detroit: St. James Press, 2003.

Heijden, Kees van der. *Scenarios: The Art of Strategic Conversation*. New York, 1996.

Heijden, Kees van der, Ron Bradfield, George Burt, George Cairns, and George Wright. *The Sixth Sense: Accelerating Organizational Learning with Scenarios*. New York: John Wiley, 2002.

Helfat, Constance E. "Guest Editor's Introduction to the Special Issue: The Evolution of Firm Capabilities." *Strategic Management Journal* 21, no. 10–11 (2000): 955–59.

Henderson, Rebecca M., and Kim B. Clark. "Architectural Innovation: The Reconfiguration of Existing Product Technologies and the Failure of Established Firms." *Administrative Science Quarterly* 35, no. 1 (1990): 9–30.

Henry, J. A. *The First Hundred Years of the Standard Bank*. London: Oxford University Press, 1963.

Herre, Franz. *Die Fugger in ihrer Zeit*. 12th ed. Augsburg: Wißner-Verlag, 2005.

Hertle, Hans-Hermann, and Katrin Elsner. *Mein 9. November*. Berlin: Verlag Nicolai, 1999.

Herzfeld, Hans, ed. *Geschichte in Gestalten*. Frankfurt am Main: Fischer Taschenbuch, 1980.

Holland, John H. *Adaptation in Natural and Artificial Systems*. Ann Arbor: University of Michigan Press, 1975.

Hope Hailey, Veronica, and Julia Balogun. "Devising Context Sensitive Approaches to Change: The Example of Glaxo Wellcome." *Long Range Planning* 35, no. 2 (2002): 153–78.

Hoppenstedt, ed. *Versicherungsjahrbuch 1997*. Darmstadt: Hoppenstedt, 1997.

Howarth, Stephen, and Joost Jonker. *The History of Royal Dutch Shell: Powering the Hydrocarbon Revolution, 1939–1973*. Vol. 2. Oxford: Oxford University Press, 2007.

Ingvar, David. "Memory of the Future: An Essay on the Temporal Organization of Conscious Awareness." *Human Neurobiology* 4 (1985): 127–36.

Jakobsen, Bjarne. "Soil Resources and Soil Erosion in the Norse Settlement Area of Østerbygden in Southern Greenland." *Acta Borealia* 1 (1991): 56–68.

Jarrell, Gregg A., James A. Brickly, and Jeffry M. Netter. "The Market for Corporate Control: Empirical Evidence since 1980." *Journal of Economic Perspectives* 2, no. 1 (1988): 49–68.

Jensen, Michael C. "The Eclipse of the Public Corporation." *Harvard Business Review*, September–October (1989): 61–74.

Jones, Edgar. *The Business of Medicine: A History of Glaxo, a Baby Food Producer, Which Became One of the World's Most Successful Pharmaceutical Companies.* London: Profile Books, 2001.

Jones, Geoffrey. *British Multinational Banking, 1830–1990.* Oxford: Oxford University Press, 1993.

Jones, Gwyn. *Vikings: The North Atlantic Saga.* Oxford: Oxford University Press, 1986.

Jonker, Joost, and Jan Luiten van Zanden. *A History of Royal Dutch Shell: From Challenger to Joint Industry Leader, 1890–1939.* Vol. 1. Oxford: Oxford University Press, 2007.

Kahn, Herman, and Anthony J. Wiener. *The Year 2000.* New York: Macmillan, 1967.

Keller, Christian. "Vikings in the West Atlantic: A Model of Norse Greenlandic Medieval Society." *Acta Archaeologica* 61 (1990): 126–41.

King, Frank H. H. *The Hongkong Bank in the Period of Development and Nationalism, 1941–1984: From Regional Bank to Multinational Group.* New York: Cambridge University Press, 1991.

King, Frank H. H., Catherine E. King, and David J. S. King. *The Hongkong Bank between the Wars and the Bank Interned, 1919–1945: Return from Grandeur.* New York: Cambridge University Press, 1988.

———. *The Hongkong Bank in Late Imperial China, 1864–1902: On an Even Keel.* New York: Cambridge University Press, 1987.

King, Frank H. H., David J. S. King, and Catherine E. King. *The Hongkong Bank in the Period of Imperialism and War, 1895–1918: Wayfoong, the Focus of Wealth.* New York: Cambridge University Press, 1988.

King, W. T. C. *A History of the London Discount Market.* London: Routledge, 1936.

Kisch, Wilhelm. *Fünfzig Jahre Allianz: Ein Beitrag zur Geschichte der Deutschen Privatversicherung.* München: Münchener Rückversicherungs-Gesellschaft, 1940.

Kölnische Rückversicherungs-Gesellschaft. *100 Jahre Kölnische Rückversicherungs-Gesellschaft.* Köln, 1953.

Kuran, Timur. "The Tenacious Past: Theories of Personal and Collective Conservatism." *Journal of Economic Behavior and Organization*, no. 10 (1988): 143–71.

Lafarge, ed. *Pavin de Lafarge, 1833–1933.* Paris, 1933.

Lafarge Coppée. "L'identité d'un groupe: Lafarge Coppée, 1947–1989, an-Goulême." Paris, 1991.

Latour, Almar. "Trial by Fire: A Blaze in Albuquerque Sets Off Major Crisis for Cell-Phone Giants—Nokia Handles Supply Shock with Aplomb as Ericsson of Sweden Gets Burned—Was SISU the Difference?" *Wall Street Journal,* January 29, 2001.

Lee, Jim. "Family Firm Performance: Further Evidence." *Family Business Review* 19, no. 2 (2006): 103–14.

Leonard-Barton, Dorothy. *Wellsprings of Knowledge: Building and Sustaining the Sources of Innovation.* Boston: Harvard Business School Press, 1995.

Levinthal, Daniel A. "Random Walks and Organizational Mortality." *Administrative Science Quarterly* 36 (1991): 397–420.

Levinthal, Daniel A., and James G. March. "A Model of Adaptive Organizational Search." *Journal of Economic Behavior and Organization* 2 (1981): 307–33.

Levitt, Barbara, and James G. March. "Organizational Learning." *Annual Review of Sociology,* no. 14 (1988): 319–40.

Logan, Donald F. *The Vikings in History.* New York: Routledge, 1991.

Macalister, Terry. "BP Goliath Plays David." *Guardian,* November 28, 2005.

Mackenzie, Compton. *Realms of Silver: One Hundred Years of Banking in the East.* London: Routledge & Kegan Paul, 1954.

Maclellan, J. W. "Banking in India and China." *Bankers' Magazine* 55, no. 735 (1891).

Mann, H. B., and D. R. Whitney. "On a Test of Whether One of Two Random Variables Is Stochastically Larger Than the Other." *Annals of Mathematical Statistics* 18 (1947): 50–60.

March, James G. "Exploration and Exploitation in Organizational Learning." *Organization Science* 2, no. 1 (1991): 71–87.

Marcus, G. J. *The Conquest of the North Atlantic.* New York: Oxford University Press, 1981.

Matzler, Kurt, Martin Rier, Hans Hinterhuber, Birgit Renzl, and Christian Stadler. "Methods and Concepts in Management: Significance, Satisfaction, and Suggestions for Further Research: Perspectives from Germany, Austria, and Switzerland." *Strategic Change* 14, no. 1 (2005): 1–13.

Mayer, Michael, and Richard Whittington. "Diversification in Context: A Cross-National and Cross-Temporal Extension." *Strategic Management Journal* 24 (2003): 773–81.

McGovern, Thomas. "Climate, Correlation, and Causation in Norse Greenland." *Arctic Anthropology* 28 (1991): 77–100.

———. "Contributions to the Paleoeconomy of Norse Greenland." *Acta Archaeologica* 54 (1985): 73–122.

Meurling, John, and Richard Jeans. *The Ericsson Chronicle: 125 Years in Telecommunications.* Stockholm: Informationsförlaget, 2000.

Miller, Danny, and Isabelle Le Breton-Miller. "Family Governance and Firm Performance: Agency, Stewardship, and Capabilities." *Family Business Review* 19, no. 1 (2006): 73–87.

Mills, C. Wright. *The Power Elite.* New York: Oxford University Press, 1956.

Mintz, Beth, and Michael Schwartz. *The Power Structure of American Business.* Chicago: University of Chicago Press, 1985.

Montgomery, Cynthia A. "The Measurement of Firm Diversification: Some New Empirical Evidence." *Academy of Management Journal* 25 (1982): 299–307.

Muirhead, Stuart. *Crisis Banking in the East: The History of the Chartered Mercantile Bank of India, London, and China, 1853–93*. Aldershot: Scolar Press, 1996.

Münchener und Aachener Mobiliar-Feuer-Versicherungs-Gesellschaft, ed. *Hundert Jahre Münchener und Aachener Mobiliar-Feuer-Versicherungs-Gesellschaft: 1834–1934; Denkschrift der im Jahre 1825 Gegründeten Aachener und Münchener Feuer-Versicherungs-Gesellschaft Anläßlich ihrer Hundertjahrfeier in Bayern*. München: Bruckmann, 1934.

Norrman, Andreas, and Ulf Jansson. "Ericsson's Proactive Supply Chain Risk Management Approach after a Serious Sub-Supplier Accident." *International Journal of Physical Distribution and Logistics Management* 34, no. 5 (2004): 434–456.

Nulty, Peter, and Jessica Skelly von Brachel. "Batman Shakes BP to the Bedrock." *Fortune*, November 19, 1990, 88.

O'Harra, William T. *Centuries of Success: Lessons from the World's Most Enduring Family Businesses*. Avon, MA: Adams Media Corporation, 2004.

Palich, Leslie E., Laura B. Cardinal, and Chet C. Miller. "Curvilinearity in the Diversification-Performance Linkage: An Examination of over Three Decades of Research." *Strategic Management Journal* 21 (2000): 155–74.

Perrault, Charles. "The Master Cat." In *The Blue Fairy Book*, edited by Andrew Lang, 141–47. London: Longmans, Green, 1889.

Pierer, Heinrich v., and Michael Mirow. "Strategie im Praxistest. Unternehmen: Welche strategische Planungskonzepte haben sich bei Siemens in den vergangenen Jahrzehnten bewährt." *Harvard Business Manager*, October 2004.

Pitt, William. "Rude Awakening." *Reactions*, May 1992, 20–21.

Quarg, Gunter, and Klara von Eyll. *Gustav von Mevissen und seine Bibliothek*. Schriften der Universitäts- und Stadtbibliothek Köln 9. Köln: Universitäts- und Stadtbibliothek Köln, 1999.

Ranger-Moore, James. "Ecological Dynamics and Size Distributions in the Life Insurance Industry." Ph.D. diss., Cornell University, 1990.

Rau, Raghavendra R., and Theo Vermaelen. "Glamour, Value, and the Post-Acquisition Performance of Acquiring Firms." *Journal of Financial Economics* 49, no. 2 (1998): 223–54.

Roberts, John. *The Modern Firm: Organizational Design for Performance and Growth*. Oxford: Oxford University Press, 2004.

Roestahl, Else. *The Vikings*. New York: Penguin, 1987.

Rosenbloom, Richard S. "Leadership, Capabilities, and Technological Change: The Transformation of NCR in the Electronic Era." *Strategic Management Journal* 21, no. 10 (2000): 1083–103.

Rosenzweig, Phil. *The Halo Effect . . . and the Eight Other Business Delusions That Deceive Managers*. New York: Free Press, 2007.

Royal Dutch/Shell Group of Companies. "What We Look For." 2006.

Rumelt, Richard P. "Strategy, Structure, and Economic Performance." Ph.D. diss., Harvard Business School, 1972.

Schoemaker, Paul J. H. "Multiple Scenario Development: Its Conceptual and Behavioral Foundation." *Strategic Management Journal* 14 (1993): 193–214.

Schumpeter, Joseph. *Capitalism, Socialism, and Democracy.* New York: Harper Torchbooks, 1942.

———. *The Theory of Economic Development.* Cambridge: Harvard University Press, 1934.

Schwartz, Peter. *The Art of the Long View: Planning for the Future in an Uncertain World.* New York: Doubleday Currency, 1991.

Seaver, Kirsten. *The Frozen Echo: Greenland and Exploration of North America ca. A.D. 1000–1500.* Stanford, CA: Stanford University Press, 1996.

Sheffi, Yossi. *The Resilient Enterprise: Overcoming Vulnerability for Competitive Advantage.* Boston: MIT Press, 2005.

Sluyterman, Keetie. *A History of Royal Dutch Shell: Keeping Competitive in Turbulent Markets, 1973–2007.* Vol. 3. Oxford: Oxford University Press, 2007.

Société des Ciments Français, ed. *Centenaire de la Société des Ciments Français, 1881–1981.* Paris, 1981.

Soloveylchic, George. *Invar Kreuger.* London, 1932.

Stadler, Christian. *Unternehmenskultur bei Royal Dutch/Shell, Siemens, und DaimlerChrysler.* Edited by Hans Pohl. Vol. 18, *Beiträge zur Unternehmensgeschichte.* Stuttgart: Franz Steiner Verlag, 2004.

Stadler, Christian, and Hans H. Hinterhuber. "Changing Companies with Strong Values: Shell, Siemens, and Daimler Chrysler." *Long Range Planning* 38, no. 5 (2005): 467–84.

Standard Chartered, ed. *Strength in Depth across the World.* 1986.

Steinbock, Dan. *The Nokia Revolution: The Story of an Extraordinary Company That Transformed an Industry.* New York: Amacom, 2001.

Strunk, Peter. *Die AEG: Aufstieg und Niedergang einer Industrielegende.* Berlin: Nicolai, 1999.

Sull, Donald N. "The Dynamics of Standing Still: Firestone Tire & Rubber and the Radial Revolution." *Business History Review* 73, no. 3 (1999): 430–64.

Teece, D. J., G. Pisano, and A. Shuen. "Dynamic Capabilities and Strategic Management." *Strategic Management Journal* 18 (1997): 509–33.

Tichy, Noel, and Eli Cohen. *The Leadership Engine: How Winning Companies Build Leaders at All Levels.* New York: HarperCollins, 1997.

Tripsas, Mary. "Unraveling the Process of Creative Destruction: Complementary Assets and Incumbent Survival in the Typesetter Industry." *Strategic Management Journal* 18 (Special Summer Issue 1997): 119–42.

Tripsas, Mary, and Giovanni Gavetti. "Capabilities, Cognition, and Inertia: Evidence from Digital Imaging." *Strategic Management Journal* 21 (2000): 1147–61.

Tushman, Michael L., and Philip Anderson. "Technological Discontinuities and Organizational Environments." *Administrative Science Quarterly* 31, no. 3 (1986): 439–65.

Useem, Michael. *The Inner Circle*. New York: Oxford University Press, 1984.

Wack, Pierre. "Scenarios: Shooting the Rapids." *Harvard Business Review* 63, no. 3 (1985): 139–50.

Wältermann, Philip. *Unternehmenserfolg in der Versicherungswirtschaft: Langfristige Erfolgsfaktoren in der Assekuranz*. Berlin: Erich Schmidt, 2007.

Wenyon, Charles M. *Protozoology: A Manual for Medical Men, Veterinarians, and Zoologists*. London: Baillière, Tindall, and Cox, 1926.

"When Lightning Strikes: How to Maintain Business as Usual in Unusual Times." *Economist*, October 27, 2005.

Whittington, Richard, and Michael Mayer. *The European Corporation: Strategy, Structure, and Social Science*. New York: Oxford University Press, 2000.

Williams, Elaine. "100-Year-Old Nokia Experiences Fast-Growth Pains." *Electronic Business* (1989): 111–14.

Winter, Sidney G. "Satisficing, Selection, and the Innovating Remnant." *Quarterly Journal of Economics* 85 (1971): 237–61.

———. "Schumpeterian Competition in Alternative Technological Regimes." *Journal of Economic Behavior and Organization* 5, no. 3–4 (1984): 287–320.

Wittgenstein, Ludwig. *Philosophical Investigations*. Oxford: Blackwell, 1989.

Wright, Richard. "How Zantac Became the Best-Selling Drug in History." *Journal of Health Care Marketing* (Winter 1996): 25–29.

Wrigley, Leonard. "Divisional Autonomy and Diversification." Ph.D. diss., Harvard Business School, 1970.

Wunderer, Rolf. "Vom Selbst- zum Fremdvertrauen: Konzepte, Wirkungen, Märcheninterpretationen." *Zeitschrift für Personalforschung* 18, no. 4 (2004): 454–69.

Yergin, Daniel. *The Prize: The Epic Quest for Oil, Money, and Power*. New York: Pocket Books, 1993.

Note: Figures and tables are indicated by *f* or *t*, respectively, following the page number.